About the author

Noel Eastwood (B.A. Psychology; Post Grad Dip Psychology; Grad Dip Special Education; Dip Teach) is a retired psychologist with a lifetime of professional experience in education, counselling, depth psychotherapy, astrology and tarot. Now a full-time author, Noel shares his lifelong interests in psychotherapy, taoist meditation, tai chi, astrology and tarot. A gifted storyteller, his fiction and nonfiction works blend ancient wisdom and contemporary themes.

Why not subscribe to his weekly newsletter?

Web: www.plutoscave.com

Facebook: www.facebook.com/plutoscave

IMPORTANT LEGAL NOTICE

This book is intended as an educational aid for students of astrology. Its contents should not be considered as a substitute for personal supervision or treatment by a qualified medical or psychological professional. The author, editors and publishers accept no responsibility for outcomes if you use the techniques described in this book. For privacy, names of individuals and any identifying details have been changed.

Copyright © 2019 Noel Eastwood

All rights reserved. Apart from any fair use for the purposes of private study, research, criticism or review no part may be reproduced without written permission of the author.
Please direct all communication to the author, Noel Eastwood.

Email: info@plutoscave.com

Web: www.plutoscave.com

Cover art: original artwork by Peta Fenton - adapted by Dar Albert, Wicked Smart Designs - www.wickedsmartdesigns.com

Dedication: to three of the most influential people in my life: Chris Turner, astrologer, who taught me how to understand myself and humanity through astrology; Simon Lim, Taoist, who handed me the key to the worlds beyond consciousness; Neville Andrews, Jungian psychotherapist, who gave me the confidence to take others within to heal their inner selves.

Table of Contents

Foreword by Chris Turner

Introduction

Chapter 1 - The psychology of astrology

Chapter 2 - Spiritual lessons in the chart - archetypal personalities

Chapter 3 - Introducing the Air Fire phenomenon, children's disorders, depression and the conflicts of adolescence

Chapter 4 - The Saturn Cycle and psychological development

Chapter 5 - Introduction to the Planets

Chapter 6 - Introduction to the 12 Signs of the Zodiac

Chapter 7 - Introduction to the 12 Houses

Chapter 8 - Planetary aspects and chart shapes

Chapter 9 - Elements, Modes and Extra Points

Chapter 10 - The amazing Luminaries

Chapter 11 – Profile of psychopath Doctor Death

Chapter 12 - Conflict and complexes in psychological astrology

Chapter 13 - Putting your chart together - chart delineation

Chapter 14 – Active Imagination and the archetypes in your chart

Chapter 15 - Introducing the five main asteroid Goddesses

Chapter 16 - Meeting the asteroid Goddess archetypes in meditation

Chapter 17 - Transits – an introduction

Recommended reading

Books by Noel Eastwood

What readers are saying

Foreword by Chris Turner

Astrology, like the archetypes it symbolises, is in a perpetual state of evolution and, I'm afraid, fashion.

When I started my serious journey into astrology more than 45 years ago the psychological aspects of its symbolism were very fashionable. Pluto was still a relatively recent discovery and Chiron was discovered around the time I decided to look into astrology more closely. It was probably the fact that astrologers were applying what they called 'humanistic' principles to it that drew me to doing at least SOME research on the subject as human (and animal) behaviour has always fascinated me. By the time of my Saturn Return I was totally intrigued by why people exhibited the emotional and behavioural differences they did.

Many professional psychologists back then were intrigued by astrology, but as astrology was very unregulated and still regarded as 'fortune telling' or something weird people did, they kept their interest very quiet and separate from their professional and psychological peers. In retrospect that did the growth of psychological astrology a great disservice. 'Pop' psychology was at its height during the 70's and 80's which meant that many poorly informed, unqualified astrologers could go to town with, sadly, more than a few very unfortunate consequences.

There was one very notable exception to this. Liz Greene, an astrologer/psychologist, rigidly kept her astrological and psychological practices very separate, never allowing one to overlap the other, was also a prolific author. Her astrology books with their psychological observations, opened the door to astrologers like myself who, although not qualified psychologists, were prepared to explore, observe and research. Many of us did go out and obtain psychology qualifications, or at the very least, counselling qualifications. When Australian astrology did become regulated, albeit by astrologers themselves through the Federation of Australian Astrologers, counselling qualifications became part of their astrological ethical and professional qualifications.

However, little did we know that astrology was about to undergo a major change in its evolution and fashion. Astrologers embraced the advent of the personal computer with glee. At the time the love affair was all about mathematics as this machine could calculate what were hours of tedious manual calculations in minutes, and by the mid naughties, in seconds. This in turn opened a whole new world for those astrologers interested in research as accessibility to birth details was not limited to local populations, but opened us up to the whole world. Data management and sorting suddenly could be done at the touch of a button.

By the turn of the century huge changes had started to happen in the astrological world, but the change relevant to this book, is that the "devolving" of astrology began to become fashionable. Many of the more intellectually motivated astrologers declared that the only way to truly understand astrology was to go back to its roots from Greek, Egyptian, Mesopotamian and Mediaeval times. The astrology of those times was very event oriented and black and white. Full of rules and regulations there had none of the grey areas that we 'humanistic' astrologers so loved. In the last 20 years this form of Classical Astrology has proliferated in spite of a few diehards such as myself stubbornly hanging in there.

One of the worst consequences of this is that archetypes and archetypal energies were slowly being forgotten, and in recent years not even taught by many astrology teachers. Fortunately, in recent years some of the older Classical astrologers have begun to realise the importance of astrological archetypes and have begun to teach them again alongside the Classical rules and regulations. I, for one, am breathing a huge sigh of relief.

Back in the 80's among my students was an enthusiastic young man, a teacher who alongside his astrology studies was also studying psychology and tarot. Noel Eastwood was a rare breed in the world of astrology and the world of scientific psychology. He saw no clash between the world of science and the world of mysticism, and in fact was able to intuitively see the connection between them all. Not only that, if necessary, he could separate the different levels of thinking as easily as he could connect them. He completed his three years of astrology study and passed his qualifying exams with flying colours.

Noel moved away from Sydney not long after that, but he made sure we kept in sporadic touch over the years. Thanks to the internet I was able to follow his career and am immensely proud of what he has accomplished.

He became a psychologist with a successful practice alongside a successful astrology practice, a reputation as a skilled tarot reader and a popular teacher of all things metaphysical.

Being a Fire sign (a Leo) Noel has always had to move on from one challenge to another. In recent years he has turned his hand to writing, and of course, has become a very successful author. Although he published his first book in 1995, it was 20 years later that the passion for writing took over, and he has published 11 successful books on psychology, health, tarot and astrology in the last four years.

This book is his latest and I love it. I admit I am a little jealous as he has accomplished with this book what I would have loved to have done. It is much harder than you would expect to write a basic book on astrology as the information available is vast. But here, Noel has managed to introduce astrologers to psychology and psychologists to astrology successfully. You will find it a simple book, after all it is an introduction, but at the same time incredibly complex. The fundamental knowledge is all there interwoven with mythology, mysticism, meditations, advice and practical applications. This book is an absolute 'must have' for every astrologer's (and psychologist's) library.

Chris Turner

Sydney, April 2019.

Introduction

This book was written to introduce students of astrology to the theory and practice of psychological astrology. As part of my work I have met many spiritually minded people on a modern mystical quest to find themselves. Finding the key to this depth of knowledge is one of their challenges. Fortunately, there are several keys and one of them is astrology.

As a psychotherapist and astrologer my goal has always been to guide astrology students to an understanding of themselves. To achieve this you first need to understand your own astrology chart, its signs, houses and planets. There are no 'ifs' or 'buts' about it, without a solid understanding of the basics of astrology you will never become an astrologer. Secondly, you need to know how to apply this knowledge in your readings for others. My Psychological Astrology series aims to provide you with the keys to this knowledge and show you how to apply it.

I understand that the majority of readers are quite conversant with the basics of astrology and that many of you are experienced astrologers so please don't think that you need to read this book starting from page one. This book is designed so that you can jump about from chapter to chapter to get a good mix of astrology and psychology according to your interests and level of experience.

In this book you will learn how to recognise the essential features and characteristics of the planets, signs and houses as used by a psychologically trained astrologer. These are the keys that open this treasure chest of knowledge.

I didn't want to write another astrology book for beginners, there are many great books already out there, so I've kept the astrology basics short and focused. The majority of this book is devoted to showing how psychology can be used in conjunction with astrology.

I wanted this book to be juicy enough to sink your teeth into but not overloaded with psychology terms and disorders to overwhelm you. I've made sure to include topics that will excite your interest so that you are hungry to put some of it into your own practice.

It includes a discussion of synastry charts and inherited family traits; what aspects trigger people to seek counselling; how you might apply psychotherapy in your astrology practice; locating the astrological significators for conflict and complexes; ADD and ADHD; astrological significators for teenage depression and suicidal thoughts; psychological disorders as a spectrum of neurological symptoms; planetary aspects and shapes; the power of the elements and modes; clues to your spiritual path in your astrology chart; the powerful Saturn cycle; the amazing Air Fire phenomenon; using Jungian archetype meditations to support your personal mystic quest.

I have made sure to include example charts to demonstrate each feature I discuss in the book. As would be expected in a book of this nature, student names and identifying details have been changed.

I believe that it is important for therapists to know themselves. Astrologers have a distinct advantage because the sign posts and companions to their mystic's quest are provided in their chart. As I always encourage my students to meditate on their archetypes I have included several encounters from my own meditations to help illustrate this.

My style of psychotherapy incorporates active imagination, clinical hypnotherapy, archetypal guided meditations and depth psychotherapy using an 'inner child' approach. My word of advice to you is to find your niche and become good at it, master your particular style of astrology or psychotherapy first. When you are ready for the next stage of your journey a teacher will appear to walk you into the next stage of your mystic's quest.

Noel Eastwood - psychotherapist, astrologer, tarotist

Australia, June, 2019

"Lost in my sorrows I didn't notice that the months and days were passing by. Is the year really over and my time in this world too?"

From: Murasaki Shikibu's 'The Tale of Genji' (early 11th century Japan)

READ THIS FIRST:- The Horoscope / Natal Chart - the following charts help demonstrate the effects of changes in birth time, date and place on an individual's chart and personality; one hour in time changes the Ascendant by 15° and every other House cusp will change too; the planets move over time, the Moon is the fastest at about 13° per day; the planets move counterclockwise while the outside chart wheel moves clockwise. The Natal Chart of an individual is like a photograph of the planets in the sky with the fixed stars (constellations aka the Signs of the Zodiac) behind them. They appear to be frozen in time. Each planet is placed at a certain degree of a Sign according to where it is in the sky, each Sign rests on a House cusp (unless it falls inside a house). Not all astrological charts are the same.

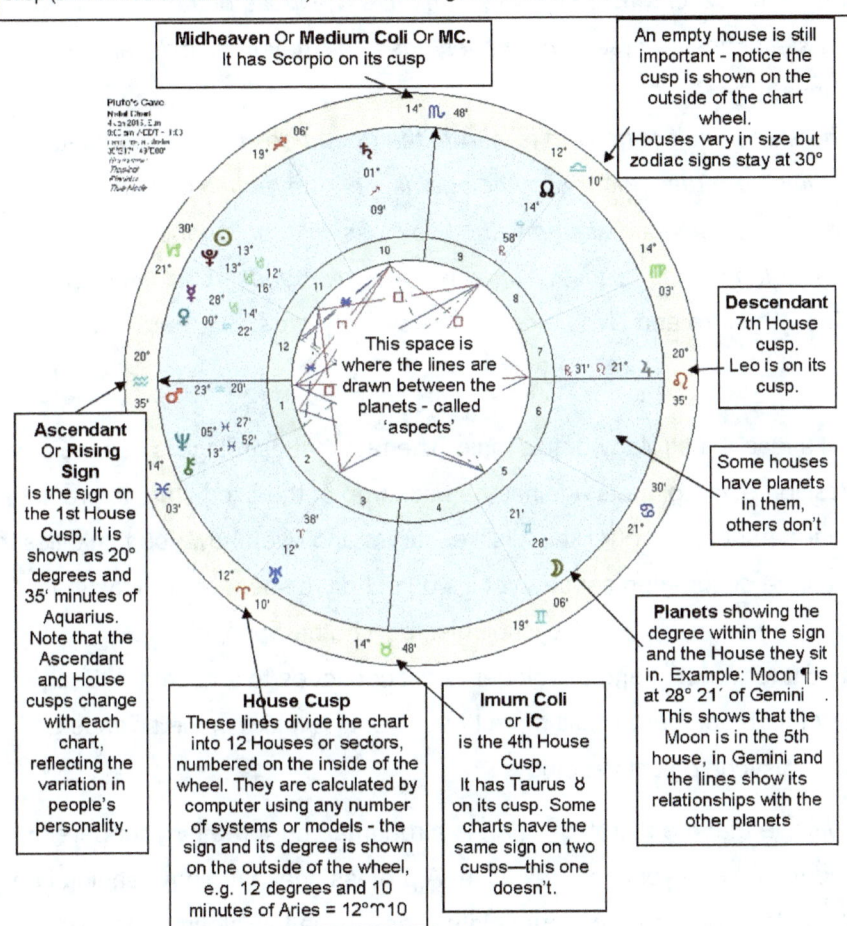

Midheaven Or **Medium Coli** Or **MC.** It has Scorpio on its cusp

An empty house is still important - notice the cusp is shown on the outside of the chart wheel.
Houses vary in size but zodiac signs stay at 30°

Descendant 7th House cusp. Leo is on its cusp.

Some houses have planets in them, others don't

Ascendant Or Rising Sign is the sign on the 1st House Cusp. It is shown as 20° degrees and 35' minutes of Aquarius. Note that the Ascendant and House cusps change with each chart, reflecting the variation in people's personality.

Planets showing the degree within the sign and the House they sit in. Example: Moon ☽ is at 28° 21' of Gemini. This shows that the Moon is in the 5th house, in Gemini and the lines show its relationships with the other planets

House Cusp These lines divide the chart into 12 Houses or sectors, numbered on the inside of the wheel. They are calculated by computer using any number of systems or models - the sign and its degree is shown on the outside of the wheel, e.g. 12 degrees and 10 minutes of Aries = 12°♈10

Imum Coli or **IC** is the 4th House Cusp. It has Taurus ♉ on its cusp. Some charts have the same sign on two cusps—this one doesn't.

Chapter 1 - The psychology of astrology

"... the characteristic alchemical vision of sparks scintillating in the blackness of the arcane substance should, for Paracelsus, change into the spectacle of the "interior firmament" and its stars. He beholds the darksome psyche as a star-strewn night sky, whose planets and fixed constellations represent the archetypes in all their luminosity and numinosity.
The starry vault of heaven is in truth the open book of cosmic projection, in which are reflected the mythologems, i.e., the archetypes. In this vision astrology and alchemy, the two classical functionaries of the psychology of the collective unconscious, join hands." Carl Jung, CW 8, 'The Structure and Dynamics of the Psyche', Page 195, Para 392.

Let's face it, astrology defies logic. The fact that astrologers use the position of the planets against the backdrop of the fixed stars to predict your personality, your likes, dislikes, fears and even how you think flies in the face of common sense - yet it works. I have spent over thirty years studying astrology as a psychologist, psychotherapist, teacher, meditator, tarotist and astrologer and it continues to amaze me. Each day I find that there is still more I have yet to explore in the science and art of psychological astrology.

I believe that the astrology chart is a roadmap nurtured by your parents and the culture you were raised in. A professional astrology reading can facilitate the learning of your spiritual lessons in this lifetime. Astrology provides a series of timed signposts that act to guide you on your journey back to your spiritual origins.

Since time birthed our species the tribal shaman, village priest and some modern era psychologists, have studied the inner and outer worlds in their effort to understand the true nature of the human psyche. The answers that they seek are clearly written in the stars above. These answers, however, are cast as a secret language that few can read and even fewer understand.

To quote Dane Rudhyar: *"Astrology is a language. If you understand this language, the sky speaks to you."*

I will start this chapter with some basic rules that will help lay your astrological foundations for reading your chart. Firstly, all birth data needs to be as accurate as possible. When someone asks for a reading they generally don't realise that an accurate birth time is absolutely essential. The Ascendant moves 1 degree every 4 minutes, therefore if the Ascendant lies at 29° Capricorn, within 4 minutes of time that will change the Ascendant to 0° of Aquarius. There is no leeway in the Ascendant no matter what anyone says. Someone with an Ascendant of 29° Capricorn will always exhibit Capricorn traits - not Aquarian traits even though it is only 1° from Aquarius. It only takes four minutes to change the tone of an entire reading.

Secondly, House Systems vary. I use the Placidus House system most of the time, but if the houses are distorted I will switch to the Koch House system. If some of the houses remain distorted, i.e. too large or small, I will revert to the old fashioned Whole Sign system where all the houses are exactly 30° wide (they are all of equal size).

A point to note: if you really want to know a person's unconscious urges and instincts then seriously study up on the houses.

Every planet has its own particular personality as does every sign. This is why I read the chart as a whole, because it is made up of a community of planets, signs and house cusps much like an extended family. Each planet and sign are known as archetypes. An archetype is a facet of your personality which represents your needs, urges and instincts. Like each person you know, each astrological archetype has specific needs, likes, dislikes, friendships, hobbies and even interests. By connecting to your astrological archetypes (planets and signs) you connect directly with the very mechanisms that forms or creates your world. I will explore this in more detail in later chapters in the book and in greater depth in my next book, *'Psychological Astrology, Jung and the Mystic's Quest'*.

I have studied the human spirit throughout my life using such means as biofeedback, self-hypnosis, meditation and psychotherapy. There is no better way to engage and gain insight into your psyche, I have found, than by meditating with the archetypes. Learn to go into a deep state of relaxation and practice doing this every day. It is easier than you think. Most of my students and clients can do it on their first attempt. Those who don't usually succeed soon after.

Knowing your astrological archetypes means knowing Roman and Greek mythology. Western astrology is based on our collective cultural heritage which is built upon the myths, legends and faerie tales of western civilisation. I suggest that you immerse yourself in the Greek and Roman myths - draw pictures, cartoons or even talk the stories into your mobile phone or computer and listen to them while at the gym. You will recognise the value of immersing yourself in mythology when you do your readings and in your meditations with the archetypes.

Thirdly, study everything about astrology - this means avoid the internet noise which is mostly rubbish published by people who are not astrologers. They have not done the hard years of formal study to know their subject properly. If you are serious about becoming an astrologer then I suggest that you study under the best teachers. Read books written by professionals and don't be afraid to email or contact them.

Also study psychology but don't try to study everything. I recommend that you stick to Jungian and Humanistic psychology. These will give you a deeper understanding of the archetypes based on Carl Jung's teaching. By studying the Greek and Roman myths and then applying it in your meditations and your readings, I believe that you will know more about human personality than most psychologists.

The ancients knew more than we give them credit for. We understand their values, beliefs and personal conflicts by examining their myths. Carl Jung spent many years studying ancient cultures throughout Africa, Europe, the Americas, the Pacific and Asia. He concluded that every culture shared the same basic myths and therefore the same archetypes. Know your myths and you will know the psychology of your culture - your family, friends, workmates and the community you live and work in. I recommend that you read Carl Jung's autobiography: *'Memories, Dreams, Reflections'*.

A point to note: astrologers of today stand on the shoulders of the great people who came before us. Among them are Liz Greene, Dane Rudhyar, Alexander Ruperti, Bruno & Louise Huber, Karen Hamaker-Zondag, Carl Jung, Robert Hand, Demetra George, Stephen Arroyo, Howard Sasportas, Glenn Perry, Richard Idemon, Greg Bogart, Noel Tyl, Richard Tarnas, Reinhold Ebertin, and many more to whom I apologise for not including as the list is enormous.

Synastry, family charts and the question of 'nature or nurture'

Psychologists have argued over this question for centuries: are humans formed and shaped by their genes (nature) or by their life experiences (nurture)?

I am sure that you already know the answer, it is 'yes' to both. You are shaped by everything about you, your genes going back several generations and by your childhood experiences. You are shaped by your parents and siblings and anyone else who has contact with you, be it brother, sister, uncle, aunt, grandmother or grandfather, teachers and carers - they impact you in unique ways. You can see this in the astrology chart.

Here is an example of using astrology to understand how family members impact each other. It is called 'synastry' which is often used to look at relationships between lovers and for prospective marriage partners. I don't want you to think that synastry is limited to love relationships, it is used for every human relationship, as you will soon see.

I have five planets in Leo so I am very Leonic (Sun, Venus, Mars, Jupiter and Pluto): I am also quite Scorpionic (Sun, Mars, Venus are all conjunct Pluto + Moon is conjunct Mercury - all six planets are in the 8th house). I also have strong Earth with a Capricorn Ascendant, its ruler, Saturn is in my 10th house and my Moon and Mercury are in Virgo. My elemental themes are Fire (Leo), Water (Scorpio being 8th house dominant) and Earth (Ascendant, Moon and Mercury).

My wife has a Libran Ascendant, an 11th house stellium, Moon in Aquarius, and a Virgo stellium. Her genetic theme is Earthy Virgo and Airy Aquarius. Two of our children have an Aries Sun (Fire) and the other is a Libran (Air); their astrological themes include Fire, Air and a strong

Pluto. They have a mixture of themes from both of us, my wife and I, yet they each have a leaning towards one of us. Two are more like me and one is more like their mother.

A point to note: knowing your family tree is of enormous benefit to your understanding of yourself and your astrology clients. I spent many years studying family trees when I was still finding my way as an astrologer. I suggest that you spend time studying as many family charts as possible too.

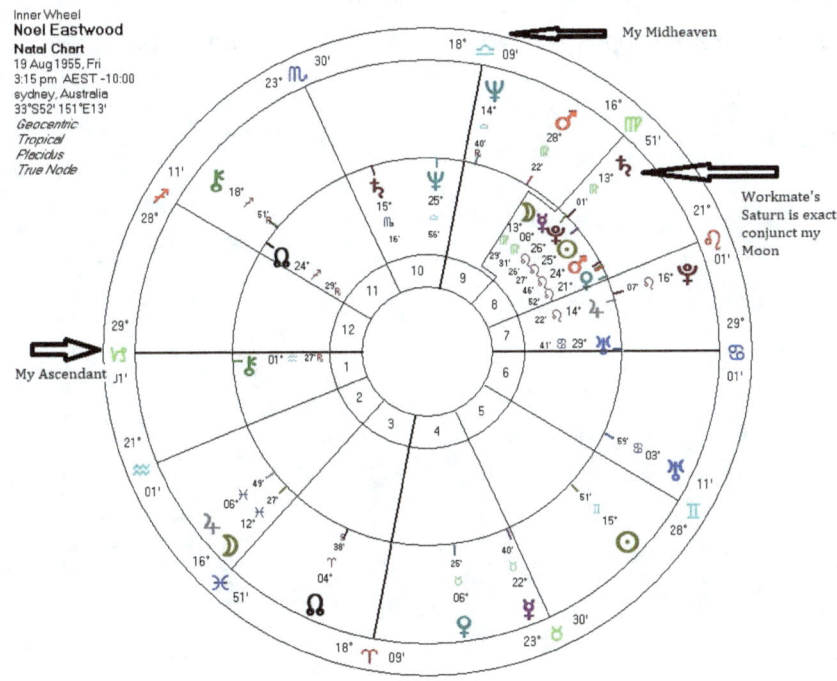

Above chart: Inner wheel Noel, outer wheel workmate.

If you have a family member, friend or workmate that annoys you, try to have a look at their chart and you will see your conflict reflected there. As an example, a man I worked with had a Gemini Sun and Scorpio Ascendant. His Ascendant was in a wide conjunction with my Saturn which suggests that he felt frustrated by my Saturn's limiting and restricting nature. In his eyes I tried to inhibit his enthusiasm and passion. On the other hand his Scorpio tried to dominate my sensible and responsible manner. My workmate's Saturn sat exactly conjunct my Moon and you can imagine what that means - he suppressed my emotional expression, in short he was a pain in the butt to work with. I would say that my workmate found me too emotional, too watery, too passionate and expressive - I needed calming down in his eyes. His Moon sat exactly opposite mine, so perhaps I triggered his Saturn-Moon opposition.

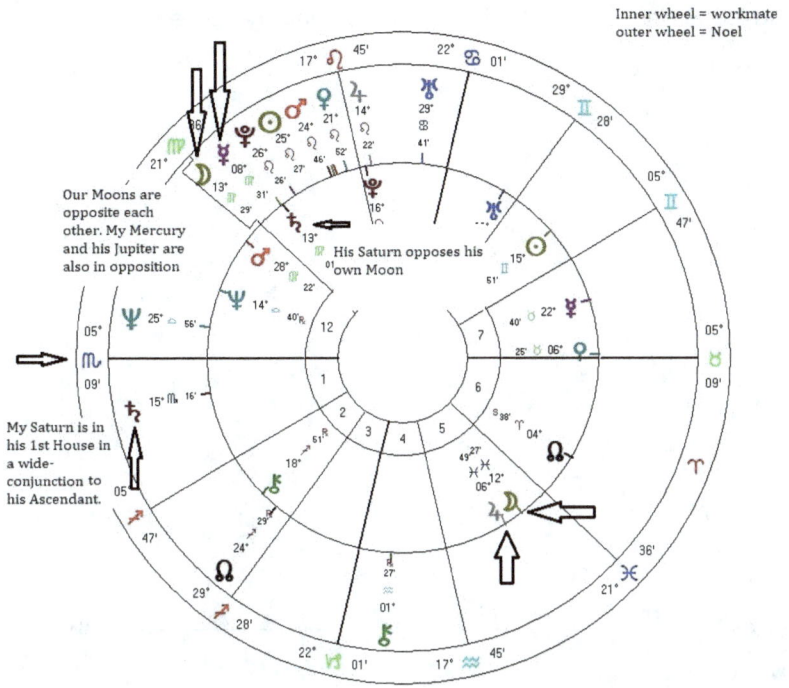

Above chart: Inner wheel workmate, outer wheel Noel.

I have 5 planets in Leo, and they are all in a tight conjunction, Sun 25°, Mars 24°, Venus 21° and Jupiter 14° who is just out of orb of Pluto at 26° Leo. I can get somewhat excitable. I can appear quite irrational with my unorthodox beliefs. When I was around my workmate I spent most of my time trying to control his excessive orthodox (redneck) behaviours and beliefs. We were very similar in that we both felt the need to control the other's excesses.

One of my friends, on the other hand, has a Saturn and Jupiter conjunction sitting on my Capricorn Ascendant. This means that he will try to limit my irrational and nonconformist beliefs and behaviours

(Saturn); then a minute later he is encouraging me to be riotously crazy (Jupiter).

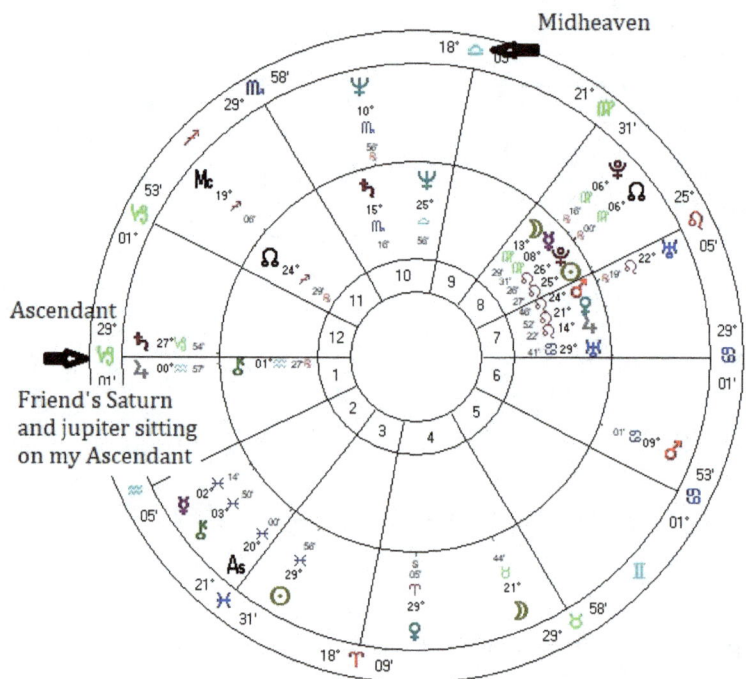

Above chart: Inner wheel Noel; Outer wheel workmate.

A point to note: using the biwheel you can check everyone you know against your own chart. You can see how you affect each other.

Someone whom you thought hates you might just be in awe of you, you won't know unless you look at their chart.

Significators and Constellations

Liz Greene, Howard Sasportas and Glenn Perry use the terms 'significator' and 'constellation' to describe combinations of planet + sign + house to define psychological patterns or disorders. This helps to categorise both astrological and psychological formations. In psychoanalytical psychology this is often called a 'complex'.

For example, Australian mass murderer, Martin Bryant, has Moon in Aries, Mars opposite Moon and Moon in the first house. These form part of his psychological conflicts that can manifest as external behaviours such as impatience, childish behaviours, temper tantrums, neediness, immaturity, emotional manipulation, bullying and psychopathology which unfortunately eventuated in multiple acts of murder. They may also constellate into a complex - a Moon or a Mother Complex, or perhaps it is a Poor-Me Complex. You will find more on complexes and psychopathology later in this book.

An example of the significators for immaturity and childish behaviour include: Ascendant, Sun, Moon, Venus or Mars in Fire and/or Air signs or the 1st house. The terms Significator and Constellation are very similar so don't worry if you get them mixed up, I often do.

A point to note: a significator is just that, a signal, I prefer to use the word 'suggests' because an astrological significator is not set in stone but rather suggests a pattern of behaviour. I would then wait until I had evidence of their behaviour which confirmed my diagnosis before labelling them with a disorder. Another thing to remember is that even though you may have these same constellations and significators discussed in this series of books it doesn't mean that you will automatically have a psychological disorder too. Who you are today can basically be traced back to your life experiences and how you were taught to manage your personal strengths and weaknesses.

Speaking of how we all see 'psychological disorders' in our own and our loved one's charts this is something for you to remember: one of the best lessons I learned from my astrology teacher, Chris Turner, was the time she asked her students to create the perfect chart, a chart that we would like to have as our own. The result - it was impossible to create the perfect chart, it does not exist.

An understanding of psychological astrology saves this young lady from disaster

This is an email I received that highlights just how useful a knowledge of psychology and astrology can be in your everyday life.

"I recently met a man online. Whilst everything seemed normal I asked him for his birth details so I could do his birth chart. Amicably, he agreed. It had Mars in Scorpio in the first house. He has an Aries Sun and Libra Ascendant. I now knew to stay away from him. Sure enough, a few days later he was twisting everything I said into something that was not true. I apologised in every way I could in case I had said something to offend him. He ended up insulting me so I stopped contact with him. Is this a sure sign of a sociopath or psychopath?"

Comment:- You did extremely well in picking this up in his chart. It means that next time you engage with someone online you will do the same. Just be mindful that the conflict seen in the chart can manifest in one of three ways - positive, negative and in-between. The in-between state is one that is yet to swing either way, perhaps the native has had no positive or negative experiences associated with that particular conflict, or, perhaps his / her other conflicts are so overwhelming that it remains unexpressed.

The significator planets may possibly be a sign of sociopathy but I'd first consider the entire chart before feeling brave enough to whisper such a label. As astrologers we must remember that everyone has some form of conflict in their chart.

Chris Turner taught her students the 'Rule of Three' to help understand what may be activated in a chart and what may not. It goes like this:

If you see significators of a conflict in the chart once it is a MIGHT be; if you see a second significator in the chart it becomes a POSSIBLY could be: if you see a third significator in the chart it becomes a PROBABLY is.

Three individual significators of sociopathy, anger, aggression, narcissism, selfishness or whatever is when you really start to consider that this person has issues.

Applying the Rule of Three to this chart I found these conflicts / significators of aggressive behaviour noted in the email above:

(1) MAYBE - Mars in Scorpio in the 1st house, this is the house that Mars rules, he is also co-ruler of Scorpio and Mars rules his Sun sign Aries - this immediately makes Mars one of his Planets of Power;

(2) POSSIBLY – his Ascendant is Libra which is in Detriment to Mars;

(3) PROBABLY – I have seen this man's chart and there are at least 3 more significators of conflict not mentioned.

We all have planets and/or points that have the potential to act out in a negative way - but they don't, they stay positive and empowering. What makes someone turn a conflict into a positive and empowering experience? They are the same factors that can turn it into a negative.

Did this man have a traumatic upbringing and did that corrupt him in some way? This would manifest as an attachment disorder of some kind. Was he over-indulged as a child? This could manifest as an 'entitlement' to be treated as special and he expects to get what he wants. Did he learn that people were placed on this planet to run after him, to clean up his mess and bow down to his every desire? This might manifest as a narcissistic or God Complex which sometimes arises in children of overly permissive parents as well as dysfunctional and/or narcissistic-type parents.

Another thing to consider in this discussion is whether he had the opportunity to practice bullying at school or at home. There is so much to consider before making a definite statement of a disorder such as 'sociopath' or 'psychopath'. These factors determine how he uses the energies provided in his chart.

I'd say that the best predictor of his personality is his past behaviour. Because you don't know his past history you have to be very observant and mindful of his current behaviour – and that was clearly exhibited when you hesitated. Fortunately you had already noticed there was conflict in his chart which suggested possible traits of bullying or sociopathy. You were prepared for a possible outburst of aggression. I believe that your insight and preparedness saved you from making a very big mistake.

I think this is a great example of how to use psychological astrology in a real life situation.

Astrologers as counsellors – psychotherapy and astrology

If there ever was a career path that best suits an astrologer it is psychotherapy but there is a caveat that comes with this statement. It is my firm belief that all astrologers who wish to provide a psychotherapeutic service to their clients should first study psychotherapy and undertake therapy themselves. The type of therapy I am referring to is called 'psychodynamic psychotherapy' which is a form of 'depth' psychotherapy. You can find out more here:
https://en.wikipedia.org/wiki/Psychodynamic_psychotherapy

This type of psychotherapy is designed to take the client deep into their psyche to uncover outdated and unhelpful beliefs. It is also used to uncover any trauma that may be lurking deep within the client's psyche. This therapeutic approach is not for everyone however. Some people just want to talk and to be heard. Others want solutions and strategies, while only a very small proportion of the population want to actually uncover the very cause of their issues at the deepest level of heir being.

I was fortunate to have been mentored by Neville Andrews, a psychodynamic psychotherapist who studied at the Tavistock Institute in London under R.D.Laing of the anti-psychiatry movement. This experience has helped inform my practice of psychotherapy. I much prefer to seek the underlying causes of my client's distress. I have been fortunate to have had such wonderful mentors in many fields be it astrology, Taoist meditation or psychotherapy and have been able to use this unique combination as a powerful force for healing and spiritual growth.

There are many ways to practice therapy, one is through meditation on the archetypes in your astrology chart. You don't need to limit yourself to the astrology archetypes though because archetypes can be found everywhere such as the tarot, fairy tales, myths and legends and even in your movies, books and TV shows.

Another approach, which is my personal favourite when working with childhood trauma and Post Traumatic Stress Disorder (PTSD), is the 'inner child' therapy made popular by John Bradshaw in his *Bradshaw On: Homecoming* series of talks on TV and his books. I have used this approach extensively and find it is suitable for almost everyone. If I had time I could tell you countless stories of how successful this approach is.

I believe that all therapists, including astrologers, should be regular meditators. There is no special form or practice, just learn to relax and your psyche will teach you the rest. You might want to read my self-hypnosis book to learn more about the many methods and techniques I use.

I suggest that astrologers who wish to use therapy as part of their practice become qualified as a clinical hypnotherapist at the very least. I also recommend that any psychotherapy or hypnotherapy qualification include a two year professional mentorship program by a qualified therapist.

As an astrologer / therapist you have a unique set of tools at hand – namely the astrology chart. I suggest that your professional reading include Existentialism, Attachment Theory, Humanistic and Transpersonal psychology, Jung and Freud. Anything written by arguably the most qualified and popular astrologer and psychologist Dr Liz Greene is well worth reading.

When starting my own private psychology practice I dedicated the next 10 years solely to becoming the best psychologist I could be. That meant my practice of astrology was put on the back burner. Be prepared that you may need to focus on just one thing and do it properly be it astrology, tarot or psychotherapy. Don't try to be superman or superwoman because 'mastery' is what I am talking about here. The mastery of psychology plus the mastery of astrology both require time dedicated to them individually and combined and that takes many years. It certainly helps to have a mentor and I believe that this single factor can cut your apprenticeship period down by half.

A few pointers on the practice of psychotherapy with your clients:

* Some people will come to you for therapy with impossibly high expectations. Don't be put off by this but clearly explain your approach and practice to your clients. Be mindful that we all have limitations and simply can't help everyone.

* Set clear professional boundaries with clients.

* Don't treat family members or friends, refer them to someone you trust.

* Study the ethics of your profession and strictly adhere to them.

* Don't take on clients with a mental illness, these clients will need to be referred on to someone qualified to treat them.

* There are laws and regulations that need to be considered and followed such as the treatment of mental illness. If you advertise that you treat mental illness it will bring the wrath of the state medical and psychology boards down on your head.

* If you want to practice as a psychotherapist then become fully qualified and join your local or state association.

* Take out malpractice insurance and any other form of legal requirement for therapists in your state.

* Talk to other therapists about forming a peer support group that meets regularly, don't try to do this alone, it is not worth it.

* An office that looks professional - you may need to rent a room in someone else's practice. You only get one chance at making a first impression so do it right the first time. Your physical appearance, dress, hair, the furnishings in your waiting and practice room as well as a secretary if you have a busy practice, all count towards gaining word-of-mouth referrals.

* May I suggest that you rent a room from another therapist starting with one or two evenings per week. This is a very common way therapists start their professional practice which can also lead to a pleasant collegial environment for you and the other staff there.

* Don't expect to become famous overnight. I suggest that you give yourself five years of part time practice. This allows you to keep your day job while continuing with your mentoring and studies to gain your qualifications. I did this for nearly 15 years before I opened my full time psychology practice.

* Have enough money in your bank to cover expenses for those five years.

* All you need is a desk and chair, a comfortable client chair (a recliner is ideal), a computer and printer, internet, soft music and minimal outside noise. A quiet and calm environment (the 'therapeutic environment') is what you should aim for.

* Charge a fair fee but also be prepared to have a percentage of free clients (pro bono) which is what I consider a way to pay back to the

universe for all it has done for us. Just be mindful that some people will lie to you about their financial status.

* Do not practice without a mentor and make sure that you fulfil all legal requirements and adopt a professional approach to your work.

* Find a way to debrief from each client and each session. Sometimes things come up that trigger your own issues. Take these to your mentor or if you have one, your own therapist. Learning how to manage stress is critical to your long-term survival as a therapist and will help you become a better practitioner.

* Work on your own psychological issues with your mentor or therapist. This means daily meditation using those processes that work for you.

* Watch your diet, drink plenty of water and get some daily exercise.

* Continue to engage in your social network, they will catch you when you fall.

Chapter 2 - Spiritual lessons in the chart - archetypal personalities

"Astrology is a naively projected psychology in which the different attitudes and temperaments of man are represented as gods and identified with planets and zodiacal constellations.' Carl Jung, Letters Vol. II, Pages 463-464

Finding spirituality in the chart is another area that fascinates me. I have spent a lot of time pondering this question in my practice of astrology, psychology and meditation.

Spirituality is not a single point, it is a synthesis of the entire chart. Fortunately, there are many excellent clues. As a psychotherapist I first look for conflict in the native's chart; and secondly, for any elemental dominance. Conflict illuminates the native's spiritual challenges while their elemental dominance shows me how they approach resolving them. These are your major life or spiritual lessons.

There are other significators I look for which includes a luminary (Sun or Moon) conjunct or opposed by any of the planets or on a house cusp. These conjunctions and oppositions will help you better understand the specific nature of your spiritual lessons.

For instance, someone with Pluto conjunct Sun shows this person has incarnated to find confidence in their Plutonic power. Confidence is their stepping stone to accessing the specific powers of Pluto. Their challenge is to develop and then harness this power to transform their life into something spiritually meaningful. They begin life with insecurity until they come to terms with their fears. By facing these fears they learn to control their environment by controlling themselves.

Pluto conjunct Sun has many other interesting features besides self control. It opens the doorway to power, real power such as astral travel, clairvoyance, flying in dreams, lucid dreaming, healing, kundalini and other psychic abilities. This person's destiny is to learn self control, but they can also access Pluto's special powers along the way. Gaining access to Pluto's power carries enormous responsibility and therefore must be earned through self-discipline and a pure heart. If the Pluto conjunct Sun person has reached this stage they are well on their journey – each day becomes another step on their mystic's quest.

This native incarnated to learn to let go of their fear while engaging with their Plutonic power at a deep psychological level. The unconscious is where Pluto lives, he rules the Underworld of the unconscious. Therefore, most of the native's spiritual lessons can be directed and resolved through specific underworld (unconscious) meditations. They may also seek out a psychotherapist who knows something about astrology, the archetypes and depth psychotherapy.

I next examine the native's Sun sign which adds a special layer to their spiritual quest. If the Sun is in an Earth sign it suggests that this person is learning to divest herself of the security of conformity and sameness. During this process she learns how dynamic change is a valid and freeing form of reality.

If in an Air sign it suggests a need for intellectual transformation as she seeks to gain clarity of thought without distractions. This may be done through social media and other forms of communication like teaching or writing. The Air sign challenge is to stop thinking so as to find clarity in silence.

If in a Fire sign it suggests a need to understand and manage the instinctive urge to dominate others. The challenge for Fire is to transform herself creatively so that she can live a meaningful life. This may be as a teacher, a musician, an actor, writer, leader or some other form of creative expression.

If in a Water sign it suggests that she is learning to understand and control her emotions. The Water Sun native needs to come to terms with betrayal, loneliness and abandonment. She can then empathically convey this sense of inner security to others.

The next layer is the house in which the two luminaries reside. There are 12 houses but I won't go into this now, that's an entire course in itself. You may wish to read my book, *Psychological Astrology And The Twelve Houses'* to learn more about the houses.

Using Henry Ford's chart below I will show you how I use the chart with people who wish to undertake the mystic's quest.

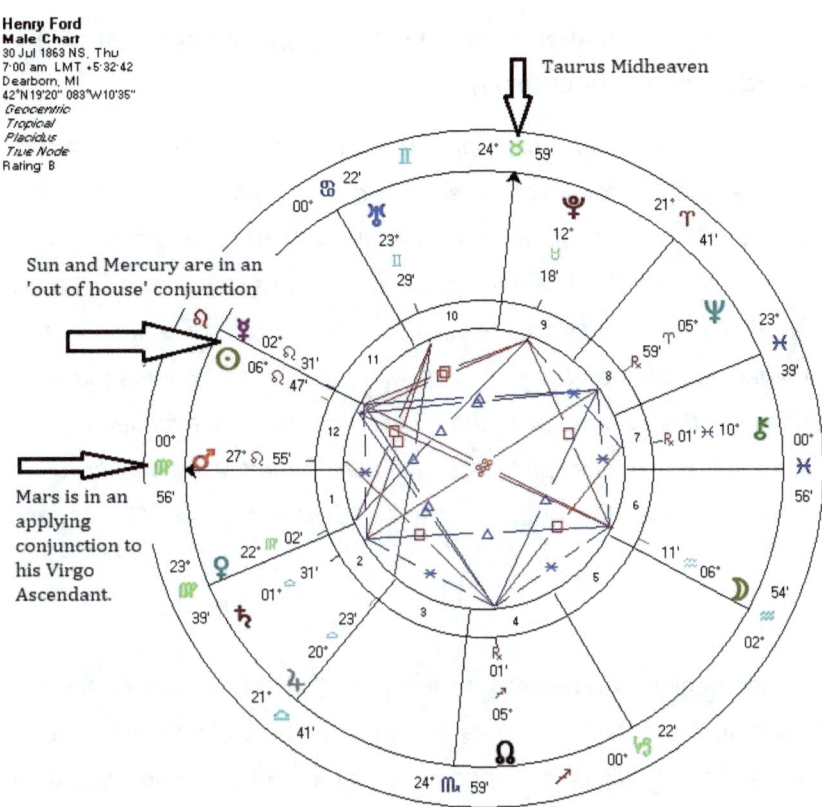

Archetypal personalities - uniting psychology and spirituality in meditation with your archetypes

"*The collective unconscious...appears to consist of mythological motifs or primordial images, for which reason the myths of all nations are its real exponents. In fact the whole of mythology could be taken as a sort of projection of the collective unconscious. We can see this most clearly if we look at the heavenly constellations, whose originally chaotic forms are organised through the projection of images. This explains the influence of the stars as asserted by astrologers. These influences are nothing but unconscious, introspective perceptions of the collective unconscious.*" Carl G. Jung, 'The Structure of the Psyche,' CW 8, par. 325.

Using the conjunction aspects in Henry Ford's chart as an example, imagine his Mercury and Sun as people. Take note of what they are wearing, their shoes, colours and tones, a hat perhaps. They would be standing together, which is what a conjunction means, together. Notice how they relate to each other. Do they engage in conversation or do they stand apart glaring at each other? Is one afraid of the other? In this example, although Mercury is sitting on the cusp of the 12th house I consider him as being part of the 12th house group of planets. Mercury and Sun are in the same house and the sign of Leo, I would generally expect them to be quite comfortable with each other.

Look at Henry Ford's Saturn and Venus conjunction. I would imagine that they are standing further apart. Venus would probably be quite uncomfortable and showing signs of frustration with Saturn. As Venus is in Virgo she may exhibit her Virgoan nature and criticise Saturn's dress or lack of cleanliness. Saturn is in Libra so he may want to state his opinion on Venus' love life or the costume she is wearing. I can imagine that Venus would definitely disapprove of Saturn's interference in her personal life.

I can't imagine Venus and Saturn on friendly terms unless Henry Ford made a conscious effort to look at how he relates with others. One shortcut for Henry Ford is to work with these two archetypes in his meditations.

Each planet and sign in the chart holds specific keys to unlock one or more of the secrets to the native's spiritual lessons. This informs them of the twists and turns in their mystic's quest to enlightenment.

Chapter 3 - Introducing the Air Fire phenomenon, children's disorders, depression and the challenges of adolescence

In this chapter I wanted to include some material on childhood, adolescent and adult mental health. This field is under-represented in astrology books and I hope that the insights I've gained through my practice of psychology and astrology will help fill that gap.

Before I dig deeper into mental health I wanted to mention an approach that you may have already heard of:

"*Psychological symptoms can be transformed when they are "re-visioned" as multi-faceted, human pathways of soul… Rather than simply trying to get rid of a symptom, one should ask, "What does this symptom want to say? Why has it arrived at this time? What kind of life am I leading that it needs this disturbance? What does soul want?" We learn that soul heals by telling itself a better story—a healing fiction that can dissolve the belief system, which keeps the soul locked in misery.'* From a discussion of James Hillmans, 'Re-Visioning Psychology' by Alison Poulsen, PhD, https://www.sowhatireallymeant.com

When I was working in schools I saw a lot of children with ADD (Attention Deficit Disorder - inattention) and ADHD (Attention Deficit Hyperactive Disorder - hyperactive and impulsive). These children had special needs that the education and medical system struggled to manage. No one really understood what caused these disorders, nor did they have a foolproof method to treat them. Behavioural programs work extremely well in most cases but medication has some nasty side-effects.

I developed learning and behavioural programs for teachers to use in the classroom and for parents to use at home, but in the more serious cases it wasn't enough. I wanted to thoroughly understand what caused these disorders so that I could find better treatments.

At that time the only thing that worked with the most serious cases was medication: Ritalin and dexamphetamine. The highly praised omega 3 fish oils only seemed to work with mild cases, just as reducing sugar did. Diet is essential to psychological health but that often meant a complete overhaul of the family's diet and lifestyle. Those who managed to change their diet made significant progress.

These days I recommend a plant-based diet high in anti-oxidants and fibre as the small and large intestines are heavily populated by nerve cells equivalent to a small brain – about the size of a cat's brain. Ninety-five percent of your serotonin, the calming, feel-good neurotransmitter, is produced by your gut bacteria.

A point to note: If you want to help increase the numbers of good bacteria who manufacture these nutrients then change to a diet that limits animal products, particularly dairy, and is high in fibre and natural anti-inflammatories. Foods like: beans, lentils, rice, buckwheat, non-GM corn, oats, potatoes (my favourite) and green vegetables plus lots of fresh raw fruit. Yes, that sounds like a vegan diet to me too. I found it easy to make the change from vegetarian to vegan over the past year and have not regretted it. There are few meals that can beat buckwheat pancakes with mashed banana and lemon juice topped with home-made cashew cream, a brilliant replacement for dairy cream. When I'm extra hungry but want to keep my calories low I have a bowl of oatmeal and dates. This is satisfying, filling and massively high in fibre and nutrients. Buy organic produce if you can.

Like the vast majority of the population most parents don't know enough about nutrition to make sound dietary choices. The volume of Big Food advertising and misinformation confronting parents is criminal. Working with these troubled children I found that no single natural remedy really helped those with the most serious of conditions.

I examined the scientific literature and spoke to professionals in other fields of science and discovered that the cause was neurological. ADD and ADHD were not due to the child's upbringing and it was not caused by psychological trauma. Upbringing and trauma can lead to the child developing an Attachment Disorder which can share symptoms with ADD and ADHD. I will examine the issue of trauma in upcoming books.

In 2001 I discovered a science podcast on neurodevelopmental psychopathological disorders – mental health disorders. It was presented by Professor John Bradshaw from Monash University, Australia on the ABC radio science show.

https://www.abc.net.au/radionational/programs/healthreport/neurodevelopmental-psychopathological-disorders/3478308#transcript

Prof. Bradshaw argued that psychological disorders lay on a neurological spectrum that was very much shaped like a wedge. The narrow end had very few symptoms while the thicker end of the wedge had most of the symptoms. To put it in simple terms, the disorders with fewer symptoms such as shyness and nervousness, lay at the thin end of the wedge;

those disorders with a lot of symptoms like bipolar, OCD and schizophrenia, lay at the thick end.

This podcast really made me think, here were the explanations I was looking for: psychological disorders are of neurological origin. Psychology equals neurology. Sigmund Freud said that one day science would prove that psychopathology had its foundations in neuropathology. What I discovered later in the practice of neurofeedback (biofeedback) confirmed this.

No longer were there questions floating around in my mind, it was quite clear: not only is psychopathology of neurological origin but there are no unique disorders, they are all a mixture of symptoms that appear to clump into groups. For instance, if there are more symptoms of anxiety then that would be called an 'Anxiety' Disorder. As the anxiety symptoms increased in number that disorder could be split off into other disorders like Obsessive Compulsive Disorder (OCD), Panic Disorder, Bipolar and even Tourettes Syndrome and Autism.

To give you a metaphor to work with: imagine a pizza, the slice with the most tomato is called 'Generalised Anxiety'; another piece has more salami and it is called 'Reactive Depression'; another piece has equal amounts of tomato and salami and that gets labelled 'Bipolar Disorder'.

I now saw psychological disorders as neurological which were possibly brought about by the child's genetic inheritance, upbringing and early life experiences. In some cases there was definite exposure to stress and trauma. It seemed that the health of the neurological wiring of the child's brain determined his or her behaviour at school and at home. With this in mind I now needed to find the corresponding astrological constellations and significators in each clinical chart to validate my hypothesis.

I examined the symptoms and charts of hundreds of children, teenagers and adults with such diverse symptoms as learning difficulties, behavioural problems, Autism, Asperger's, Tourettes, ADD and ADHD. I also collected and examined the charts of the diverse forms of psychological disorders that I encountered such as Bipolar, Adjustment Disorder, Major Depression, Generalised Anxiety Disorder and Obsessive Compulsive Disorder.

I discovered that there were specific astrological significators and constellations that suggested the neurological/psychological disorders I had previously considered untreatable.

I call this astrological constellation the 'Air Fire Phenomenon' because it is highlighted by these two elements more than any other significator in the chart. The astrological community had known of the unique qualities of these two elements for some time but what I found took the conversation to another level. To discover that the astrological significators of a psychological disorder could be seen in the chart was mind boggling, even to me.

I will be examining this phenomenon in more detail in my next book, *'Psychological Astrology and the Signs of the Zodiac'*.

A point to note: psychological problems and disorders are not a mystery, the potential for developing these issues can be seen in the chart. A disorder is but one possible expression of one of these constellations – they are NOT the only expression. Not everyone with these constellations and significators develop a psychological disorder. Whether or not a psychological disorder is triggered is determined by many other factors.

I later discovered that psychological disorders could be successfully treated with a non-invasive training program called biofeedback - specifically Neurofeedback. This drug-free training program is frequently called 'brain-training'. It is non-invasive, drug-free, has no side-effects and can potentially provide a cure. I found those who used neurofeedback accompanied by a good diet, nutritional support, a good social network, relaxation and meditation made the fastest recovery. You can read more about neurofeedback and biofeedback in my book, '*Self Hypnosis Tame Your Inner Dragons*'.

A point to note: the Autistic Spectrum is simply that, a spectrum like every other so called 'disorder'. It ranges from extremely severe autism with a complete lack of verbal and non-verbal communication, minimal comprehension and often the result of severe brain damage and physical disability such as co-ordination and movement. This is where I started my teaching career, with these children. The spectrum rises though a range of those physical and cognitive limitations to eventually reach the top of the spectrum becoming 'high functioning autism' which is what we call 'Asperger's Syndrome'. People diagnosed with Asperger's Syndrome have minimal intellectual limits but they do have a narrow focus and a limited range of emotion. They often suffer high anxiety in new situations, lack the ability to reflect and struggle to read social cues. We see some Asperger's Syndrome types in the scientific and mathematical based fields and academia.

Astrological Significators for Depression

Depression is a complex and frequently misunderstood disorder. There are 2 main types of depression: Endogenous Depression which forms part of your personality, melancholia. It is sometimes known as a 'constitutional disorder'. These days it is called a Major Depressive Disorder or Clinical Depression and is characterised by persistent and intense feelings of sadness for extended periods of time. In other words it is episodic, which means it is not constant sadness, it comes and goes.

The other common type is Reactive or Situational Depression. It is formed as a reaction or response to a serious trauma or crisis. Often this is a natural reaction to trauma or witnessing a traumatic event. If symptoms continue beyond what we consider 'normal' it is then labelled a 'disorder'.

Both feature the symptoms of hopelessness, helplessness, sadness, episodes of crying, bereavement, grief and loss, lack of motivation, meaninglessness, amotivation, listlessness and loss of energy.

A point to note: looking at this list, I believe that everyone will experience these symptoms at one or more points in their life. Episodes of depression and anxiety are quite normal because life is darn tough.

Clinical depression is a neurological slowing of the dominant hemisphere of the brain, generally the left side. When you also feel symptoms of restlessness, anxiety and irritability it is no longer just depression but is a mixture of anxiety (hyper or high neurological arousal in the non dominant hemisphere) and depression (hypo or low neurological arousal in the dominant hemisphere).

I find that people with Reactive Depression present for counselling after or during a crisis. Those people who have experienced depression for many years, as in Endogenous Depression, generally require a different approach to those with other forms of depression. They usually present for counselling when urged by their doctor or friends and relatives.

People experiencing an Existential depression, which means they are depressed by the meaninglessness of life, are sometimes in need of spiritual healing. The mystic's quest is often an important component in their healing. This is a fascinating topic that I will examine in a later book.

I find that depressed people have one or more strong significators in their natal charts. In fact all of the powerful outer planets have the potential to signal mental health challenges. The most common significator for depression is Saturn and the outer planets Chiron, Neptune and Pluto conjunct the personal planets and points - Sun, Moon, Mercury, Venus, Mars and Ascendant.

I find that Uranus is quite different. He tends to signify anxiety, worry, restlessness, excess mental ruminations and hyper-vigilance. Uranus winds you up while Saturn, Chiron, Neptune and Pluto can swing your mood both up or down which can be quite disturbing.

I'll mention Jupiter here because he does influence your mood. I have seen Jupiterian symptoms in ADD and ADHD, the Air Fire Phenomenon highlights Jupiter's effects. In terms of mental health Jupiter isn't really a depressive, he winds people up with enthusiasm, excitement, delusions of grandeur and extreme gregariousness. When their dreams and delusions aren't realised the native can swing into depression, but generally it isn't for long. I consider Jupiter to be more commonly associated with narcissism more so than depression or anxiety.

A point to note: if you have a dominant Jupiter it is important that you recognise that there are many positive ways that he can manifest in your life.

I will add here that sometimes a dominance of trines can increase the native's sensitivity to stress. It can trigger episodes of depression and anxiety when things become tense. In my experience squares don't seem to contribute all that much to developing depression. In fact squares appear to be protective in most instances.

A good example is a Grand Cross. It is a complex pattern which shows that the native may experience depression but they have such strong barriers that they don't notice it. These people simply put their head down and keep walking into the heavy downpour that life dumps on them. If you ask them whether they feel depressed they will say, *"No, should I be?"* But when you examine their life it is filled with situations that would make you cry. They, however, just put their head back down and keep going.

Strong Earth charts can be quite emotionally inhibited. This may be eased if they also have a strong Fire element which tends to lift their mood a little better than the other three. For example, I will sometimes see depression with Capricorn Moon people, though they don't recognise they have depression. Life for them has always been tough so feeling down is quite normal for them. The Moon in Taurus and Virgo doesn't seem to contribute to feeling low and depressed but rather they seem to add emotional stability.

I have noticed that some Capricorn Moon people favour listening to emotionally evocative music. This is probably therapeutic, perhaps it is how they connect and heal their bruised and buried emotions. Venus in

Capricorn can sometimes experience depression as well because it impacts the native's social and love life. On the other hand Moon and Venus in Capricorn can be a positive experience. It can add stability and structure to the native's social, love and family life which allows them to limit any feelings of negativity.

A point to note: psychologically aware astrologers will always consider the chart as a whole. They won't rely on a single planet or point until there are other factors to support their hypothesis. Please don't be upset if you find that what I have written here describes your chart. My experiences working in the mental health field means I see a lot of wounded people. These are the people that present for counselling, tarot and astrology readings, they form the basis of what I am relating to you in this chapter. If you have a Capricorn Moon it does not mean that you are going to be depressed. Please read on and you will see that every sign and element has its mental health weaknesses and strengths.

The Air signs generally struggle to understand emotions so they rarely present for counselling for depression. They are good at ignoring their feelings so they don't feel anything. They can detach so effectively that people might consider them cold and uncaring. Even when sympathising with someone's problem they do it in a very cerebral way. They can listen and suggest practical advice, but you won't catch them crying in sympathy. They don't even cry for themselves. What they do experience is anxiety, neurological over-arousal, they worry excessively, and that is when they present for counselling. They will say, *"I can't talk to you now, I'm too stressed."*

The Water dominated person experiences depression in a unique way. They get depressed when someone lets them down, betrays and abandons them. Their form of depression is loneliness, they feel grief and loss very strongly. They will say, *"Why doesn't anyone call or visit me?"*

Even though I have stated that people with a strong Earth element are prone to depression I'd like to add that the same goes for those dominated by the Fire element. Fire signs need to be seen, to be noticed, praised and their efforts recognised. They need all the attention they can get because when they feel neglected they feel depressed. A depressed Fire sign is far more miserable than any Air, Water or Earth sign. The Fire element rules the drama queen... need I say any more? The depressed Fire sign will say, *"But what about me?"*

While the distressed Air type drinks to manage their racing mind, the Water signs drink to feel less alone. Their friend is their bottle. The Fire signs drink to get drunk so they can manage their sense of neglect, perhaps someone will laugh when they fall over? This is an example of how the drama queen emerges in their need for attention. The Earth signs drink because it makes them feel numb and numb is a comfortable feeling.

One of the most common astrological triggers for people to seek counselling, astrology and tarot readings is when Saturn transits their natal Ascendant, Sun or Moon. The same may be seen with transits of Neptune, Pluto and Chiron - they each bring their own particular type of depression.

A serious look at mental health in adolescence

I have included this section to help build a bit of a picture for my readers: teenagers, parents, grandparents, astrologers and therapists. A background in mental health isn't necessary but this information may help you in your practice of astrology and/or psychotherapy.

Adolescence is sometimes described as a roller-coaster ride of hormone driven mood swings, poor life choices and rebellion. Muscle bulk and tone, fat and skeletal structures, body parts, hair and skin all make a dramatic transformation from child to adult in these few years of puberty.

Children as young as 8 years of age are now entering puberty where as traditionally the average was around 16 years. It is suggested that the consumption of factory farmed animal products containing naturally occurring growth hormones (such as IGF1), antibiotics and introduced growth hormones (like rBGH in dairy cows) as well as man-made chemicals such as plastics (particularly BPA) has pushed puberty to occur at such an early age.

An adolescent must contend with changes in their attitudes, values and beliefs as their brain shifts from basic survival to a steady myelination of the frontal lobes. Myelination is the hardwiring of the nerves which have basically lain dormant since birth, much like a new house is internally wired but has yet to be connected to the power pole.

The myelination process allows the young adult to make decisions based on conscious and deliberate consideration of every option available to them. With the myelination of the frontal lobes the adolescent can consider the impact of their decisions on others, the environment, future consequences and reflecting on what had happened in the past. Their thoughts are more structured and there is a growing ability towards strategic planning. In other words the Executive Functions, primarily based in the frontal lobes, are finally wired into the brain. Unfortunately the myelination process does not seem to help the teenager clean up their bedroom.

With puberty's tsunami of hormones the adolescent becomes interested in sex and love. The physical urge for sexual union becomes painful, but it is the emotional urge for union, the 'soul mate' thing we feel, which pushes the adolescent beyond reason. Not only do they have to contend with issues of sexuality and love they are also at the critical stage of 'identity formation'.

With the arrival of puberty the well ordered family is only one argument away from fracturing. All too often this is the result of tantrums, dominance issues and outright rebellion.

I sometimes think of puberty as a sailing ship caught in a violent storm. Each massive wave and savage wind blast pushes it closer to the rocky cliffs which represents their family, school, social and sports groups, and other authority figures. The adolescent usually tries to escape the controlling clutches of these institutions by rebelling against them.

Some adolescents manage their family's expectations and sail between the rocks unscathed. Some gain a sense of identity and freedom through rebellion. Those who fail to adapt or escape can become broken souls. Sadly, in this struggle for control, many parents feel as though they are the losers.

How do we deal with this rebellious adolescent storm? Traditionally tribal mentors adhered to a prescribed 'rites of passage' to initiate the child into adulthood. In the western world we had Boy Scouts and Girl Guides, sports clubs, church and school also played a major role. Our adolescents of today don't have these time-honoured and tested signposts to lead them to a mature and secure adult life.

Our challenge, or barrier, to our children's transition into adulthood is 'time'. With mum and dad at work trying to make ends meet they simply aren't home to monitor their children. The uncle, aunt and grandparent mentors of yesterday-year are also too busy trying to survive to assist. Today's adolescents have had to turn elsewhere for their rites of passage. Their initiation into the adult world is now through drugs, alcohol, sexual promiscuity and dangerous behaviour. Their mentors are TV celebrities and sports heroes who are as lost as the adolescents who worship them.

I hope that the following is of some assistance when counselling your adolescent clients and their parents.

The most critical time for a mental health crisis is generally from 15 to 21 years of age. Psychologists and medical professionals tend to avoid diagnosing depression in younger people because it is so very difficult. Psychologists would find it much easier to help their adolescent patients if they had the aid of an astrology chart. I will examine the Air Fire phenomenon and mental health, particularly in the adolescent years, at length in my next book.

Males tend to be at risk of early death because they undertake dangerous acts like driving cars too fast and when drunk; use drugs and alcohol to excess then go swimming or diving off bridges. Males also avoid seeking help because of the traditional masculine model which they are taught to adhere to from birth. Traditional males are programmed not to seek help, not to admit they are incompetent at a task and not to tell anyone what is really happening inside them. To speak out publicly is to ask for ridicule and humiliation so they don't, to admit incompetence is shameful.

Girls generally don't ask for help either, at least not from their parents. They do, however, talk to their friends, a school counsellor or a favourite teacher. This is where grandparents can be helpful. They generally have time to listen and understand. They can be open with their grandchildren about their own issues and how they overcame them when they were that age.

This story helps illustrate just how wise grandparents can contribute to our teenagers in crisis:

A grandfather spoke to his grandson who came to him with anger at a schoolmate who had done him an injustice.

"Let me tell you a story. I too have felt a great hate for those that have taken so much with no sorrow for what they do. But hate wears you down and does not hurt your enemy. It is like taking poison and wishing your enemy would die. I have struggled with these feelings many times."

He continued, "It is as if there are two wolves inside me; one is good and does no harm. He lives in harmony with all around him and does not take offense when no offense was intended. He will only fight when it is right to do so and in the right way. But the other wolf, ah! He is full of anger. The littlest thing will set him into a fit of temper. He fights everyone, all the time, for no reason. He cannot think because his anger and hate are so great. It is helpless anger for his anger will change nothing.

"Sometimes it is hard to live with these two wolves inside me, for both of them try to dominate my spirit."

The boy looked intently into his grandfather's eyes and asked, "Which one wins, Grandfather?"

His grandfather smiled and said, "The one I feed, son, the one I feed."

~ Author Unknown, sometimes attributed to Native American mythology (Lenape or the Cherokee) ~

Sadly, many of today's grandparents are too poor to have time to spare. Without an adequate pension or some form of income our culture's family unit is a poor reflection of what it was a few generations ago. Most elderly people are living on the edge of poverty working until they are no longer able. Grandparents are generally palmed off to nursing homes or live alone in a unit or shelter far from their children and grandchildren.

I worked for a year in a juvenile justice prison (adolescent males and females). I undertook a study of psychopathology in the juvenile justice setting as a research project.

This is a summary of what I found: "*Of the residents with identified mental health illnesses some have several diagnosis. It is common for a resident with ADHD to be co-morbid with depression, conduct disorder or bipolar disorder. One resident reported that he had a diagnosis of ADHD, Bipolar and Oppositional Defiant Disorder. A snapshot of the resident population: 20% are on the child and adolescent psychologist's caseload, 50% have a parent with substance abuse, 90% report having regularly used drugs and / or alcohol, 20% are at risk of significant psychological illness, 20% have a parent with a diagnosed mental illness, 30% report sexual assault, 20% have a parent with a criminal record and 5% are diagnosed with Fetal Alcohol Syndrome.*"

A point to note: it is quite rare for an adolescent to be brought before a judge or magistrate and sentenced, even in Australia. The situation cited above is for the most serious cases who continued to re offend, sometimes up to 30 times before they were sentenced. The most common offence was related to car theft and being a passenger in a stolen car. Once they were caught they were given conditions of bail. Those who breached their bail conditions, and most of them did, were eventually sentenced to serve time in juvenile prison.

Back to the general population, Australian studies estimate that almost 20% of children and adolescents meet the criteria for a clinical diagnosis of a mental illness. More boys (20%) than girls (15%) were identified as having mental health problems. These young people are at an increased risk of drug and alcohol abuse. Children and adolescents with mental health problems experience depression, anxiety, first onset psychosis, self harm and suicidal behaviour, eating disorders, disruptive and dangerous behaviours. They are six times more likely to have suicidal thoughts and three times more likely to abuse drugs and alcohol than their peers.

The suicide rate in male adolescents is higher than their female counterparts. Males accounted for just under four times the female suicide rate. They also make up 19% of all male suicides and 15% of the total suicide population.

If you wish to look up the US CDC statistics please visit:
https://www.cdc.gov/childrensmentalhealth/data.html

It is argued that high unemployment rates increase adolescent male suicide risks. Changes in the labour market create fewer options in life for unemployed young males than those with paid work. Men have been traditionally socialised to earn money, gain power and attend to their family's needs, just as women are traditionally expected to raise children.

Adolescent males identifying with the traditional male role may be more inclined to measure their manliness by their employment status. If they remain unemployed they are at a higher risk of becoming depressed leading to thoughts of suicide.

The modern female adolescent tends to develop their identity by conforming to what their friendship group considers important. Conformity equates acceptance. It is important for the young person to belong to a friendship group, to wear the right clothes, hair style and having the same interests. Young girls are also caught up in the heavily promoted traditional expectation that 'slim and attractive' is equated with social acceptance. Seeking peer and social acceptance through physical beauty may lead to other mental health issues.

The pressure on young people of both sexes to conform to their peer group or cultural expectations and standards can be overwhelming. No longer do our children have role models in their home. Young boys no longer go to work on the farm or hunting with their father, uncles, grandfathers and cousins. No longer do young girls learn how to cook and care for the family from mom, aunts and grandmothers in the communal kitchen and homestead. The mentoring and bonding between young people and their elders has all but disappeared in our modern world.

Our children no longer have elders as mentors to look up to, they now worship media heroes. Unfortunately many of these heroes are, like adult children, blindly seeking their own identity. Humans are voyeurs, we like to watch how others live their lives so that we can determine how we should live ours. Big Brother and other reality shows have become our children's mentors. Is it any wonder that we have a mental health crisis on our hands?

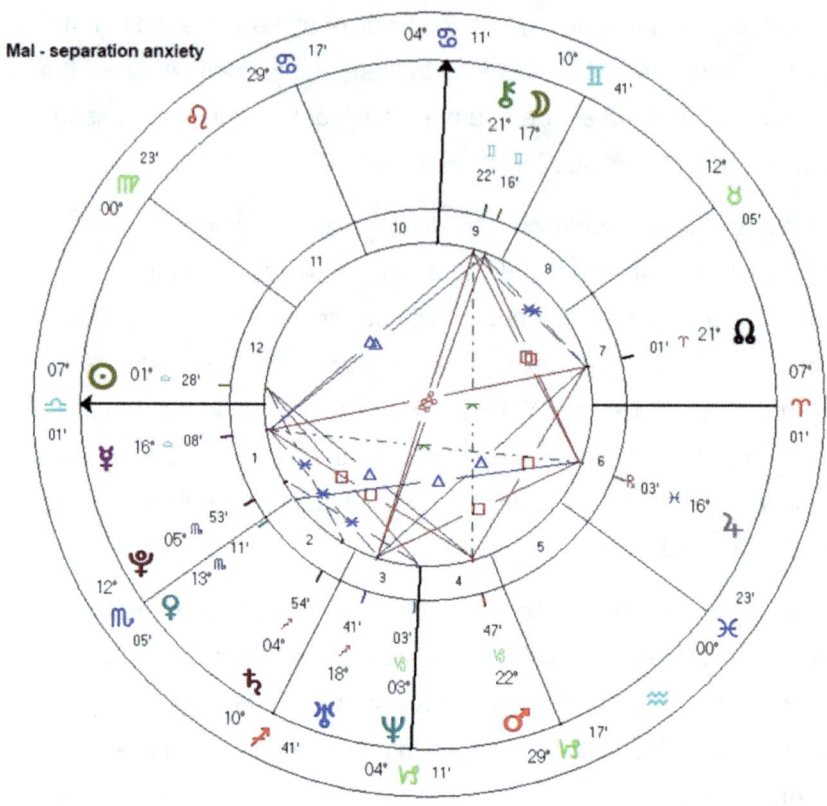

Case study of teenage depression - Mal

Mal was a teenage boy I once worked with who had a diagnosis of Depression, Separation Anxiety and Attachment Disorder. Refusing to attend school and very able to manipulate his mother, he successfully hid from the truant officers each time they pulled into the driveway to take him to school. Instead of attending class he played computer games at home all day long. This started when he was about 13 years of age, which is the start of high school.

If we examine the research material on Separation Anxiety, Depression, Attachment Disorder and School Refusal we see quite a few common symptoms. These disorders are more common in males than females; one parent families; one parent families where the parent is the mother; single child families in which that child is male; families where the mother suffers from a high level of anxiety or agoraphobia—fear of public places; and it is more common when the parent places a low priority on education.

In some situations the child bullies and manipulates the single parent to stay at home. Mother bashing by teenage boys and girls is a growing concern in the western world. It appears that the single mother unconsciously treats her child as a surrogate partner or friend. This is a form of projection in which the child takes on the responsibility for the mother's happiness by attending to their emotional needs. Often, as the father is absent, the child can develop an attitude and belief of entitlement. When the child grows older and stronger they find that they can manipulate their mother by yelling at her and threatening her with physical violence. Mother is basically empowering her child while disempowering herself generally because she is isolated, lonely or has emotional needs of her own.

Unfortunately the situation described above is not confined to boy children, girls are becoming increasingly violent towards their siblings and parents Single mothers are particularly vulnerable to bullying from their children especially when they only have the one child. Single mothers with a single child is the most common situation of parent bullying that I have seen in my counseling room.

A point to note: please don't think that this phenomenon is isolated to mothers and male children, it is quite common for males to bully and bash their fathers too. I have also seen situations where girls bully and assault both their mothers and their fathers. Bashed fathers rarely seek help from police or welfare providers like counselors and psychologists. The statistics cannot measure and reflect what they don't have hard data for.

Parents who don't know how to parent are quite common particularly among those who have experienced poor parenting from their own parents. Problems arise in families when parents are 'overly permissive'. This means that they are sensitive and vulnerable and thus unable to set firm, sensible boundaries and limits on their children's behaviour. They give so much love and attention to their child that the boundaries between child and adult are blurred and the child, with so little maturity, easily exerts dominance over the parents.

I might mention two main complexes here: the Oedipal and Electra complexes. The Oedipal Complex describes how the male child sides with the mother to disempower the father. The Electra Complex basically describes how the girl child sides with the father to disempower the mother.

When two family members oppose one other member within the family it creates enormous tension and dysfunction. Sadly it can happen in any family and is quite common between one parent and a selected child whereby they dominate and humiliate the other parent. In fact it is common to see two members of a family unite to disempower a third, the 'targeted person' or the victim. If this becomes an established pattern then I would suggest the targeted family member seek counseling as it can really destroy a family and all three individuals involved.

To sum up, childhood depression and anxiety is commonly linked to an emotionally needy, single parent with a single child. This can lead to a collusion between the parent and child to avoid attending school or other situations that the child wants to avoid. In some cases the single parent keeps the child at home to comfort him or her because they are lonely. Strategies for avoiding stressful situations may be learned by watching how others do it – like their parent. It can also be genetic. In some cases of depression, separation anxiety and attachment issues the relationship between the parent and only child could be described as 'co-dependent'.

Delineating Mal's chart

· **Focus on Air**—as we know people with a lot of Air have difficulty coming down to earth to get into their emotions, their feelings, they can live in their head. Mal has Libra Ascendant, Sun in Libra, Moon in Gemini (in 9th house) and Mercury in the 1st house—all point to a loaded Air chart.

· **Out of touch with his feelings & manipulation of mother**— Moon is in the Air sign Gemini and is conjunct Chiron, the 'wounded healer'. Here we see that Mal is wounded by his mother, he argues with her and possibly dominates her physically, intellectually as well as emotionally.

This conjunction suggests that his mother is wounded herself (which she is), so she would probably have permitted Mal to stay home from school to care for her own needs. She is a single mother, lonely and in psychological pain so having her only son at home satisfies her emotional comfort needs. The conjunction between Chiron and Moon suggests that Mal is well on his way to developing serious depression issues.

· **Mal's Sun is in the 12th house conjunct the Ascendant** - Mal is afraid of going out, of being exposed, he hides in the 12th house. This is also seen with North Node (social security—feeling safe with others) in the 7th house of 'other people'. He therefore may be afraid of going out in public and may signify symptoms of agoraphobia. This also shows North Node opposite Mercury suggesting difficulty communicating with others. Mercury in the 1st house shows a need to communicate, but it is poorly aspected and part of a T-Square with North Node and Mars. It suggests that he argues and perhaps, given the Moon Chiron conjunction, he also yells and screams at his mother. He sacrifices his Mars needs to express by staying away from situations where he has to assert himself, like school. He instead uses his Mars against his mother. Sun in the 12th house also indicates an 'absent father' which would indicate that he relies on his mother for security.

· **Neptune is conjunct the 4th cusp applying from the 3rd house** – this is an applying aspect and therefore powerful. This shows us a fear of abandonment and because Neptune rules the 6th house he is unable to apply his sense of responsibility. Instead of service to others he demands that they (mother) serve him.

· **Pluto is conjunct the 2nd cusp and Venus** - personal security and friendship is another issue that he is confronted with.

What also can be seen in this chart is Mal's strong intellect which he uses to manage his insecurity through yelling and dominating his emotionally vulnerable mother. Overall Mal has significators that indicate depression arising from insecurity. He has learned that he can use his intellect and physical size to manipulate the situation as the only male child to his single mother. Interestingly his father (represented by the Sun) is not poorly aspected, being in the 12th house it shows that Dad is not present, and that Mal probably has an idealised image of an 'ideal father'. Unfortunately I cannot discuss his father as I have not met him nor do I know anything of the mother's relationship with him.

Summary of teenage depression and separation anxiety

In the many children and teenagers charts that I have studied there are some commonalities I can share with you. The Fire and Air elements are dominant; there is a poorly presented Moon; and a strong 12th house; in many charts Pluto is either conjunct or opposite the Moon. Their charts show links to the scientific research: Moon represents emotional and mother issues; anxiety is represented by the 12th house of avoidance; there are symptoms of ADD and ADHD; and in some cases the child is verbally violent towards the mother.

What I would have expected in astrological terms was a strong Water chart, but what we see in Mal's chart is a strong Fire (1st house is strong with Mercury, Pluto and Venus) and a disconnect between intellect and emotions from his strong Air element (Libra Ascendant, Sun and Mercury in Libra, Moon and Chiron in Air and Mercury in the 1st house). Mal's Water element is signaled by Sun in the 12th house, Chiron conjunct his Moon, Neptune conjunct his 4th house cusp and Pluto in the 1st house conjunct Venus.

In summary we might expect to see strong Fire and Air elements, a conflicted Moon (sometimes with Pluto) and a conflicted 12th house. There is also some significance with a strong 1st house. The Water element is definitely there and is frequently quite conflicted.

A point to note: these significators are strong indicators of depression even though many disorders are labeled as 'anxiety'. That is the problem with psychological labels: they rarely accurately explain the cause or the symptoms.

Overall summary of adolescent mental health

- Adolescents undergo massive physical and emotional transformation during puberty, they seek to develop a new identity that evolves from their childhood. Developing a strong identity in the teenage years is essential for survival in the adult world.
- It is important that teenagers are supported to make this transition to become a mature, functioning member of our community. Sadly, most people never achieve that level of maturity. These failed youths weigh heavily on the rest of the community who eventually are needed to support them.
- A psychologically oriented astrologer seeks to understand their client's inner child needs. This allows you to describe their needs in your readings and suggest a suitable therapeutic approach which can lead your client to inner healing and spiritual awakening.
- Having your adolescent's chart analysed by a professional astrologer may help them prepare for possible mental health challenges in the future.

- Medical assistance can be useful in many cases but sadly the symptoms of anxiety and depression require more than medication. If you wish to explore this option please do your research and get a recommendation to see someone who really knows what they are talking about. An experienced psychotherapist trained in neurofeedback and nutrition is a good place to start.
- If you are a therapist, an awareness of teenage depression combined with your studies in psychological astrology will certainly help you assist your clients.
- Astrologically, when I see the Ascendant, Sun, Moon, Mercury, Venus or Mars conjunct or opposite any of the outer planets I am drawn to it as a possible source of conflict. This is quite common so please don't think that makes you or your teenager psychologically conflicted. There are so many other factors that need to be considered before coming to any conclusions. If in doubt contact your mentor or teacher and discuss the chart before you say anything. Astrologers see countless clients who are happily expressing the positive aspects of such a constellation so please be mindful that conflict is only one possible expression.

A point to note: if you consider the symptoms of anxiety and depression as opportunities for spiritual growth then you have shifted your thinking beyond the currently orthodox medical model to a metaphysical one. Every symptom of psychic pain is an opportunity for spiritual growth. Many people have made the giant leap into a more satisfying spiritual and physical lifestyle by escaping the clutches of Big Pharma. I will be exploring these options in my book, '*Psychological Astrology, Jung and the Mystic's Quest*'.

To conclude this chapter I would like to tell you a story to illustrate why it is important for us as professionals to be mindful of the power we hold.

A child was walking along the beach early one morning and noticed that the tide had gone out leaving thousands of starfish stranded on the sand. Being mindful that she was the only person on the beach the child picked the starfish up one by one and began throwing them into the water.

After a short while a young man and his girlfriend came by and called out: "what's the point of throwing the starfish into the water, you'll never save them all."

The child looked at the two adults as she lifted another starfish in her hand and called to them over her shoulder: "It makes a difference to this one."

Chapter 4 - The Saturn Cycle and psychological development

One way to understand the psychological and developmental issues faced by your client is to take note of the clearly marked signposts of the 'Saturn Cycle'.

Have you heard of the '*7 year itch*'? It is considered a time when lovers become restless and look outside of their relationship for better options. Astrologers believe that every 7 years you experience some sort of personal crisis or find yourself at a crossroads wondering where to go next. This is an opportunity to make significant changes that will improve your life.

Saturn takes 29.4 years to make a complete orbit of the sun. Astrologically that means every 7 and a bit years he forms an important aspect to his natal position in your chart. At the first 7 year point he forms a separating square (90°); at 14 years he forms an opposition (180°); at 21 years he forms an applying square (90°) and at between 28 and 30 years he forms a conjunction (0°) with his natal position. This both ends the cycle and starts a new one.

The aspect Saturn forms at each 7 year milestone is a hard or challenging aspect. This provides you with the opportunity to examine your life and try to structure it in a more functional way.

When Saturn returns to his natal position in your chart at 28-30 years of age it is called the 'Saturn Return'. This can be one of the most pivotal periods of your life. It is a time when things seem to get out of control requiring a serious examination of your life and how you are living it.

Most astrologers would agree that the Saturn cycle is the most significant cycle of them all. Yes, there are lots of important planetary cycles in astrology. For instance, Jupiter has a 12 year cycle which impacts some people very strongly; then there is the North Node cycle that I have seen have a major impact too; another is Uranus which creates an opposition to its natal position at around 40 years of age known as the 'mid-life crisis'. Because the horoscope is a circle everything is cyclic. You might want to pick a planet or a point in your chart and follow it to see how it impacts your life.

The Saturn Cycle provides the opportunity to convert an emotional crisis into insight and transformation. Importantly for us these ingredients form the cornerstone of personal growth. Unfortunately very few psychologists understand this simple fact. This is why we value such amazing people as Carl Jung, Michel Gauquelin, Isaac Newton and Liz Greene, professionals who had the courage to stand up and share their knowledge despite the massive backlash from their professions.

Saturn's tribal pathway through the lens of evolutionary psychology

To help you understand the Saturn Cycle I'd like to take you back in time to look at the gender roles, identity formation and the life progression of our ancient tribal ancestors. You can do that by looking at the fossil records but that can only tell you part of the story. Another way is to examine current hunter-gatherer tribal cultures that still resemble how life was lived prior to the modern era.

In a traditional tribal setting the infant boy and girl, from birth to around 7 years of age, were encouraged to play. This was their time to learn about themselves, their environment and their place in the tribe. As they grew older they would begin to mimic their same-sex elders. Each member of the tribe was responsible to help raise the children. With such high child mortality rates among all native cultures it was a rare individual who didn't relish spending time with their precious children.

Our ancestors were nomadic hunter-gatherers, they lived with the constant threat of famine, starvation, predation by wild beasts and attacks from other tribes. As one tribal area was hunted out and the available tubers, fruits and vegetables were consumed, the tribal elders would determine when to move onto the next hunting ground.

Community and unity was precious as it still is today but many westerners simply don't realise nor value it. Each tribal member was responsible to ensure that their children were kept away from the fire, didn't play with poisonous snakes and scorpions, and especially to be kept well away from water holes, rivers and any expanse of water. The safety of their children was paramount as this ensured the future security of the tribe. The more babies they had the more workers, hunters, gatherers, mothers and warriors for the tribe's ongoing survival. However, there were constraints on how many children a nomadic tribe could support. In times of famine the tribe recognised that if their infants, elderly and injured couldn't keep up then they would all perish. Infanticide and euthanasia was considered a way of life in times of hardship.

The typical nomadic family was small, only what could be carried by the women was carried from camp to camp. The men would only carry their weapons. This allowed the men to remain unencumbered so as to kill game and ward off enemies. A warrior who carried a baby on one hip and the family grinding stone in his free hand left his family, and thus the tribe, undefended and vulnerable to attack.

Women could only carry one baby in arms at a time. Any other small infants would either be carried by another tribal member (usually an aunt or big sister) or they walked by themselves. Anyone who couldn't keep up was left behind. This meant that women would wait until their youngest child could walk long distances without having to be carried before falling pregnant. The other limiting factor on family size was the availability of food.

It must be remembered that there were no shops or stores fifty thousand years ago. If you didn't hunt or gather food every day you died and so did your family. Security of food and protection from predators and enemy warriors was always the tribe's top priority. A family group is most vulnerable when leaving one food area and walking to another, often several days away.

To ensure the tribe's ongoing survival certain rituals, rites of passage and cultural rules were established. This is where the Saturn Cycle can help us better understand how astrology and human evolutionary behaviour come together.

From 7 years to 14 years the child was expected to help their elders with the basics of daily life: collecting firewood and tending the fire; carrying belongings when on walkabout; and assisting the women to gather food. This was also a time when they observed and assimilated their tribe's customs, social norms and gender roles.

Young boys would be responsible for securing resin, animal tendons, bark string and sand for the warriors and old men which was needed to repair and sharpen their tools and weapons. The young girls would tend their mother, aunts and grandmothers in preparing the food that required threshing, beating, grinding, washing and soaking. They brought water to the kitchen area, helped make flat bread and cook the roots and other vegetables. Tending to their family needs was strictly a gendered role.

Each boy or girl was mentored by an uncle or aunt on their journey to become a valued member of their community. Anyone who failed to conform to their role could jeopardise the safety of others. Boys who let the cooking fire go out, for example, would be punished for neglecting their duty thus jeopardising the welfare of their family and therefore the tribe.

A girl that failed to watch the babies while the women were gathering lilies in the lake was also a threat to the tribe's future. A lost baby was one less provider, one less warrior or one less hunter.

At around 14 years of age the boy child transitioned from childhood to manhood through ritual and initiation. His manhood ceremonies reinforced his role as a warrior, a hunter, a provider and protector of the tribe. A girl child would hand her dolls to her sister or cousin on the day of her first menstruation and prepare for initiation into the sacred rites of womanhood.

The young warrior would generally spend the next few years living apart from the tribe in special locations to learn 'secret men's business'. Young women were generally married off to their promised husband while still undertaking 'secret women's business' in special ceremonies led by the older women.

When the warrior or woman reached the age of 21 years they had other responsibilities that came with their growing maturity. They were expected to provide for the tribe as a fully initiated adult, no longer as a child or novice. The boys were now men, the girls were now women. They had the responsibility of producing and raising children for the tribe. Their roles may diversify, for instance as healer, shaman, dancer, spear-maker, basket weaver, or any other role the individual excelled at.

As the man or woman matured they would take on further roles such as mentor to the youngsters. Uncles were generally responsible for mentoring their nephews while aunties took on the role of mentoring their nieces. This is a time honoured tradition that continues in many cultures today.

At their Saturn Return at around 28-30 years of age these adult men and women were expected to actively contribute to their tribe's safe continuity. They had now reached full maturity and were in positions of responsibility. As fully initiated adults they were responsible for making important decisions that affected the whole tribe.

Each adult helped maintain the tribal culture through ceremony and stories of the tribe's history. The passing down of knowledge through myths and legends ensured tribal unity and continuity. It taught such values as loyalty, honour and respect for specific behaviours, beliefs and laws. A tribe united in a common bond was a tribe that survived the hardships of famine, warfare, threats from wild animals and disharmony within the tribe itself.

Most of this bonding was done around the campfire. Here they would sit of an afternoon or evening sharing gossip while preparing food, repairing their tools, broken baskets and weapons. Stories of the days hunting and gathering were told amid laughter and jokes. This helped build unity and trust while reinforcing the individual's role in the community.

When the night grew cold and the tribe gathered around the fire it was time for their myths and legends. Again this was an opportunity to build and reinforce the qualities and traits necessary for the tribe's survival. Sometimes everyone gathered around a communal campfire while the master story-teller told his stories. This was often accompanied by the tapping of sticks, the singing of songs and the dancing and pantomime of the actors - it was corroboree time.

In summary, Saturn is the teacher of tradition and the role that each of us must play in order to protect and perpetuate our culture. You will have noted that Saturn's keywords are tradition, culture, continuity, structure and conformity.

Saturn's personal psychology pathway

Within the safe space of their mother's womb the human foetus experiences almost everything that the mother does: her anxieties, her joys and her sadness. The unborn child remains quite unconscious to these experiences until around 5 months of gestation. At this time the unborn baby starts to encode his or her experiences in the womb. This remains quite limited as their nervous system has not developed enough to do more than very basic encoding.

At the moment of birth the baby is thrust from the security and warmth of the womb to enter what is usually a cold and sterile hospital ward. This sudden introduction to the outside world can be quite a shock. We know that first impressions are important in forming beliefs and in this case the baby learns what to expect from life by their entry into the world.

A traumatic birth may lead to an expectation that life is about hardship and pain, as opposed to an easy birth and an expectation that life is safe and comfortable. This first impression is powerful and can impact in specific ways on how the native will live their life.

At 7 years of age transiting Saturn forms a separating square to its natal position - the child begins to awaken in consciousness. No longer needing mother's warmth and security the child begins to explore the world beyond mother's apron strings. At this age the child seeks to experience their father's world. The square aspect formed by Saturn to its natal position at this age shows a desire for independence. This is noticed especially at school where children are allowed to enter junior primary sports competitions and to travel more independently. Expectations are higher and they begin to work with less supervision.

At 14 years of age transiting Saturn has moved further and now forms an opposition to its natal position. The child wishes to know even more about the world beyond home and family. Now that they have been exposed to the world of adults the adolescent wants to experience the world of the teenager. The adolescent enters puberty and begins to experience massive surges of sex hormones that, in some cases, scream for some sort of release and expression.

It is said that children up to the age of 14 years require nurturing and containment. The child has an initial need to be and to feel safe. It is during these first 14 years that they are taught the rules and limitations of being in a community of others. They have yet to fully develop emotional maturity and self control which comes with the myelination of the nerves in the Frontal Lobes which begins at around 12 years of age.

The opposition aspect is a sign of rebellion that is commonly seen in teenagers. To put it in simple terms the opposition leads to conflict or what we call 'oppositional' behaviour. The native lashes out against those that stand in their way screaming, *"Don't oppose me, get out of my way!"*

From age 14 to 21 years the adolescent begins the slow and often painful process of separating from their parents which will eventually lead to their raising a family of their own.

The adolescent now seeks to understand themselves as an individual outside the confines of their family. This stage is called 'identity formation' by Erik Erikson in his theory of the stages of psychosocial development. To parents it seems that their adolescent child pays more attention to their friends than from their own family. It is a time when their need to belong and be accepted by their peer group is stronger than those same needs from their parents and family. Adolescents who cope well with this stage of development are already emotionally secure individuals and will get by in life with little support. Those that struggle as teenagers often have security needs that may require support from family, friends and their community. Today this could be from membership of a church or community youth group or the school counsellor.

In our western education system where students are placed in classes according to age, those students who are younger than their peer group (often up to 12 months younger) may need more support. Being older than your peer group gives you a distinct advantage by having greater life experience, emotional maturity, size and strength. Younger, smaller and weaker youths struggle to compete with their older, more experienced and sexually mature peers.

At 21 years of age transiting Saturn forms an applying square to its natal position. This is when the adolescent begins to accept the fact that life is no longer the Garden of Eden they enjoyed as an infant and hoped for as an adolescent. It is a time when they learn to accept responsibility for their actions; a time to engage fully in their employment; and to start their own family.

This final 7 year stage is often difficult as the Saturn cycle is not quite complete. Often the 21 year old holds on to expectations that the world will continue to provide for them.

As parents we want our children safe and happy but we also want them to be independent. With the way things are in the world today this isn't always possible. Adult children often live at home with their ageing parents, playing video games and on social media. They often fail to contribute to the family well being and become a financial drain on the families' scant resources. This causes friction between parents and their adult child. Without the traditional rites-of-passage discussed in this chapter the modern world is fated to raise generations of adolescent adults who never grow up.

At around 28-30 years of age transiting Saturn has completed its cycle around your chart and has returned to its natal position. This is called the Saturn Return, a very significant astrological event. The individual is now faced with reality, a coming-of-age after completing the difficult challenges of the Saturn Cycle. It is at this point in time that the native is driven to assess and review their childhood expectations and beliefs of existence.

This confrontation forces them to decide in which direction they should turn and what they need to leave behind as they begin an entirely new Saturn Cycle. This is the age at which the native is confronted by reality: life is not as easy as they had expected and that the wrong decisions of the past may one day need to be righted.

The Saturn Return is often a time when people seek counselling or make major changes to their lives. Look around at the people you know in the 28-30 age group and you will see them making decisions they would not have been able to make a few years earlier. Look at your own life, what were you doing around this age, the time when Saturn returned to his natal position? This is often the most important period of your life and can show you how to manage your Saturn transits in the future.

For older people their next Saturn Return is at around 56 and another at 84 years of age, are you prepared for it?

Chapter 5 - Introduction to the Planets

Astrology's Golden Rule

Planets are the WHAT – these are the key characters in your chart much like actors in a Shakespearean play. They are also called 'archetypes' in psychological astrology. For example, Mars is your basic drive to move forward and conquer. Mars is the archetype of drive, assertiveness and energy.

The Signs are the HOW – they show how the planets react. For example, Mars shows your level of energy, HOW you express this energy is seen in his sign. Mars will be more reactive in a confrontation when he is in Sagittarius or Scorpio than if he were in Pisces or Taurus. Another example is how Mars' energy can appear dispersed when he is in Cancer yet more focused when in Capricorn.

The Houses are the WHERE – this shows where the planet reacts to situations. For example, Mars in Scorpio in the 3rd house would be more inclined towards being argumentative and eager to get into a verbal fight just for the heck of it; Mars in Scorpio in the 5th house would be far more competitive and aggressive in sport.

A point to note: I like to consider the chart as a Shakespearean play: it has characters, a stage and costumes. Planets are the WHAT of astrology - what character is performing now? The sign shows HOW the character is demonstrating his or her qualities which can be identified by their costume, masks and make-up. The houses are WHERE the characters are acting out their performance and that is formed by the scenery on the stage.

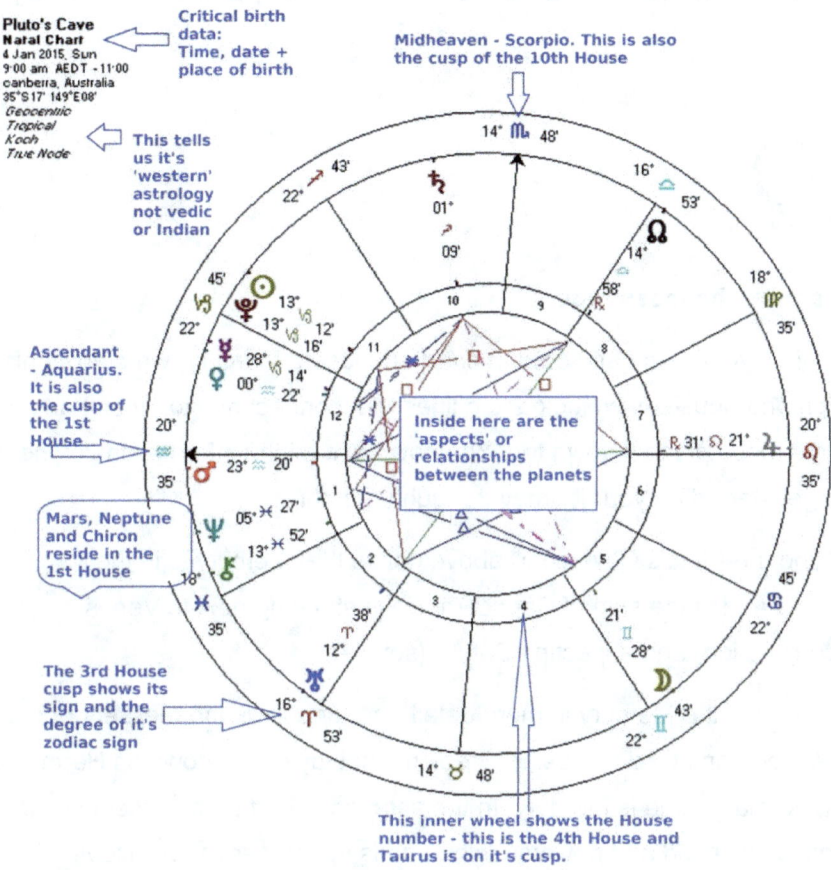

Above chart: highlighting the major features of the chart.

In this chapter I'm going to show you one way to examine each planet in your chart. To get you started on your journey I'm going to take you on a walk through your chart accompanied by Mercury, your inner messenger.

Mercury the messenger

Look at your own natal or birth chart and locate Mercury; write down his sign and house. Next look at the lines that connect him to other planets, write those planets down too. You now have all the information you need to get started on your journey through your chart.

Using the Pluto's Cave chart above notice that Mercury is in the 12th house and in the sign of Capricorn. He is standing next to Venus (conjunction) and aspecting Saturn (sextile).

Let's examine Mercury in more detail - he, or she, is the messenger of the Gods and Goddesses. In Greek mythology he is known as Hermes, his Roman name is Mercury. In the astrology chart he represents your conscious mind and how you think - he is spontaneous conscious thought.

Mercury also has character, in other words Mercury, the God, is wily, witty, clever, smart and sometimes a trickster. I've never actually met a trickster Mercury though. I think Mercury is way too serious about his role as minder of your mental processes to want to make your life miserable by tricking you.

Mercury is an Inner and Personal Planet, this group includes: the two Luminaries, Sun and Moon; Venus and Mars. I don't include Jupiter and Saturn with the Personal Planets. The inner planets move fast. Mercury will sometimes move more than one degree per day, sometimes he will stop and move backwards. When a planet goes backwards relative to the earth it is called 'Retrograde motion'. A retrograde Mercury can feel as though your mind is foggy and sluggish.

Your inner planets are sometimes visible to you and those around you. For instance, you may notice Mercury in action when you are thinking and processing your plans for tomorrow. Pluto's Cave has Mercury in Capricorn which suggests that he thinks things through thoroughly and won't rush into making a decision without due consideration. He likes to take his time before saying something and will often say nothing rather than say the wrong thing.

Mercury is next to Venus in Aquarius and we could say that these two archetypes get along quite well. Venus is interesting, instinctively clever, chatty, sociable and likes to engage and connect socially. Mercury enjoys clear, Capricornian-style communication with all of the astrology archetypes depending on aspects and rulerships within the chart. These two planets will sit over a cup of tea together and chatter every day.

Mercury is also sextile (a 60° angle) with Saturn. A sextile is a pleasant aspect and reinforces that these two planets will get along fine. In fact they support each other primarily because Saturn rules the sign that Mercury is in, Capricorn. If you combine the two planet keywords you will get: solid, resourceful and disciplined mental activity and communication. You would conclude that Mercury certainly thinks things through before he speaks. His Venus connection suggests that he is sometimes quite charming and sociable.

You have the WHAT - Mercury; and you have the HOW - in Capricorn. By putting these two factors together you get: '*Mercury communicates carefully and orderly*'. Next you are going to look at WHERE the actor, Mercury, dressed conservatively as would be appropriate for Capricorn, acts out his particular style of mental processing.

Mercury is in the watery 12th house where you can see there may be some trouble. I consider the 12th house very much like a cave where the planets go to rest, meditate and recuperate before they end their cycle around the chart. The 12th house is the last house of the chart. Once they have completed this cycle they start a new one - the 1st house cusp is the start of the next cycle.

Sometimes the 12th house also suggests that the planet has matured and is ready to enter the next level.

Mercury in the 12th house suggests that he can sometimes get caught up in a daydream - the 12th house is often referred to as the house of 'dreams'. The 12th house is generally not considered the best place to try to communicate from. For the chatty, witty Mercury this 12th house placement might be the last place he wants to be.

It is the astrologer's challenge to delineate Mercury with all these different forces impressed upon him. This is why astrologers study hard to thoroughly learn the keywords and blend them together. I will walk you through how you might want to practice delineations in a later chapter. There is a shortcut though and that is to close your eyes, drop into a light meditative state and have a good chat with Mercury.

Introducing the archetypes in my meditation with Mercury in the Pluto's Cave chart:

I sit back in my lounge chair and relax. I slowly calm my mind and body by breathing in and out to enter a light trance state that I use for these types of meditations. I can see Mercury standing inside the chart. He appears old and mature, like a wizened elder. He also presents as very smart, knowledgeable.

He and Venus are standing outside the cave of the 12th house. The grass is green and it is evening or early morning - *"It is morning,"* he tells me. They like to sit and chat outside as they watch the world go by. The 12th house is sometimes like that, it seems to be quite separate from the rest of the world.

I ask Mercury if he would take me for a walk through the chart and introduce me to the other archetypes. He is delighted. Sociable Venus wants to go with us but I tell her that this is not her time.

Mercury walks me to the Pluto's Cave Ascendant, Aquarius. Aquarius is turquoise green and female, she is watering the gardens of the Ascendant. She sees herself as keeper of the chart and extremely important to Pluto's Cave. Mercury tells me that Aquarius is very active, she's not so active right now but she's ramping up and preparing for intense activity soon – thus why she is watering the gardens, to prepare them for a fruitful harvest.

Standing beside Aquarius in the 1st house is Mars, fiery and strong. He is watching her work in the garden. He too is showing some interest in us as we walk through the chart. Mercury has become much more animated with Mars beside him. I can see that he enjoys taking me through the chart and he likes being out of his 12th house cave too.

Mercury explains that Mars is drive and energy, essential for a successful business. These two archetypes work well together, Mars and Aquarius, to drive forward and create a powerhouse of energy for the other archetypes. They are the face of Pluto's Cave and take that responsibility seriously.

Next is Neptune. An ocean greets us, we are at the beach, it is nice and sunny. There are no people to be seen, the beach is empty. It is so clean though, pristine, and the smell is fresh and invigorating. But there is a sense of loneliness here and I feel it. Mercury tells me that Neptune sometimes comes to the beach for a break. He likes it like this, quiet and completely free of people and problems.

"But humans like warmth, human contact, friendship and social support," I say to Neptune.

"I am all those things too," says Neptune, he sounds like he is a little annoyed at me. *"Look at my planetary aspects before you judge me."*

I open my eyes to look at the Pluto's Cave chart: there is a square to Saturn and a trine to the Moon. Actually, I think that looks pretty darn good. The Saturn anchors Neptune and although a square aspect can be uncomfortable, in generational planets (the outer planets from Jupiter out to Pluto) they tend to cooperate much better than with the inner planets. The trine is an easy flowing aspect. Neptune's trine to the Moon shows love, socialisation, nurturing, affection and an ability to show it.

"Yes, I can see that, Neptune. Thanks for reminding me." I'm always fascinated when the archetypes interact with me and bring things like that to my attention. I haven't studied the chart for some years and I deliberately didn't look at it for this meditation. I wanted it to be as close to a fresh adventure as possible for this chapter.

Neptune explains that Pluto's Cave, my astrology and tarot business, sometimes becomes overwhelmed with activity.

"Look at Aquarius and Mars, they drive the business like two hydrogen bombs, they don't know when to stop. They'll wear you out if you don't come and spend time on this lovely beach. Here, sit down on the sand with me."

Neptune pats the sand next to him. He now appears as a suntanned figure, a surfer of the 1960's perhaps. Mercury and I sit with him.

"Now be quiet and watch the waves roll in. And don't fuss, the chapter will soon be written and finished, just relax."

I do as I'm told. A memory begins to form... when I was a child my family would spend every school holidays at the beach. With my brothers and sister we basically lived among the waves and sand dunes. I remember being alone most of the time, I like being alone. I would wander off exploring the sand dunes, up into the bush and along the primeval sandy beaches. Back in those far off days there were few visitors to the south coast of NSW, often the beaches were completely deserted - just us kids, the sun and the sea.

I remember sitting for hours watching everything: waves, sand moving in the wind, insects, crabs, seagulls, you name it I watched it. It's hard to describe but it was like stepping out of the world for a time to watch life - as though in a separate dimension.

Neptune doesn't often present in a solid human form like this. Sometimes he is a merman cartoon character wearing a king's crown, at other times he is just a nebulous shape. This time he is real and I guess it's because Mercury is here with us. Mercury nods affirming my unvoiced question.

Neptune now leans over and stares into my eyes and I feel myself experience a deeper state of relaxation. He wants to impress upon me the calm I experienced at the beach in my childhood. I'd forgotten what it was like.

"Remember and do this more often."

After a few minutes of peace Mercury stands and invites me to walk with him over to Chiron. Chiron is half horse and half human, he looks just like Chiron on the cover of my *'Astrology of Health'* book. He is virile and powerful, like a stallion. He tells us that he gives Pluto's Cave depth of character and wisdom. As a healer he exhibits purpose, a powerful driving force that drives my teaching. He lives in a cave hidden among the sand dunes. He helps bring spiritual transformation as well as stability to my work.

Chiron walks with us to the 2nd house cusp, Pisces, and introduces us. Pisces is the deep unconscious and is ruled by Neptune, so the two are very similar. Pisces is a twin, here in my meditation there are two Pisces. They are not fish but very much like two sailors. They take my hands in theirs and I feel warmth flowing into me. It is weird but it feels nice. They are sending me some kind of energy. Aha, this is the 2nd house of security. It represents spiritual, material and emotional nourishment and that is what the two sailors are giving me - nourishment. Nourishment can be considered a form of security. The two of them hold hands with me. I want to invite Chiron and Mercury to join us but Pisces says no, their gift is for me alone.

Mercury has been very quiet, just as I would expect from a Capricorn Mercury, quiet and careful in his manners and speech. I remind myself that he resides in Pluto's Cave's 12th house, very much the underworld, the deep unconscious.

I am going to stop our little adventure here. I'm tired and this journey around my chart would take me several days to complete. I just wanted to show you how I work with the astrological archetypes. This is very personal, as I expect yours will be too. I believe that astrology can be used just like this to reinforce the foundations of depth psychotherapy. Astrology and psychology are one and the same thing for me these days.

A point to note:

Luminaries - Sun and Moon.

Inner Planets - Sun, Moon, Mercury, Venus and Mars (sometimes called Personal Planets).

Bridging Planet - Jupiter (sometimes included with the Inner and Outer planets).

Outer or Generational Planets - Saturn, Chiron, Uranus, Neptune and Pluto. I usually include Jupiter with this group.

Exercise for this chapter

Your homework for this chapter is to start your own inner journey around your chart, just like my one above. Close your eyes and find your Mercury, ask him to take you on a walk around your chart to meet every planet and house cusp sign. Write your meditation down in your journal when you have finished. Don't try to do it all at once though, go slowly over many days, weeks and months. In fact don't stop as this meditation can open your mind to marvels undreamed of.

WARNING: if you have a diagnosed mental illness you are advised to discuss these meditations with your psychologist or mental health specialist before attempting them. I always tell my students that if they feel uncomfortable they should just open their eyes, splash their face with water, go for a walk or have a shower. In thirty years I have never known anyone to have a negative experience with these meditations. But just in case please find someone to guide you if you do feel uncomfortable.

A good web site to visit for more information on the planets and signs is: http://www.wikiwand.com/en/Astrological_symbols

Signs	Symbol	Glyph	Planet	House	Element	Modes
Aries	Ram	♈	♂	1	Fire	Cardinal
Taurus	Oxen	♉	♀	2	Earth	Fixed
Gemini	Twins	♊	☿	3	Air	Mutable
Cancer	Crab	♋	☽	4	Water	Cardinal
Leo	Lion	♌	☉	5	Fire	Fixed
Virgo	Virgin	♍	☿	6	Earth	Mutable
Libra	Scales	♎	♀	7	Air	Cardinal
Scorpio	Scorpion	♏	♇	8	Water	Fixed
Sagittarius	Centaur Archer	♐	♃	9	Fire	Mutable
Capricorn	Seagoat	♑	♄	10	Earth	Cardinal
Aquarius	Water Bearer	♒	♅	11	Air	Fixed
Pisces	Two Fish	♓	♆	12	Water	Mutable

Table: rulerships, elements, modes, symbols and glyphs.

The Planets

Sun - Luminary, rules Leo, Inner or Personal Planet

The Inner or Personal Planets show the native's innate personality.

The Sun, a Luminary, takes 30 days to travel through one sign, travels 1° per day, it is the centre of our Solar System.

Symbol - the saviour, Christ, Sol Invictus, Mithrais, giver of unconditional love through light and warmth.

Myth – as with all the astrological archetypes there are multiple myths so I will only include the most popular in this book. The myth commonly used for the Sun in astrology is the Greek God Apollo who drives the radiant chariot of the sun across the heavens. I will explore the various planet myths in my upcoming book *'Psychological Astrology and the Planets of Power'*.

Glyph - the circle represents unlimited potential it also represents the conscious principle of spirit. The dot represents consciousness and the realisation of spirit and soul into matter. The Sun presents as the reason we incarnate at this time.

In the chart (WHAT) - represents father, husband and strong male influences on the native, success, vitality and self-esteem. It can represent the mother when she is the dominant parent in the family.

In the signs (HOW) - it represents how the native reflects their basic soul urge.

In the houses (WHERE) - shows where the native will express their soul urge, their reason for incarnating.

Appearance - strong, radiant and powerful ego, physical strength and willpower.

Psychologically – the Sun is everything about you particularly your self-esteem and confidence. Those with a strongly placed Sun tend to be a bit too egotistical or overly sensitive to criticism. Sun in the 1st, 5th and 9th houses tend to need a lot of attention, the term 'drama queen' fits them quite well. The more fire in your chart the more your Sun is emphasised. I look at the Sun in the chart to note its house position, sign and element. I next note the aspects it makes with the other planets. As the Sun is basically your reason for incarnating the connections it makes to other planets will tell you more about how you manage self-esteem, needs for attention and recognition, criticism and how you shine when in company.

Rules - heart, general health and vitality, fathers, leaders, rulers, nobility, royalty, the spine.

Keywords – soul, creative, honest, loyal, self-esteem, vitality, nobility, success, selfishness.

Moon – Luminary, rules Cancer, Inner or Personal Planet

The Moon takes 27.3 days to orbit the Earth and is related to the human female ovulation cycle. The Moon takes 29.5 days to travel from New Moon to New Moon which is called the Synodic or Lunation cycle. It takes roughly two and a half days to travel through one sign and travels between 11° and 15° per day. Also known as Luna, she is the largest known moon in our Solar System. The Moon creates the tides and cycles of nature and reflects the Sun's light.

Symbol - the unconscious reactions and instincts of the native, anima or feminine principle.

Myth - Luna, Diana and Artemis, the huntress of the night, she is the twin sister of Apollo. She hunts the forests, is chaste and is never seen without the viewer being killed or made an example of. She rules the human life cycle from birth, fertility and death.

Glyph - the half circle represents soul and the receptive feminine principle, also described as the unconscious principle - a mirror to the Sun.

In the chart (WHAT) - shows mother, wife and other strong feminine influences, family, the social side of the native, the general public, inherited or genetic traits.

In the signs (HOW) - represents the emotional reaction of the native, how others perceive them, how they nurture others and accept nurturing from others.

In the houses (WHERE) - where the native's moods are inclined to fluctuate, where they will experience and express their feminine traits.

Appearance - round face and large breasts in women and a barrel chest in men.

Psychologically – the Moon shows your ability to nurture others, how you allow others to nurture you, and how you were nurtured in childhood. It also shows your mother or primary carer in childhood illustrating how you were cared for. The Moon is also your feelings, it highlights how you relate to others emotionally. I look at the Moon and Sun to see the foundational qualities of the individual. The Moon shows the native's feelings, whether they are caring and nurturing or cold and disconnected from others and thus themselves.

Rules - breasts, stomach, female reproductive system and cycles, lymph system and body fluids, emotional and mental health.

Keywords – mothers, older women, nurturing, loving, emotions, family, social, protective, moody, irrational, emotional blackmail, cyclic behaviour, sensitivity, feelings, fluids.

Mercury - rules Virgo (passive) and Gemini (active) - Inner or Personal Planet

The smallest planet in the Solar System, is never more than 28° from the Sun, has an 88 day year, varies between 3 - 5 weeks to travel through one sign, goes retrograde often. Travels roughly 1° per day.

Symbol - symbolises the intellect and conscious mind, the mental activity of the native. It is also known as a convertible planet as it has both male and female traits. It can be androgynous or hermaphrodite both male and female. It bridges between Moon and Sun - spirit and soul.

Myth – Mercury (Greek Hermes) is the messenger of the Gods who never grew older than Peter Pan, ageless, active and can represent the alchemist or magician.

Glyph - crescent of receptivity above the circle of spirit and the cross of matter.

In the chart (WHAT) – the conscious mind, children of the native, siblings, youth in general, short distance travel.

In the signs (HOW) - shows how the native applies their conscious mind, how they think and what stimulates them, their style of communication, also shows if they worry excessively.

In the houses (WHERE) - shows where the native uses their mind and where their creativity comes from.

Appearance - thin and active manner, quick moving with darting, active eyes.

Psychologically – this is your conscious mind, that part of you that thinks out loud as it processes what is going on around you. There is nothing hidden with Mercury, he simply illustrates how you think. He is your style of cognition which includes your higher level Executive Functions of planning, problem solving, being about to think forwards and backwards in time and to learn from your past experiences to then project them into the future. Mercury's element tells me almost everything I need to know about how the native mentally processes each moment of their daily life. It shows whether they process unconsciously like a dream and then forgets what it was they were thinking about (as in Attention Deficit Disorder – inattentive, daydreamers) or whether they can process rapidly while multitasking like someone with the Mercurial mind of a genius. Mercury shows how the native manages small talk, their tolerance of small irritating interruptions in their day to day activities and their ability to stop internal dialogue to relax and fall asleep.

Rules - the five senses, hands, fingers and skin.

Keywords - communication, conscious mind and thought processes, intellect, worry, intellectual pursuits, creativity, youth, children.

Venus - rules Taurus (passive) and Libra (active) - Inner or Personal Planet

Never more than 48° from the Sun, also known as the Morning and Evening Star, rising and setting before or after the Sun as it races in front of and then behind the Sun in its journey around the sun. It takes approx. one month to travel through one sign and travels roughly 1° per day.

Symbol - love and society, how the native relates, relating and connecting, benefic or 'good fortune' planet.

Myth - Venus (Greek Aphrodite) is the most beautiful of the goddesses, ruler of love, beauty, music, the arts and social graces.

Glyph - the circle of spirit over the cross of matter, the universal sign for 'female'.

In the chart (WHAT) - women, particularly young women, shows the cash flow of the native and how they relate with people, friends, lovers and in general social situations.

In the signs (HOW) - shows how the native relates to others, what they are attracted to and their attractiveness to others.

In the houses (WHERE) - shows where the native expresses their talents, where they go to seek relationships, where they are most charming and where they spend the most money.

Appearance - beautiful, graceful, vain, may either have beautiful or problematic skin and hair.

Psychologically – Venus is the social animal of astrology - she can be the ideal beauty who must remain untouched and flawless, or the husky beauty who inflames your desires. Venus shows how the native interacts with others. She is not the planet of love as many people seem to think, rather, she is the planet of attraction. Venus shows us how the native attracts others, what it is that is attractive about them, as well as the type of person they are attracted to. If you want love in the chart there is much more to look for such as the 7th house, the Moon and Sun as well as the aspects they make with the other planets, houses and signs. When I turn to Venus in the chart I look for the native's personality in social settings: how shy they are, how easily they meet and greet strangers, how comfortable they are with a small group or out in public at the shopping mall. Venus is a wonderful planet that tells an astrologer so much about how this person manages their interactions with others and how comfortable they are. Look at the aspects Venus makes with the other planets as this will give you deeper insights into the native's personality.

Rules - beauty, the arts (music, craft, graphic art), diplomats, mediators, parathyroid gland, glands in general, kidneys, skin and veins.

Keywords - relationships, beauty, artistic talent, jealousy, charm, attractiveness, mediating, relating, connecting, money as cash, comfort, peace, harmony.

Mars - rules Aries - Inner or Personal Planet

Orbits the Sun every two Earth years which means that it takes two years to complete one cycle of your chart; appears red in the night sky and is known as the Red Planet; takes two months to travel through a sign. Travels roughly 1° every two days.

Symbol - energy and drive, shows natives direction as indicated by the arrow in its glyph, requires goals otherwise he can become directionless and an over-active nuisance.

Myth – (Greek Ares) the God of war, governing warriors, heat, fevers, blood and pestilence.

Glyph - the arrow of will exalted and directed on the circle of spirit, the opposite of Venus; both operate as the male and female archetypes (male / female polarity).

In the chart (WHAT) - represents boys and young men, energy, aggression, temper outbursts, ambitions and drives of the native.

In the signs (HOW) - shows how driven the native is and whether they have low or high energy levels, sexual vitality and endurance.

In the houses (WHERE) - shows where the native expresses their enthusiasm.

Appearance - generally muscular and energetic, red colouring to hair and face flushed, restless.

Psychologically – this is the planet that acts like a hyperactive child at school swinging off the ceiling fan. Mars in the chart provides important clues as to how driven the native is and how they go about achieving their goals. After examining Mars I will look at the Midheaven to see if these qualities are reflected to confirm what I see with Mars. Some people have Mars in houses and signs as well as aspects to other planets that restrict his innate drives and urges. This may manifest as a frustrated, angry, disempowered and disillusioned Mars. An outgoing Mars is riotously funny, a real pleasure to be around. They are always planning or having an adventure that oozes fun, danger and plenty of play and partying. I rarely see a dangerous Mars simply because Mars is not aggressive or dangerous, he is just looking for an outlet to his energy. Thwart that expression of his archetypal power and you get internal disharmony, illness, depression and frustration with outbursts of anger and aggression. Look at the sign, element and house that Mars is in and the aspects he makes with the other planets to determine whether your client is going to achieve their desires and goals. Mars is a vehicle we all use to get what we want, he is not malicious or nasty, he is just energy. If you can remember that simple tip then it will be easier for you to interpret his placement in the chart.

Rules - blood, muscles, sinus, adrenal glands, external sex organs, sexual drive, surgery, weapons, blood pressure and fevers.

Keywords - drive, strength, sex act, aggression, energy, temper, impatience, surgeons, military services, fights, tools and weapons, accidents, danger.

♃

Jupiter - rules Sagittarius - Bridging Planet as it can be both Personal and an Outer or Generational Planet.

The largest planet in the Solar System, takes 12 years to circle the zodiac which means that it takes roughly 1 year to travel through a sign. Jupiter helps bridge or link the personal with the generational planets.

Symbol - symbolises the expansion and expression of self through wisdom and fun, the major benefic or 'good fortune' planet.

Myth - Jupiter is the Roman Jove (Greek Zeus), son of Saturn and King of the Gods, he fathered many of the other gods and goddesses. Also includes the myths of Bacchus and Dionysus.

Glyph - the crescent of soul over the cross of matter.

In the chart (WHAT) - shows the native's level of knowledge, wisdom and expansiveness, generally represents the native's uncle, teachers or guides. May indicate addictive and gambling habits, narcissistic and irresponsible behaviours and a lack of morals.

In the signs (HOW) - shows how the native uses their charm, wisdom, religious and moral aptitude, their level of generosity and outgoing nature, how they give in life.

In the houses (WHERE) - Jupiter's house position is as important as his sign position, shows where the native uses their Jupiterian qualities, where they will be successful, most optimistic, indulgent and happy.

Appearance - often overweight or tall and slim, noble or overbearing appearance.

Psychologically – Jupiter and I have a love-hate relationship. I have Jupiter strongly placed in my chart where he has enormous impact on what I achieve in my life. His cycles have determined when and where I will be successful in achieving my dreams. I struggle to manage his hyperactive, gregarious and friendly nature simply because I have so many planets in Fiery Leo, and Jupiter, as the ruler of Sagittarius, is also fire. I admit that I have a soft spot for him but when I look at the charts of people in crisis I sometimes see Jupiter's unpleasant side. He is the ruler of addictions, drugs, gambling, sexual promiscuity, irresponsibility and of using people to gain what they want. Jupiter rules many professionals that have the power to manipulate and immorally gain from other people's weaknesses - lawyers, religious leaders, corporate leaders, crooks and cheats. I have written about Jupiter's unpleasant side many times and will be exploring this in my next few books because he just amazes me with his versatility and duplicity. One moment he rules the morally just person helping them find a foothold in life, but the very next minute he tempts the weak minded corporate manager with sex, money and fame. Jupiter is more of a trickster than Mercury ever could be. Jupiter is Zeus, the King of the Gods of Mount Olympus, as such he has a history of affairs, temptation and breaking the rules. Yet once he finished siring his many children he grew up. With age Jupiter becomes the wise elder, the magician, the wicca and the shaman. He is the judge, the hierophant and the teacher. The simple lesson of Jupiter is that he needs to grow up, he needs lessons in life that knock him down so that he learns that life is not just one big party. His irresponsible behaviour as a youth can lead to his becoming a valued member of the community. Look at Jupiter's aspects with the other planets in the chart, sign and house placement to determine how the native manages their wayward desires, their propensity towards immoral, addictive and harmful behaviours. This is one planet every astrologer needs to get a handle on and to do that I recommend you spend time in meditation with your own Jupiter.

Rules - liver, obesity, gall bladder, arterial system, lungs, spleen, blood quality, growth hormone, law, advisers, judges, religion, addiction, gambling, teachers, wealth, middle age spread.

Keywords - philosophy, law, religion, morality, wisdom, success, expansion, abundance, culture, business, addictions, indulgence, narcissism, self-interest, food addiction, drug use, alcoholism, gambling.

♄

Saturn - rules Capricorn - Bridging Planet as well as an Outer or Generational Planet.

Saturn takes roughly 28-30 years to complete its journey around the zodiac and is perhaps the most important of the 'cyclic planets' as it rules the 7 year cycle of human spiritual evolution (29.4 years to complete one full cycle, it forms a mini-cycle every 7 years). Saturn takes roughly two and a half years to travel through one sign. Saturn, like Jupiter, helps bridge the personal and the generational planets.

Symbol - the ruler of time, karma and fate, the 7 year cycle, the tester of those on the path to knowledge, possibly the most important planet as it consolidates your life lessons and prevents you from moving forward before you are ready.

Myth – Saturn (Greek Cronus) ate his children until his son, Jupiter, conquered him; also known as Cronus, the King of the Titans and the God of Time (Father Time).

Glyph - the cross of matter over the crescent of soul.

In the chart (WHAT) – authority, tradition, conservative views, often the parent who teaches the native self-discipline, older people, grandparents, old age, the lessons to be learned.

In the signs (HOW) - how their self discipline, determination and sense of responsibility is used, types of lessons the native must face to move forward.

In the houses (WHERE) - more importantly shows where the lessons of life are, where the native will apply their ambitions and feel the most need to order and structure their lives, where they are the most disciplined or in need of discipline, where they are the most inhibited and afraid.

Appearance - generally thin and bony, tall, sometimes with poor skeletal structure.

Psychologically – here is another of my favourites, Saturn only wants one thing: for you to be the best organised and structured person you can be. Unfortunately Saturn is very heavy handed, he won't let you out of the house until you've cleaned your teeth, mopped the floors, scrubbed the bathtub, painted the spare bedroom, cleaned up the mess in your bedroom and studied for that exam in two months time. This is the reputation Saturn has and it is well deserved, he is a terrible task-master who wields a cane to smack you with if you don't complete your tasks. Saturn is well known to hold you back in the classroom until you have finished your lessons, he makes you sit at the dinner table until you have finished your nasty spinach and dry, stringy meat. Saturn instils discipline but only because he wants you to take responsibility for your life. He is cautious and will wait patiently until the right moment which can be very frustrating if you have a bus to catch. I see Saturn in the chart as a pointer to where the native needs to sort their life out. He clearly illuminates your weaknesses and these are usually bad habits, poor organisation and laziness. I believe that Saturn is perhaps the most important planet in the astrology chart because he is the one who will make you a better person.

Rules - skeleton, teeth, nails, the ground and its minerals, the public service, positions of responsibility, ambition, organisations and institutions.

Keywords - structure, organisation, culture, tradition, limitation, consequences, consolidation, inhibition, ambition, achievement, fear, fate, karma, destiny, lessons, isolation, loneliness, determination, discipline, age, time, sadness, depression.

Uranus - rules Aquarius - Outer or Generational Planet.

Uranus, discovered in 1781 takes 84 years to orbit the Sun and the same period to orbit the chart; it takes 7 years to travel through one sign; is the archetype of rebellion, revolutions and freedom from suppression; twice the size of Saturn and twice the distance from the Sun. Its eccentric orbit was so disturbed that astronomers came to think that there was another planet beyond it – this was Neptune.

Symbol - the unpredictable element within our psyche.

Myth - in Greek mythology Ouranos was Heaven and Gaia, his wife, was the Earth; he was castrated by his Titan son Saturn; our original patriarch and sky God. It has been suggested that he may also represent Prometheus and the Fool card in the tarot.

Glyph - the cross of matter between two crescent souls over the circle of spirit, to fully utilise your spirit you must first embrace matter with your soul.

In the chart (WHAT) – is the higher octave of Mercury and connects your intuition with your conscious mind; is similar to Mars because of his ruthless nature; represents the intuitive 'lightning bolt' moment of awareness, illumination and instantaneous reaction of the mind. Uranus demands freedom to express one's opinion and will. Introduces elements of tension, stress, nervousness, dynamic change and can sometimes manifest as psychosis as well as exhibiting moments of pure genius.

In the signs (HOW) – in what form the native exhibits their needs for freedom.

In the houses (WHERE) - more importantly this shows where the native is in need of freedom, where they express their intuition and intellect, their needs for independence and change, originality and where they act the craziest.

Appearance - dignified and eccentric, often appear aloof as they seek to grasp the fleeting moments of genius within their stream of consciousness.

Psychologically – I remember when Uranus crossed my Ascendant while I was studying psychology at university. During his transit I wrote my first book on self hypnosis, I worked three jobs and drove three hours a day to get to my classes. I also had three children, a wife and mortgage, it was a busy and stressful time. I owe a big thanks to Uranus for putting me under so much pressure to succeed because those years changed my life. Uranus has the wonderful role of forcing the native to come up with plans and strategies to improve their life and that of others. My natal Uranus is conjunct my Descendant (7th house cusp) and I see him as a dynamic actor who continually introduces new situations through the people I meet. He is the planet of activity, much like Jupiter, he agitates your psyche to bring out the best in you through inspired ideas, plans and urges you to manifest them. His down side is that he can over-stress you, he brings too much worry, too many stressful situations into your life, more than you can handle. A poorly placed Uranus forces the native to dwell on their negativity. This can make them feel as though they are forced into a corner, trapped with no way out. Their mind can sometimes spiral out of control. I see a lot of people with disturbed sleep and racing negative thoughts with a poorly placed Uranus. He is one archetype that needs to be managed in meditation. I suggest you negotiate to get the outcomes you need from him. Uranus is actually very friendly and helpful, amazingly so for such a powerful archetype so don't be put off by his enormous power.

Rules - biological cycles, nervous system, brain and spinal cord, eccentricity, geniuses, mind, intellect, inventors, electricity, computers, scientists.

Keywords - eccentricity, naive, manic behaviour, bipolar, illuminating, inventions, intuition, brilliance, genius, freedom of disruption, change, opportunity, expression, rebellion, revolutions, impulsive, logic, excitable, tension and nervousness.

Neptune - rules Pisces - Outer or Generational Planet

Discovered in 1846 as the western world was discovering alternative belief systems. At this time philosophers were challenging the dogma of religion and strict scientific empiricism with its facts, logic and the tunnel vision of the left brain. The western world turned to embrace new forms of spiritualism, magic, hypnotism, psychotherapy, dreams, drugs and drug therapy. Neptune has an orbit of 165 years, spends roughly 14 years in the one sign, travels about 2° each year.

Symbol - symbolises the passive escape from the limitations of our logically minded society, the development of mind exploration through meditation, alternative religions, spiritualism, hallucinogenic and prescription drugs.

Myth – is known by the Greek name Poseidon, like the oceans he rules Neptune knows no limits and cannot be contained or moulded.

Glyph - the cross of matter entering the crescent of soul, the gaining of wisdom by joining matter with the soul.

In the chart (WHAT) - the native's connection with the unconscious, illumination, dreams, visions, compassion, psychic connection, illusion, sensitivity, disconnection, loss, grief, confusion, abandonment, betrayal, disillusionment.

In the signs (HOW) - shows how the native expresses their connection to spirit.

In the houses (WHERE) - most importantly shows where the native will need most grounding, where they are most disillusioned and confused, also where the native will apply their true spiritual nature, where the native is most idealistic, imaginative and most sensitive to the outside world.

Appearance - fluid, puffy skin, attractive in an etheric way, vague and dreamy.

Psychologically – the planet of dreams, illusions, mystery and confusion is so very different to that of the other outer planets like Pluto and Uranus. When I take my students into trance to work with Neptune he rarely manifests in a human form or even in a solid form. He most often takes on a mist or an energy form but sometimes he will switch between an energy form and a human form. Neptune is just one heck of a strange planet, a mystery in so many ways. In the chart he shows where and how you aspire to spiritually align yourself with your destiny. He does this by making things interesting. I find that his lessons are the hardest to understand simply because he is very much like a crossword puzzle using cryptic clues to help you find the answers. His transits are almost as bad as Pluto's and that says something. He can cause you to experience a mystery illness that no one knows how to fix let alone what the problem really is. Neptune hides and disguises himself and his methods in his desire to help you find spiritual harmony. I think the best way to understand Neptune is to see him as many aspects or facets of the one archetype, He uses a multitude of sounds, feelings at many layers, images and tactile sensations, all are clues to illustrate his lessons. In the chart he can help you guide your client to make solid and grounded decisions. When I see a poorly aspected Neptune I advise my client not to make any decisions before seeking the advise of someone they trust. I also advise them to get counselling by a trained therapist who is well versed in astrology and depth psychotherapy. When Neptune is out of balance the native simply can't see their way forward. I will often describe this as being in the forest when the mist comes in and the cliff is somewhere off to the right... or was that to the left... or is it right in front? In other words the native is lost and floundering with no idea of how to help themselves. This is why astrology and counselling are so important to this person.

Rules - body fluids, aura, pineal gland, solar plexus, infections, influenza, hidden and mysterious illnesses, sleep, dreams, addictions, psychologists, artists, fishermen, ocean workers, film industry, imagination and fantasy.

Keywords - sensitivity, illusion, disillusionment, abandonment, confusion, dreams, spirit, idealism, compassionate, escapism, addiction, sleep, deception, psychosis.

Pluto - rules Scorpio - Outer or Generational Planet - dwarf planet

Pluto takes 248 years to orbit the Sun and the same period through your chart. Its time in each sign can vary from 12 to 32 years due to its elliptic orbit. It is smaller than Mars and is in co-rotation with its moon, Charon. Together they are less than 1/5 of our Moon's mass and can almost be called a double asteroid. Pluto is the most powerful of the planets and as such its discovery, at the time of the arrival of the atomic era in 1930, announced another archetype into our consciousness: total destruction. As of 2018 astronomers have discovered 528 Trans-Neptunian Objects orbiting the sun beyond Neptune.

Symbol - Pluto symbolises the complete evolution and transformation of the soul through annihilation. This may be the product of an existential or spiritual crisis, by harnessing the awakening and flow of kundalini, or by a personal crisis precipitating massive changes to the native's life. Pluto can also represent the spiritual or mystic quest for enlightenment.

Myth - Pluto is the Greek Hades, ruler of the Underworld and keeper of the land of the dead. He walks the Earth under a veil of invisibility, no-one escapes the Grim Reaper.

Glyph - the circle of spirit over the crescent of soul on the cross of matter joining the three showing their importance in descending order.

In the chart (WHAT) - represents spiritual transformation through crisis often of a psychological or health origin; regeneration at a cellular level and healing.

In the signs (HOW) - shows how you manage psychological transformation, evolution and crisis. Shows how the native undertakes their mystic's quest for enlightenment.

In the houses (WHERE) - most importantly it shows where you are most susceptible to crisis and in need of deep and long lasting psychological and spiritual transformation. It shows the depth of character needed to undertake the psychological and health challenges of the mystic's quest. Also shows the native's level of spiritual, psychic, occult or esoteric development; can be associated with physical and mental health crisis.

Appearance - intensity of gaze and manner, dark piercing eyes.

Psychologically – this is the planet even astrologers are afraid of. Pluto is the ruler of the underworld, the unconscious is his domain and he has complete sovereignty over it. Your past hurts and pleasures reside there, your belief systems were born there, your wounded inner selves (children, adolescents and adults) are still suffering inside his dungeons. Pluto is the most important psychological healer of all the planetary archetypes. To learn how to heal yourself you must enter his domain, the underworld. I see this as a dungeon, a series of caves and caverns hidden deep underground. That imagery allows me to go somewhere tangible, like a cave. That is why I called my business Pluto's Cave, it is the portal that opens me to where my issues can be found and thus healed. Throughout my practice of psychotherapy, meditation, clinical hypnotherapy and astrology I have focused on introducing people to a means of psychic healing that was tactile and real. When someone can feel their small, wounded inner child huddled in their arms then that can lead to genuine healing. Pluto is your psychological wound, from birth or perhaps brought over from a past life, as well as the wounds you receive in this incarnation.

You will see this by his placement in your chart by sign, element, house and the aspects he forms to the other planets. When I view the psychological profile of my client I will look at Uranus, Neptune and Pluto in relation to the aspects they make with Sun and Moon first. Then I will look at Pluto's aspects with the inner planets Mercury, Venus and Mars. These aspects will tell me what the native is struggling with in their life. It shows what their conflicts are and where they expend most of their energy. Pluto has the potential to crush you or your client. Knowing the nature of that trauma will lead you to finding a way to heal it. I always turned to inner child meditations for healing trauma at the level Pluto delivers. I have never had a failure when my client continued their practice. Most often they would say, *"At last I can sleep without nightmares. I really feel so different now that I can hug my inner child."*

This is Pluto's gift: he will welcome you into his cave and allow you to visit his dungeons. This is where you will find and rescue your inner children. You will learn more on how to do this in my self-hypnosis book.

Rules - politics, underworld crime, theft, the regenerative power of the body to heal itself, immune and defence system, sexuality, orgasm, thymus gland, eliminations of toxins, the healing crisis, tantra, kundalini, astral travel and life-force.

Keywords - collective unconscious, betrayal, regeneration and elimination, power, intensity, control, transformation, evolution, secrets, kundalini and tantric sex for enlightenment, invisibility, destiny, karma, fate, extreme violence, annihilation.

Chiron - Outer or Generational Planet, no rulership, asteroid / dwarf planet

Discovered in 1977, it has an orbit of 50.76 years and is about 1/5 the mass of our Moon. It resides between the orbits of Saturn and Uranus. Its orbit is on an angle to all the other planets similar to Pluto's. It once came as close to Saturn as his moon, Phoebe, in 1664. Chiron is so small that it is also called a planetoid or a large asteroid, however due to its orbit, like that of a planet, it is known as a planet by astrologers. It takes roughly 4 years to travel through each sign.

Symbol - symbolises the emergence of the new age healing phenomenon, links your inner with your outer consciousness. Shows your psychological blind-spot which can disguise symptoms and delay healing. The fundamental wound you receive at birth.

Myth - Chiron was the wise ruler of the centaurs but rather than debauchery and fun he chose the path of teaching and healing. He taught the sons of the gods but when Hercules shot a poisoned arrow into his foot he discovered that he was unable to heal himself. He eventually traded his immortality to free Prometheus from punishment for giving fire to humanity.

Glyph - the K of its discoverer (Kowal) over the circle of spirit.

In the chart (WHAT) – psychological and health crisis, anguish, is strongest when in conjunction with the angles and conjunct or opposite an inner planet.

In the signs (HOW) - shows how you learn and use your innate wisdom and healing potential.

In the houses (WHERE) - shows where you are wounded and in need of healing, where your fundamental wound lies; where your wisdom and charisma are most evident, shows where you are able to give of your healing nature.

Appearance - inconclusive.

Psychologically – Chiron is the wisest of the centaurs who have a reputation for rowdy and outrageous debauchery. After suffering great pain from a wound by his student Hercules, Chiron is finally permitted to retire from his sojourn on earth. The lessons he had to learn were compassion for others through personal experience and to ask for help. This planet is one that I have sitting just below my Capricorn Ascendant and appears to have signalled my own traumatic birth. He was instrumental in my finding Pluto's portal to the underworld via his cave in the mountains. You can read more about this in my first psychological astrology book, '*Psychological Astrology And The Twelve Houses*'. The keyword I find that best fits Chiron is 'anguish' which describes what it feels like when a catastrophe is approaching but you are powerless to stop it. Chiron can be extremely brutal in handing out his lessons. I think he is, in some ways, more brutal than Pluto. Chiron is the teacher of the zodiac. He does this through hardship and physical illness.

If Chiron is strong in your chart then you will know exactly what I mean. He forces you to learn your lessons by bending your arm up behind your back until it either breaks or you give in and learn the lesson. The tension that builds can manifest as a physical and even a psychological crisis. I've not done any research on his transits but I have seen him play a major role in all forms of health crisis. To gain an understanding of

Chiron in your client's chart examine his house position and then look at the aspects he makes with the inner planets. I look particularly for Chiron powerfully placed on an angle (1st, 4th, 7th or 10th house cusp) or conjunct or opposite any of the inner planets (Sun, Moon, Mercury, Venus or Mars). Meditating with Chiron is highly recommended particularly if your natal Chiron is powerfully placed or if he is transiting a sensitive point in your chart.

Rules – no rulerships as yet, some astrologers prefer Virgo others as the co-ruler of Sagittarius, personally I don't think he needs to rule any sign. Chiron is a free and eccentric planet most powerful when touching a sensitive point in the chart.

Keywords – anguish, wounded healer, charisma, hands-on healing, healing crisis, teacher, new-age healing, emotional or psychological wounds, religious or cult evangelists, prominent in wise healers and teachers.

The North Node - the Dragon's Head

This shows the native's destiny similar to a compass needle. Read its sign and the house it resides in as well as the aspects it makes to the other planets. The North Node is called the 'Dragon's Head', exactly opposite is the South Node or 'Dragon's Tail' at the same degree but in the opposite sign and house. For instance, if the North Node is at 12° Taurus in the 3rd house then the South Node will be at 12° Scorpio in the 9th house.

Psychologically - the North Node shows social skills and social ineptness, whether the native is sociable or tries to avoid going out in public. North Node in the 7th can be interpreted as the native eventually meeting their soul mate, though I don't believe that there is only one person on the planet that we are most compatible with. A strongly placed North Node shows a positive person destined to do positive things. Look at the North Node's house position, sign and element as well as the aspects he makes with the other planets to gain more insight. A negatively placed North Node suggests someone with less capable social skills and possibly inclined to be quite shy. The North Node also shows the native's ultimate destiny. If you meditate with your North Node you might ask him to act as a compass and direct you towards your goals. He may even do this in your dreams but first learn how to program your dreams to help that happen. Meditating with the archetypes is explained in greater detail in my *Self-hypnosis Tame Your Inner Dragons* book.

South Node - the Dragons Tail

This is directly opposite the North Node and shows the natives past, their childhood and possibly the past life traits brought into this life. If this is strongly aspected then the native could be inclined to live their past over and over again. If there is focus on the South Node it could indicate that they were especially comfortable in their old habits and they much prefer to continue with them. This can be negative if the native is always relying on their past to manage their future.

How fast do the planets move?

The Ascendant and Midheaven enter a new sign every 2 hours.

Moon completes an orbit of the Earth every 27.3 days and the same to complete a circuit around your astrology chart.

Earth orbits the sun in exactly 1 year (365.26 days) which is exactly the length of time the astrological Sun takes to complete its path around your chart.

Mercury orbits the sun in 88 days but takes roughly 12 months to complete a circuit around your chart.

Venus orbits the sun in 225 days but takes roughly 12 months to complete a circuit around your chart.

Mars orbits the sun in 1.9 years (687 days) but takes roughly 2 years to complete a circuit around your chart.

Jupiter orbits the sun and your chart in 12 years.

Saturn takes 29.5 years.

Chiron takes 50 years.

Uranus takes 84 years.

Neptune takes 165 years.

Pluto takes 249 years.

Chapter 6 - Introduction to the 12 Signs of the Zodiac

The signs are the HOW of astrology, they represent HOW a house or a planet interacts with the rest of your chart and in your psyche. Staying with the Shakespearean play analogy, the planets are the actors while the signs are their costumes, make-up and the masks they each wear.

There are 12 zodiac signs that Tropical astrologers use and they are all exactly the same size - 30°. I won't confuse you trying to explain the differences between the Tropical system that western astrologers use and the Vedic system which is called 'Sidereal' astrology. Western astrologers predominantly use the Tropical system and we 'fix' the 12 signs of the zodiac at exactly 30° each. I explain this in more detail in my book '*Psychological Astrology and the Twelves Houses*'.

You can also read more about the two systems of astrology on Wikipedia: https://en.wikipedia.org/wiki/Sidereal_and_tropical_astrology

The zodiac signs or 'constellations' are formed by the fixed stars. The stars above us only move fractions of minutes of arc over time which is why they are called 'fixed stars'.

Astrologers only use 12 of the 88 constellations we see in the night sky. Astrologers don't bother with the others, 12 is plenty enough for us to work with. Anymore and we'd never finish a reading because we'd have too much information to sift through.

The signs of the zodiac are important, they show us the colours and flavours, traits, qualities and characteristics of the planets and houses. They are much like the clothing a person wears which tells us so much about someone's personality. We can determine such qualities as whether they have a sense of adventure, are traditional in their tastes, are romantic or pedantic, eccentric, dreamy, free thinking or conservative.

You will always find a sign sitting on each of the house cusps in your chart. Look at the cusp of the Midheaven (10th house cusp) in the Pluto's Cave chart – it is Scorpio. Scorpio adds his unique personality to the chart's ambitions for itself and those it is responsible for. If Scorpio were a person how would he or she behave? Please note that in theory the signs have a fixed gender but in practice they don't, they could be either, both or no gender.

The charts in this book show the styles I use in my practice. I like to keep things simple so that I am not overwhelmed by too much information in the chart. The clutter of too many asteroids, midpoints, Arabic Parts or Lots, theoretical points and aspect lines can become way too distracting when trying to do a reading. I need to be able to focus, look at certain key points in the chart and then the native's personality begins to leap out at me. I can't do that with a cluttered chart. If I need to add more points like the asteroid Goddesses, Dwarf Planets or the Centaur asteroids I will make up a series of separate charts.

Psychologically the signs represent HOW the various astrological archetypes manifest and interact in their various combinations in both your inner and outer worlds. Going back to Scorpio on the Midheaven we could say that Pluto's Cave manifests his drive to achieve in the world (which is the Midheaven's role) in an intense, passionate and controlling manner.

With Scorpio on the Midheaven, the cusp of the 10th house, it suggests that the native seeks to control their fear of losing control by expanding their sphere of influence outwards and upwards particularly in terms of the 10th house. It also suggests that the native will turn inwards to seek spiritual insight and inspiration to help them achieve their ambitions. This is generally associated with crisis and transformation as this is the sphere Scorpio operates within. You cannot separate Scorpio, Pluto and the 8th house from an innate urge towards transformation, spiritual evolution and crisis, they go hand in hand unlike any other sign, planet or house.

The Midheaven is the place, WHERE the native strives to achieve their Scorpionic goals. By combining the HOW and WHERE (sign and house) you can see that the native has a desire to passionately control the outer environment to better understand the meaning of their existence. To see whether they will turn inwards to find spiritual inspiration as well requires an examination of Scorpio's ruler, Pluto, his house position and the aspects he forms with the luminaries and inner planets.

If you look at the native, Pluto's Cave, you can see that it strives to understand the very mechanics of life and death, to go beyond this mundane world. These are all in the domain of Scorpio. It uses the theory and practice of the Jungian form of depth psychology and Taoist meditation to experience the life and death struggle as a mystic on his quest to enlightenment. Pluto's Cave also uses the signposts of astrology and tarot to guide students to the worlds beyond consciousness. This is all suggested by that single point in the chart - the sign of Scorpio sitting on the 10th house cusp. But, the story of Pluto's Cave's astrology chart does not end there, the Midheaven is only a sign post, it isn't the journey.

Did you think that you would find that amount of information from just a single point in a chart? Did you know that studying single, double and then triple combinations can help illuminate almost everything you need to know about a person? It can be done but requires dedicated practice with many hundreds of charts over years of study. However, if you are dedicated to becoming an astrologer it won't seem half as bad as I sometimes make out.

I use a 4 key-point method in my readings which can uncover the most important features of the native's personality. I learned to focus my readings when I only had a few minutes to examine a chart. At that time I was busy studying full-time while running my practice as therapist and astrologer.

I was fortunate to have had a solid foundation in astrology from my teacher, Chris Turner. She was lovable but tough and her students became the very best astrologers. This is why I said at the beginning of this book that if you really want to be a competent astrologer you need to study the basics thoroughly under the very best teachers. Study and sound practice earns you the right to have access to this incredible depth of knowledge. So please, do your exercises and practice as often as you can with as many charts as you can get your hands on.

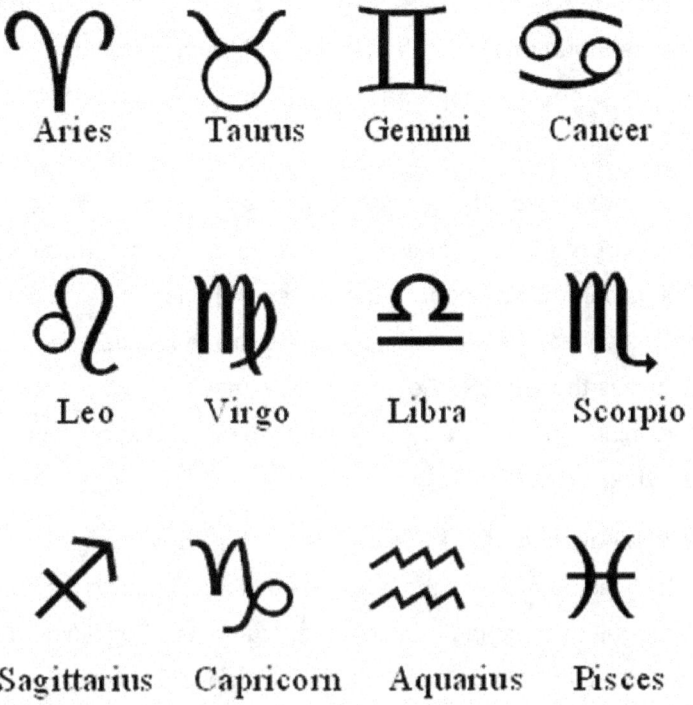

Above: the glyphs or symbols for the zodiac signs.

Pluto's Cave chart - look at the sign on the cusp of the 3rd house, it is Aries. To be more accurate it is 16°53' of Aries. This tells you that Pluto's Cave communicates enthusiastically, processes its thoughts quickly (which is Aries), can be hot tempered (Aries) and likes to argue the point (Aries). He enjoys winning an argument but if he doesn't he will quickly accept defeat and move on.

What does Aries on the 3rd house cusp look like in meditation? He would probably be dressed in an Aries manner - war-like perhaps, ruggedly handsome, sunburned maybe, muscular and bright minded. It is usually the archetype's physical appearance that you would notice first in your meditations.

Aries is a dynamic archetype, male or female, depending on how your psyche interprets this form of energy. Aries loves action and expressing himself physically, he probably gesticulates with his hands a lot. But it is his mind, his conscious active mind that we are most interested in because this is the WHERE he expresses himself. The 3rd house is the conscious mind, communication, early childhood and schooling, and his preferred style of learning.

If I were to meditate on the Pluto's Cave chart I would imagine I could walk up to Aries standing at the cusp. He might be holding a book, bouncing a ball or swinging a sword - he might even be twirling a globe of the earth in his hands. If I spoke to him his speech would be pronounced and emphatic, more so than almost anywhere else in the chart.

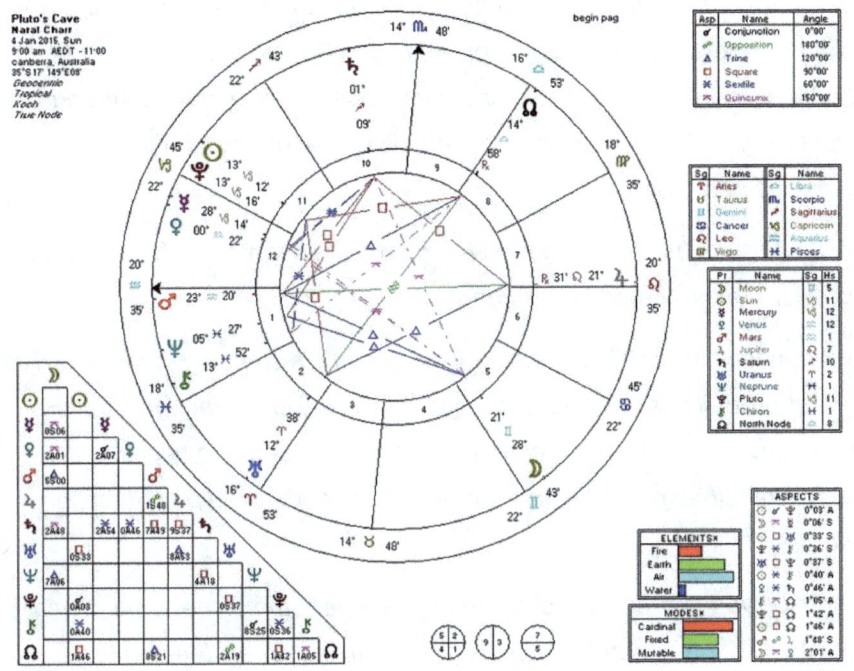

Above chart: the various formats and extra data that you can configure from your computer software.

This is my meditation with Aries on the 3rd house cusp: *Aries is standing at the cusp of the 3rd house, dressed in a short skirt like a Roman soldier. His sword is short and he is twirling a globe of the earth on the tip of his sword. The archetypes have a sense of humour and I would say that he was watching me writing that description in the previous paragraph.*

With a flick of his wrist he slices the globe into segments, 12 segments, to illustrate the theme of this chapter.

I can smell his sweaty body odour because he's standing in the sun. The ground is quite flat and reddish here. Aries is excited, though, excited that I have finally begun creating my books and courses because that allows him to express himself through my fingers as I type out these words.

Did I tell you that every archetype in your chart, the planets, signs and points (like the Ascendant, cusps and North Node) all demand to be expressed in their own particular way? Well, you really will be doing psychological astrology when you work with your own archetypes in this manner.

Aries wants his piece of the action just like every other sign and planet in the chart. He wants me to manifest him in the real world. He's not stupid, he knows he's a cusp ruler in Pluto's Cave's chart. Aries has been restless for some time and wants to see some action. Now he is expressing himself, through me and soon through you, his students.

Aries stops swinging his sword when I say that, now he's even more interested. "Students?" he asks.

"Of course, Pluto's Cave represents students too," I tell him.

Aries stands still for a moment. He's thinking, and that is what he does because he sits on the 3rd house cusp which rules cognition. He is Pluto's Caves' conscious mind and his role is to 'think' more so than to 'act'.

He tells me that he doesn't want to frighten the students so he won't try to dominate my writing. That is comforting, there are another 20-30 archetypes who want to be expressed in these books and courses and I'm not sure I could make them all happy. If one or two wanted to dominate I'd be exhausted trying to keep up with them.

I come back to the world and type up these notes.

A point to note: this method of meditating is an incredibly powerful way to 'know thyself' through the tarot as well. Have you seen my books on the tarot yet? I thoroughly recommend you have a look if you are interested. I've been working hard at developing each suit's elemental theme throughout the Tarot series and I'm blown away with what comes from the meditations for those books.

Your exercise:

1. Write down the signs on each of your own house cusps:

Sign on my Ascendant (1st house cusp): _____

Sign on my Midheaven (10th house cusp): _____

Sign on my other house cusps - etc: _____

2. Next, try to understand some of the features and qualities of your chart by talking with the archetypes in your meditations each day. Record

everything you do in meditation as well as in your dreams. As Freud said, *'dreams are the royal road to the unconscious'*.

3. Write down as many keywords for the signs as you can find, research high and low, immerse yourself in your study and write them all down.

Signs of the zodiac

I am quite mindful that most readers already know a lot about the signs of the zodiac and more information may simply annoy you. There are already so many excellent books and websites out there on the signs. I am also in the process of writing my next book, *'Psychological Astrology and the Signs of the Zodiac'*. This book will allow me to go into much greater depth with each sign. In this section I will add the keywords I use and insights into the psychology of each sign that I find most useful in my practice.

Aries - Cardinal Fire:- chauvinistic, stelliums, forceful, aggressive, energy, drive, wilful, fight against injustice, what you see is what you get, honest and brutal in defence, courageous, cheerful, strong, competitive. Aries rarely holds a grudge and will forget an argument almost immediately, they can't be upset for too long, life is just too fascinating for them to keep looking backwards. Aries can also be: selfish, childish, greedy, egotistical, impulsive, argumentative, restless energy.

Taurus - Fixed Earth:- practical, persistent, reliable, hardworking, sensual, loyal, pleasant friendships, jolly, musical, artistic, patient beyond reason, possessive, materialistic, lazy, over-weight and slovenly, stubborn with tunnel vision, opinionated, inflexible, food loving, pleasure loving, hoarder, collector, comfort eating and drinking, impatient and rude. If you want someone to work above and beyond their pay grade employ a Taurean. I see Taureans working 14 hour days and then some more because they never know when to say 'no, stop'. A good employee, partner or community member is someone who will take on a task and complete it on time and competently, this is where Taureans excel.

Gemini - Mutable Air:- adaptive, quick thinking, intelligent, bright, generous, quick witted, humorous, gossip, communicative, sharing, social, friendly, unreliable, con-artist, superficial, erratic, changeable, bored, disorganised, mental anguish, worry. Of all the signs of the zodiac I am always amazed by how clever Geminis are. They can juggle a social life, a party life, a job, their household, children, a part-time business and then come back the next day and do it all over again. They are charming, witty and have the ability to complete tasks with flair. One thing that trips them up though, is their tendency to become fixated on detail. They can fuss over a single sentence for hours to get it to read 'just right'. The very next day they will come back and change it.

Cancer - Cardinal Water:- emotions, moon phases may affect Cancerians (especially at the Full and New Moon), intuitive, loving, compassionate, nurturing, motherly, faithful, breasts and ovaries, stomach, oversensitive, manipulative, gain through cunning, sideways motion to achieve goals, vulnerable, controlling, clinging, moody, menstrual cycle, can't let go of their children, fear not being needed. These are the stay-at-home mums and dads who love family, love cooking and they love to feed everyone even more than anything else. A Cancerian without a family will go out and create a 'family' from their friendship group, workplace or social club. They love being needed too. If you ignore showing your appreciation for the Cancerian's pea and ham soup with home-made bread rolls you can really upset them. Don't try to break up their family either, that will really bring out their crabbiness. They will fight tooth and claw to bring everyone back to the warmth and comfort of their home.

Leo - Fixed Fire:- individualistic, independent, leadership, proud, noble, confidence, self-esteem, sensual, romantic, attention seeking, heroic, generous, loving, loyal, dramatic, drama queen, actors, arrogant, authoritative, domineering, lazy, over-the-top, indulgent. There are two main types of Leo. The first type is the gentle, generous and loving lion who protects and cares for everyone in his pride. He goes out of his way to make people feel special, loved and appreciated. This Leo is loyal to his friends and shares his bounty freely with them. The other type is the bossy, obnoxious bully who dominates others in his desire for glory, attention and recognition. This type is not very common but it can be seen with those who have a strong fire element in their chart. I have explained this in greater detail with the Air Fire Phenomenon.

Virgo - Mutable Earth:- service, perfectionism, practical, hard working, helpful, dependable, nagging, unadventurous, cleanliness, nit-picky, narrow minded, pedantic, generous, caring, kind. I like positive types of the Virgo archetype, they like to serve and always go beyond what is expected of them to help others feel comfortable. Some Virgo types can be nit-picky and pedantic but they do make good editors who can see the detail without the distracting fluff surrounding it.

Libra - Cardinal Air:- mediation, compromise, negotiation, relationships, balance, harmony, charming, diplomatic, attraction, beauty, art, music, appreciation, balanced objectivity, indecisive, selfish. Librans have a tendency to give in when they become stressed. I have worked with a lot of domestic violence victims, both male and female, who have compromised so much that they have nothing left to give. These Librans need to learn how to set boundaries and to enforce them.

Scorpio - Fixed Water:- evolution and transformation of spirit, crisis, destructiveness, revenge, creativity through rebirth, regeneration, energy healing, death defying, kundalini, tantra, sex, secretive, moody, aggressive, intensity, controlling, passionate, resourceful, sarcastic, jealous, abandonment, libido, betrayal, cruel, occult interests, psychic, astral travel, self destructive tendencies, power seeking, domineering, intuitive. The sign of Scorpio is often misunderstood because we tend to focus more on their external behaviour like sexuality, jealousy and their nasty aptitude for revenge. The Scorpio I see is the one who has so much internal need for union with their soul that will go to great pains to destroy anything that gets in their way. Sometimes they will even destroy themselves if that helps them achieve unity. The problem with this powerful soul-urge for spiritual unity is that it is extremely one-sided, no one can do all that by themselves. I think of a Scorpio dominated person as having just the one paddle in their canoe. Those who paddle on just one side of the canoe will end up going in circles. Scorpios need to learn to seek help, but it needs to be the right kind of help. They, of all the signs, are so focused that once they get started on the wrong path they can't stop until it ends which is often in disaster. On a positive note, once Scorpios learn that there are other ways to live besides pushing everyone out of their way, they can let go which allows their canoe to float freely down the river without any effort at all.

Sagittarius - Mutable Fire:- philosophy, morality, ethics, religion, police force, lawyers, knowledge, honesty, independence, fun loving, party animal, generous, irresponsible, tactless, wisdom, gambling, alcoholic, addictive, narcissistic, open minded, gregarious. There are two types of the Sagittarian archetype as well, The first is the wild centaur who indulges in self interest, greed and apathy towards those beneath them. These Sagittarians can be found in the judicial system, all religions, corporations and criminal organisations. Where ever there is money to be made you will find a centaur as its head. The other type of Sagittarius is the satyr Crotus, a loving and kind half-human half-goat. Crotus is much like Pan and Chiron. He is the opposite of the centaur and can be found as the philanthropist giving what he has earned through his talents in business to those who are needy. His interests include music, art and he is a swift hunter. It is said that Crotus invented the bow and arrow.

Capricorn - Cardinal Earth:- ambition, conservative, traditional, achievement, goals, reality, determined, resourceful, reliable, dependable, responsible, organisation, pragmatic, boring, insecure, fearful, domineering, controlling, bossy, tunnel vision, moralistic. Capricorn is the sign of 'slow and steady', just like the story of the 'Tortoise and the Hare'. You will find two types of Capricorn too, the one who is hard working, sticks to the rules and eventually, after a life-time of doing the right thing, achieves his or her goals. The other is the public servant who invents rules to thwart those he or she is supposed to serve. Capricorns are particularly aware of time and have a tendency to think in terms of *'tomorrow is almost upon me so I shall prepare for it today'*. Probably the best way to highlight Capricorn's traits is this Taoist story: *A man was hiking through the mountains when he came upon an old man planting an almond tree seedling. Knowing that almond trees take many years to mature he said to the old man, "It seems odd that a man of your advanced age would plant such a slow-growing tree." The old man laughed in replied, "I like to live my life based on two things: one is that I will live forever. The other is that this is my last day."*

Aquarius - Fixed Air:- humanity, intuition, originality, ingenious, need for freedom, rebellion, eccentric, independent, inventive, revolutionary, solitary, rebellious, unconventional, worry, stress and tension. When I see the Ascendant or a personal planet in this sign I am always on the lookout for excess and hyperactivity of any kind. If it is Venus I look for their need for unusual relationships be it with friends or lovers. If it is Mars then this person is driven to exceed anyone else's achievements usually accomplished via strange and usual means. If it is the Moon then it might manifest as an emotional roller coaster that is either way up or way down or both at once. The Aquarian Moon type can also appear aloof switching their feelings on and off at will which is ideal when handling a crisis. Aquarius dominant people are fascinating because they can take-on or adopt a variety of personalities. Like a consummate actor they play these roles without even trying. This is not the phasing in and out of people's energy like a Pisces who have no control over it. Aquarians do this to impact those around them or to achieve a uniquely Aquarian outcome. Aquarians can be the truest of friends. They have the capacity to forget your faults to focus on your strengths bringing out the best in you - but you will certainly have to work for it. Of all the signs Aquarius is most like the Alchemist of ancient times. Just remember that these qualities are always going to be modified by many other factors in the chart and should never be taken alone.

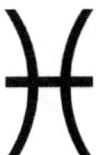

Pisces - Mutable Water:- disillusionment, confusion, illusion, dreams, spirituality, delusion, martyr, sacrifice, sensitivity, idealistic, sympathy, compassion, lost, imaginative, addictive, sleepy, unrealistic, abandonment, betrayal, suffering, morality and immorality. The watery sign of Pisces is what many people think is the most psychic sign of the zodiac. Yes, it rules the 12th house of the world of psyche but the Piscean must earn the right to access this form of spiritual proficiency. To swim in the waters of the unconscious without drowning takes years of dedicated training and self-discipline. Most Pisces just want to get on with life, as one Pisces said: *"I spend all my time trying to stay in this world while most of my friends are trying to get out of it."* The mundane world we share can be way too harsh, uncaring and painful for the Pisces dominated person. Their sensitivity is sometimes so raw that it simply hurts to go out in public. When you see planets in the sign of Pisces remember that this is someone that has depths few will ever understand. Most often the native just thinks that life is all about hardship and that is what it is meant to be. If they have Pisces strong in their chart they may need to be trained to use their sensitivity in other ways. If their usual mode is to take life head-on then they may be able to learn to engage while also disengaging, something like tai chi would be ideal for these people. Sheltering and protecting the Pisces from the harsh outer world is sometimes required allowing them time and opportunity to develop skills to manage life without drowning in it. Helping them convert sensitivity into activity is another approach. This allows Pisces dominated energy healers, musicians and artists to spread their wings and soar above the rest of humanity.

A good website on astronomy, which forms the foundations of astrology, is Christopher Crokett's site:

https://cosmoquest.org/x/365daysofastronomy/author/christophercrockett

Chapter 7 - Introduction to the 12 Houses

This chapter introduces you to WHERE the action takes place in your chart and thus your life. It is there in your houses. The first astrology book I wrote was *'Psychological Astrology and the Twelve Houses'*. I specifically wanted to write that book first because the houses are so important yet often poorly understood. Funny isn't it, we learn that the planets and signs are important, however, examining the houses has always been my starting point in chart delineation. *'Know thyself'* through the houses and the rest starts to fall into place is my thinking.

Let me now introduce you to one of the most confusing and complex fundamentals of astrology and that is the House Systems. As well as the signs your chart is also divided into 12 segments called the 'houses', it makes your chart look a bit like a pizza.

In a Whole Sign or Equal House system each house is exactly 30° wide. However, astrologers have a habit of doing crazy things and over time have played around with the way the houses are created. Some house systems, like Placidus, which is the most common Tropical house system, will cause some of the houses to become larger than the others. This means that some houses will need to be smaller so that all 12 houses fit into the 360° circle.

As the chart is a circle representing the movement of the planets through the heavens above us whenever a planet makes a full circuit of the chart this is called a 'cycle'. If you consider the Moon, which travels completely around the zodiac as well as around the earth in one month, you will see that it touches every planet and house cusp once during its cycle. If the Moon starts at 0° Aries today, in 27.3 days it will return to 0° Aries.

Before I go further, click the link to the houses in wikipedia below. It shows just how complicated calculating the house cusps can be. This shows why we now use computers to do all those complex calculations.

https://en.wikipedia.org/wiki/House_%28astrology%29

Back in ancient times astronomer astrologers used the Whole Sign system based on the 12 signs of the zodiac - the same 12 signs that we use today. Each Whole Sign horoscope (the word 'horoscope' means 'hour') is divided equally using the 30° segments for each zodiac sign. You can learn more about the Whole Sign house system from Hellenistic Astrologer Chris Brennan's podcast - www.theastrologypodcast.com - or here: https://www.youtube.com/watch?v=A_Vw0uy1mtM

A point to note: each **sign** of the zodiac is fixed at exactly 30° however, each **house** can be any size. This is one astrology fact you do need to remember – the signs are fixed at 30° but the houses aren't fixed to any size unless you use the Equal House or Whole Sign house system. The Placidus and Koch house systems are the most common House Systems used by western (Tropical) astrologers. These two house systems adjust the house size according to your place of birth north or south of the equator.

When you look at the Pluto's Cave chart you will notice that it was 'born' on 4th January 2015 at 9:00 am in Canberra, Australia. At the top left corner of the chart you will see the essential details necessary to draw up a chart: time of birth; date of birth; and place of birth.

Its 1st house has Aquarius on the cusp, therefore Aquarius is the Ascendant or Rising sign. Inside the 1st house you can see that it contains some planets: Mars, Neptune and Chiron. Keywords for the 1st house include: personality, mask, physical body, health in general.

The 2nd house cusp is Pisces – its keywords include: money, security, safety, material possessions, earning ability, values, attitudes, beliefs, ability to support others, anxiety due to insecurity.

The 3rd house cusp is Aries – its keywords include: communications, siblings, socialisation, mental activity and the conscious mind, intellectual pursuits, speaking skills, mental hobbies, daydreamer or critical thinker.

If you wanted you could include the actual degree of the cusp sign. For instance, Pluto's Ascendant is at 20° and 35' of Aquarius which is sometimes written 20°35' Aqu or 20°S35'. This tells you that the constellation of Aquarius was sitting on the eastern horizon at the time of Pluto's Cave's birth and it would be two thirds through its 2 hour sojourn at the Ascendant line.

The Ascendant moves 1° every 4 minutes of time. In 2 hours the entire 30° of your Ascendant sign changes to the next. Your Ascendant shows the 'face' or 'mask' you wear in public. Ask your friends if they can recognise your Ascendant sign's traits.

The Pluto's Cave chart shows that he likes to be seen as smart, independent, eccentric and intuitive - these are Aquarian traits.

Your Ascendant contains only some of the personality traits you project out into the world. Other traits will be found in your 7th house as well as your inner planets (Sun, Moon, Mercury, Venus and Mars).

The rest of your chart is made up of the other 11 houses, some have one or more planets inside and others have none. Does an empty house mean anything special? Not really, as you learn more about astrology you'll find that empty houses can still tell you a lot about your personality.

The sign on the house cusp leads you to its planetary ruler which is another important factor in reading or delineating charts.

A point to note: I often hear people complaining that they already know everything about this basic astrology stuff. I've studied and practised astrology and psychology professionally for 30 years and I still go back to the basics. I suggest that you continue to visit these foundational keywords and qualities at every opportunity.

Below are the house keywords that I used to start my own astrology journey. You are encouraged to collect as many keywords as you can and add them to your personal list.

Houses - keywords

1st house:- physical appearance, early childhood years, ego, personality, vitality, health in general, the mask, persona, self.

Psychologically – I always start with this house when examining a chart. Any planet that sits just inside or just above the Ascendant line is going to affect almost everything in the native's psyche. A planet that is applying or approaching the Ascendant from the 12th house will leak its specific form of energy into the native's consciousness. In other words they will have unconscious material from their 12th house enter their conscious mind. This material will be associated with the particular planet or planets involved. It can be triggered by events and situations, generally traumatic ones. A planet that is separating and sitting just below the Ascendant in the 1st house is going to manifest freely and consciously as part of the native's general personality. A planet in the 1st house will manifest quite clearly as part of their personality and this is why the 1st house is so important to me as a psychotherapist – it clearly shows the immediate qualities of the native. Anything in the 1st house is important, very important.

2nd house:- money, safety, material possessions, earning ability, values, attitudes and beliefs about your safety and needs for security, ability to support yourself and others, anxiety due to emotional or financial insecurity.

Psychologically – this house is triggered into action when the native's security is threatened. These threats are generally of a material nature more so than emotional or psychological. We all know how distressing it is when we don't have the cash for that special meal we promised our family; or when we can't drive over to our friends on the weekend because we can't afford to put fuel into our car. We will also see this house heavily involved with hoarders who are threatened with a court order to clean up their cluttered house – they end up in a panic. Material security is essential to our survival: without a roof over our head or the means to put food in our stomach and that of our family we are forced to do things that can challenge our fundamental morals and principles. I was reminded of this while watching the movie, *'Les Miserables'*. Actress Anne Hathaway as Fantine, has lost her job in a factory. To keep her daughter from the same fate as hers she turns to the only means of income available to her – prostitution. She eventually has to sell her beautiful hair and teeth as well. When we are forced into a corner, trapped, we become desperate and will do just about anything.

3rd house:- communication, siblings, mental activity and the conscious mind, intellectual pursuits, speaking skills, excessive worry, early schooling, daydreamer or acute hyperactive mind.

Psychologically – this is the house where I see those suffering from insomnia, excessive worry, racing negative thoughts and extreme irritation over the smallest of things. It is the house of your conscious mind which means little things can get stuck inside your head. When this house contains personal planets I am very conscious that this native needs to learn to relax, to practice 'thought stopping' techniques. These people have incredible minds. They can spot a mistake a mile away, they can structure a thought or a speech and recall it a week later. They can construct thoughts consciously while doing a hundred other tasks. Their challenge is to stop thinking when they need to switch off and get some sleep or to have a break. You will find many alcoholics when this house is populated by personal planets. They drink to stop their mind racing. When this house contains outer planets it is less constricted and not so excessive, however, it can manifest in a more unconscious way. Personal planets will express very clearly and consciously, you will see them in action in this house. Outer planets will be less visible, hidden and manifest less clearly. You will need to examine rulerships and aspects to understand their impact on the native's conscious mind.

4th house:- psychological past, upbringing, childhood to about 7 years, primary carer, family, house and home, inherited traits, conditioning.

Psychologically – this house highlights the native's childhood and upbringing. The 3 psychological houses, the 4th, 8th and 12th houses, are all associated with the native's management of their psychological issues. Those issues generally stem from their past which is primarily childhood, family, relationships with parents and siblings, schooling and their relationships with others during these early years. The 4th house is the key to these issues. Well aspected personal planets suggest that they were raised in a supportive and caring family environment. It shows that they will make a home very much like the one they were brought up in. When I see outer planets here I will check to see if there was stress of some sort or perhaps domestic violence in their childhood. Not all outer planets in the 4th house suggest violence or trauma. They may indicate that a parent was rarely at home perhaps because they were working to pay off a large mortgage or were studying at night school. In a single parent family absence is quite common. It could also mean that one of the parents had a mental illness and was mostly unavailable to their children. It could suggest that the parents were busy raising a troublesome child or needed regular hospitalisation. Perhaps a family member had a physical, intellectual or mental disability. Poverty plays an enormous role in this house too due to its impact on how the children were raised and cared for. Is the 4th house also a reflection of past lives? Maybe, I am more of the opinion that the entire chart is a reflection of past lives.

5th house:- individuality, creativity, speculation, addictions, sports, hobbies, imagination, friendships, need for fun and sex, talents, children, energy levels.

Psychologically – here is the house of adolescent fun, dangerous and risky joy-seeking behaviour, alcoholism, drug use, sex and excesses of every kind. It is also the house of the creative and imaginative mind as well as friendship. What an enormous combination of personality traits and behaviours this house is responsible for. When I see a loaded 5th house I am aware that this person will sometimes struggle controlling their urges to do something outrageous. I am also aware that they may have addiction problems and that having fun is a priority. These traits, however, are not the 5th house's only expression. Counselling someone with a loaded 5th house is a challenge because these behaviours are self fulfilling – they give the native great pleasure. How do you take something like that away without causing grief, loss and a powerful urge to fill the gap with something just as exciting? You don't take their pleasure away, instead you slowly ease a substitute in its place. This is also the house of spirit which contains an unconscious drive to fulfil what is missing in their life. It is the house of meaningful existence. Natives with a loaded 5th house are on a quest to find meaning to their life. I can't stress enough how important meaningfulness is to these natives. They are usually highly intelligent and will sometimes respond when shown that there is an alternative path, that of the mystic. With this as an alternative they can maintain their sense of adventure while also eliminating the dangers of heart attack, stroke and accidents. Rather than ruining their own life as well as those they take with them, they can embark on a safer and more meaningful adventure.

6th house:- responsibility, physical health, reliability, self-discipline, determination, service, work environment.

Psychologically – so many times I've looked for my client's health problems in the 6th house only to be disappointed, because this is not just the house of health. It can point to issues but it is a very general pointer. Health is complex, it is constructed from every planet and point in the chart and no single point holds the secret. It does, however, highlight the qualities that lead to good health: reliable, responsible behaviour, dedication to healthy pursuits and disciplined actions. It shows how the native will organise their life around good habits and sensible choices. This is the house of service as well and shows quite clearly how well the native gets along with their co-workers, employers and employees. If someone asks about their career this house will show you how well they stick to their tasks, how well they work in a team or independently and whether they will turn up to work at all. A very important house that highlights the native's attitudes to life, dedication to serve others as well as their personal cleanliness and habits.

7th house:- lovers, partners, enemies, marriage, romance, partnerships in business, court actions, legal contracts, customers, clients, others, projections and shadows.

Psychologically – as an astrologer you will always be asked about someone's love life, their future partner and their marriage. You will find those answers in the chart and this is the house I will turn to first. The 7th house does not have all the answers though, you will need to also look at what Venus, Sun and Moon as doing and particularly if they have hard aspects to the outer planets. But generally speaking any planets in the 7th house will be major players in the native's choice of partner and how things play out in their marriage. I have frequently counselled people who continually enter relationships with the wrong types. Over and over they choose the wrong man or woman who hurts them yet they keep coming back for more repeating the same mistakes every time. The classic is someone with Jupiter conjunct the 7th house cusp or inside the 7th house. Some will have Sagittarius on the 7th house cusp as well. These are the natives who fall for someone who is a party animal, showy, generous and who appears to have it all. The excitement of being with them and enjoying their alcohol, drugs and parties is just too alluring. When this is pointed out to them they must decide whether to continue like this or make a wise and sensible choice and walk away. Counselling people with a loaded 7th house will challenge you like no other.

8th house:- passion, intensity, serious sex, tantra, kundalini, transformation, crisis, psyche, occult, destructive tendency, power, fascination with death and the afterlife, the mystic's quest for self knowledge, the urge to balance emotional and psychic disharmony.

Psychologically – I have said a lot about Scorpio, Pluto and the 8th house already so I won't go into great depth here. Basically this is the house of crisis, anyone with a loaded 8th house is going to stagger from one crisis to the next. In fact they can recall every wound that they have ever received in life. This continual state of crisis is what forces them to seek a way out. They eventually realise that they must transform or die. It is also the house of death, the occult and a fascination with the afterlife. The native can be guided to embark on a spiritual journey - I call it the mystic's quest. This can potentially redirect destructive crisis while fulfilling their obsession with the occult. By providing such a pathway the native can find what they are looking for: a means to escape the torment of life while also discovering what lies beyond the curtain that separates life and death.

9th house:- wisdom, law, morality, irresponsible behaviour, higher learning, long distance travel, philosophy of life, life experiences, addictive personality, immorality, criminals, religion, an appetite for more of everything.

Psychologically – this is the house of the moralist, the lawgiver and the wise philosopher. The 9th house shows us where the native goes to find his moral compass and highlights how and where they seek wisdom. When this house is loaded with planets, particularly the personal planets Moon, Sun, Mercury, Venus and Mars, the native is often a full time student, an academic, lawyer or someone involved with religion. It means that they never stop learning be it at university, night school or surfing the internet. When this house contains outer planets you will see the native take their studies so much more seriously than anyone else. They anchor their self-esteem and personal beliefs on knowledge. This applies to occultists like tarotists and astrologers as well as those involved with the hard sciences. Anyone who can't let go of their studies, who can't write that book because they still have to learn one more thing, they are the ones most affected by the 9th house. It is also the house of the immoral and the criminal. I will be exploring this in greater depth in my next book, *'Psychological Astrology and the Signs of the Zodiac'*.

10th house:- ambition, achievement, direction, destiny, career, public image, authority figures.

Psychologically – the house of the ambitious and the blessed over-night success story. Have you ever wondered why it is that some people are so successful? Everything they touch turns to gold. Look to the 10th house for success in every endeavour be it writing, business, friendships, study and anything to do with setting and achieving goals. I like to see the Sun in the 10th house, the closer it sits to the Midheaven the better. Sun in the 10th house shows that the sun shines through this person and touches everyone they meet. This is the charm and gregariousness of the Leo shining at his best. Everyone likes a person who makes them feel good about themselves and this is what this placement does. The native with their Sun in the 10th house can make those around them feel special. Then there is Saturn who suggests that this person is driven to work hard and shows dedication and self-discipline in the pursuit of their goals. These are important qualities for success. Next is Venus who manifests similarly to the Sun in the 10th house. Venus is attractive and everyone is attracted to attractive people. All the research on beauty and success shows us that shop attendants, for instance, will always seek to serve the most attractive customer first. We bend over backwards for those who are physically or sexually attractive. This is what Venus brings to the native who has it sitting in their 10th house, the closer to the cusp the better. It doesn't necessarily mean that the native uses those qualities to consciously manipulate others. It means they unconsciously ooze these qualities and that is what makes them more inclined to get what they want. I would not say that these natives are selfish or narcissistic. They are simply blessed with good genes, good manners and oodles of charm.

11th house:- humanitarian, dreams and wishes for the future, friends and associates in clubs and other organisations, ideals, helping the environment.

Psychologically – this is the house of the humanitarian be it to save the planet from climate change, to save starving children or to serve on the local community committee. A person with a loaded 11th house, especially with more than one personal planet residing there, takes life seriously. They see things most of us ignore and pass by. Rescuing a bird with a broken wing on the side of the road is an example of their keen sense of humanity. They also rage against injustice and you will find these people in organisations that struggle against strict orthodoxy and dogma at every level. They don't necessarily have a religious view but attack injustice with religious vigour. These people also have difficulty getting in touch with their emotions. They can easily talk about how they feel, or better still, about how others feel. When it comes to discussing their own feelings and experiences that led them to seek counselling they struggle. It isn't that they want to avoid talking about how they feel, they love to talk, it is because they can't quite connect to their emotions. The native with a loaded 11th house needs to be coached, taken by the hand and walked through how to engage in therapy. They love it when they can go within and get in touch with their wounded selves and their sad inner children. Once they understand what is needed they are off on another campaign, another crusade. This time the crusade is to save those facets of their psyche that have been splintered off through trauma and remain hidden within.

12th house:- deep unconscious, higher self, haunted by memories of the past, extreme sensitivity, escapism, hidden strengths and weaknesses, imprisonment, secrets, karma, the deep waters of the unconscious.

Psychologically – as I have said before, the 12th house is the very last house of the chart. For me it is like a cave where you can visit the archetypes who are resting there. If you don't have planets within the 12th house then you can talk to the sign sitting on its cusp. Those who have a loaded 12th house, that is with one or more personal planets, Moon, Sun, Mercury, Venus and Mars, will often struggle to find a way to express that planet's energy. Planets applying to, or within 8° of the Ascendant are strongest. I mentioned earlier that these planets tend to leak into the 1st house, it is like a ceiling that leaks when it rains. These people struggle with unwanted thoughts and memories. The specific qualities of the planets in the 12th house can be triggered by external events or situations. These people do well in therapy but they are often the ones who drop out the soonest. Life is hard for them and unless you can provide a suitable therapeutic approach that matches their needs they will run. Avoidance is one means of surviving their inner world of the 12th house. They do that by sleeping all day, missing appointments, prescription drug and alcohol use and failing to attend school or work. They need someone who knows how to work with their depth of trauma and the very rawness of it. Inner child therapy is what works best for them.

Further reading: *'Psychological Astrology and the Twelve Houses'* by Noel Eastwood.

Chapter 8 - Planetary aspects and chart shapes

Major aspects and harmonics

Aspects are the lines in the middle of the chart that join the planets. These lines are called aspect lines or just 'aspects' for short. They show the geometric angle between the planets which astrologers use to understand their relationships with each other.

I know that I've said this before but I'll say it again: I view the chart as a community of characters. The planet and sign archetypes become real people with real needs, urges and interests. I ask them questions about how they can help me, what they need from me and even to negotiate with those planets in conflict so that they can be at peace with each other to support our common needs. They are my inner guides, healers and counsellors.

All aspects are harmonics found by dividing the 360° of a circle by any number. Simply divide 360 by 1, 2, 3, 4, 5, 6, etc. and you will get a harmonic.

For instance, the first harmonic is obtained by dividing the circle by 1 which is the Conjunction at 0°.

The 2nd harmonic is found by dividing the circle by 2 = 180°, the Opposition.

The 3rd harmonic is the circle divided by 3 = 120° which is called a Trine.

The 4th harmonic is the circle divided by 4 = 90° which called a Square.

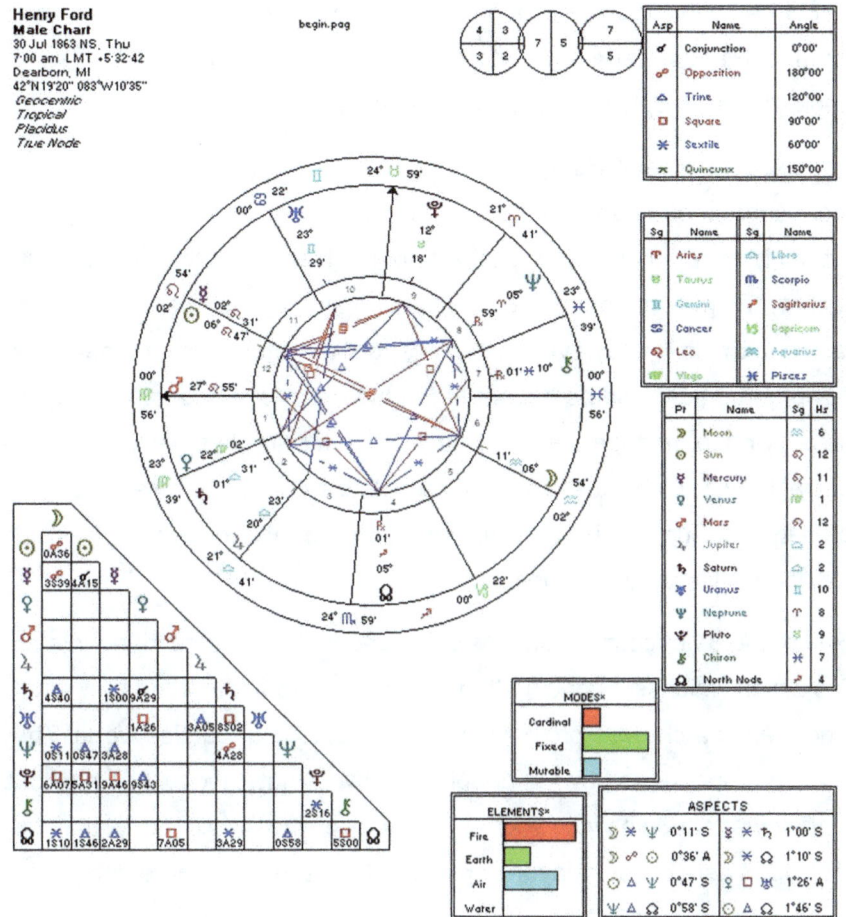

Above chart: Henry Ford.

Look at Henry Ford's chart and you will notice that there are a number of lines in the middle circle. These are the aspect lines, the energy relationships between the planets. Using Henry's chart you can see that his Sun is in Leo and so he would probably have a mane of hair that would shine brightly in the light, a strong face and stance. His personality would be Leonic too, exhibiting charm, strength of character and a noble bearing. Pluto in Taurus would be dark, powerful in build and appearance, deeply secretive and somewhat foreboding.

The aspect between Henry's Sun and Pluto is a Square (90°) which means that the relationship between them is somewhat challenging, probably not a comfortable relationship. In other words the Sun and Pluto archetypes may not get along very well. They may stand apart while you talk to them, they may even play power games against each other. This power struggle would be happening within Henry's subconscious while he is trying to manage the many stresses in his life. At times it would distract him from his tasks. In other words the conflict between the two archetypes, Sun and Pluto, could sabotage Henry and his enjoyment of life and his life purpose - destiny.

One of the defence mechanisms of psychoanalytic psychotherapy is Projection which is a concept that you can use to understand how and where each archetype projects their urges onto your outside world. They could be represented by the people you love & hate; those who play out their power struggles with you; or even those who are kind to you. If you look upon aspects as relationships then it is easier to understand.

Calculating Aspects

Basically you take the degree of each planet and check it against every other planet. When I was studying astrology this was done by hand. It was very easy to make mistakes, many a time I had to redo them, more often than I would have liked. These days you can use a computer to print out the aspect grid and study it at your leisure.

Let me give you an example of how to read the aspects. If the Sun is at 15° Leo it will form a conjunction, square, opposition or trine aspect to almost every planet that is also at 15° of a sign. It will make a conjunction, trine, opposition or square aspect to any planet when they are within an orb of 10°. The 'orb' is like the 'error' in statistics, plus or minus 10°. Orbs are important and I'll explain them in more detail through this chapter.

In this example, if the Moon is between 5° and 25° of a fixed sign like Leo is, then it would form a square if in Scorpio or Taurus and an opposition if in Aquarius. If the Moon is in a fire sign (Aries or Sagittarius) it would be in a trine aspect to the Sun. If it is between 5° and 25° of Leo it would be conjunct the Sun.

I use an orb of 10° for all of the planets. Some astrologers use an orb of 15° while others use an orb of 8° or even 5°. Every astrologer has a preferred orb that they use in their calculations. The closer the two planets are to each other the stronger the aspect / relationship.

Applying Aspects < > Separating Aspects

When a faster moving planet is approaching an exact conjunction, square, trine, opposition, etc. we call it 'applying'. In other words this planet is moving towards the slower one. Using Henry Ford's chart you can see that Mercury is applying towards the Sun. It is moving towards an exact conjunction with the Sun. The Sun on the other hand is 'separating' which means that it is moving away from the exact conjunction with Mercury.

Knowing whether a planet is applying or separating helps the astrologer determine if the aspect, and therefore the relationship between the planets, is getting stronger or weaker. An applying aspect is developing energy and will remain active and dynamic throughout the native's lifetime. Separating aspects, however, have already spent their energy and are easing off. These applying and separating aspects are most important when you learn about Transits and Progressions.

The further a planet is from Sol, the sun, in our Solar System, the slower it moves around your chart. Therefore Mercury, the closest planet to the sun, moves faster around your chart than Pluto which is the furthest planet from the sun. The two planets inside the Earth's orbit, Mercury and Venus, will always travel roughly the same speed around your chart as the astrological Sun which is about 1° per day. Sedna, a trans-Neptunian planet discovered in 2003, completes her orbit around the sun in 11,400 years. Obviously Sedna is a very long way away completing its cycle around your chart in 11,400 years - so don't hold your breath waiting for it.

The Major Aspects

☌ **Conjunction - 0°- orb of 10°–** when two planets are close to each other their energies blend. This can be likened to playing two notes of a musical scale to create a harmonic. Some of these harmonics will sound quite pleasant while others won't.

The planets in conjunction in Henry's chart are Sun and Mercury. The Sun at 6°47' of Leo and Mercury at 2°31' also in Leo. They are within 4° of each other which is well within your 10° orb. This is a tight conjunction showing that the two planets have a strong influence on each other. Both planets are in the same sign and house which makes it easier to read too.

I also notice that Mars is conjunct Henry's Ascendant from the 12th house by 3°. This has significant impact on Henry because it is applying to the Ascendant from the 12th house.

A conjunction between Sun and Mercury is quite common because Mercury never moves more than 28° away from the Sun. This is because it is inside the Earth's orbit. Venus is also inside the Earth's orbit and is never more than 47° from the Sun in the chart. All the other planets are outside the Earth's orbit and do not travel along with the Sun in the chart like Mercury and Venus do.

☐ **Square - 90° - orb of 10°** – the square aspect is formed when two planets are 90° apart. I use an orb of 10° which means that their angle can be between 80° and 100°. This aspect is traditionally a hard aspect, one that requires you to work at to overcome the lessons it throws at you. It presents as a psychological challenge that is difficult to notice, like a feather sitting on top of your head, you don't notice it but others can.

Looking at Henry's chart you can see that Venus is square Uranus. Venus, being the faster moving planet, is applying to an exact square with Uranus. You can see this by looking at the slower moving planet's degree. Uranus is at 23°29 while Venus is at 22°02. Within 24 hours Venus will make an exact square aspect with Uranus. At the moment they are within 2° of arc, Venus only has to travel just over 1° to form an exact square aspect with Uranus. You would say that *'Venus is applying to Uranus but is yet to form an exact square'*. This aspect is quite dynamic, it hasn't lost its momentum which will happen when the two planets begin to separate.

Square aspects are difficult, they require committed effort to understand and resolve. They are also your most powerful allies in self development. They force you to improve or else you become stuck in a rut. Henry is at risk of being quite impossible to live with as Venus is sociable while Uranus is tense and restless - together they indicate social tension and irritability.

Squares give you character, they can force you to recognise your faults which provides you with opportunities to improve yourself. If you use the analogy of trying to look on top of your head you will begin to understand. You can't do it, you simply can't see up there, you will just keep turning around like a dog chasing its own tail. Your problems are just not visible to you until you actively seek to understand yourself.

☍ **Oppositions - 180° - orb of 10°** – two planets opposite each other at 180°, you will see them on opposite sides of the chart. It has the same orb as the conjunction and square - 10°. Oppositions are not as hidden or disguised as the square. In an opposition you can see the problem, it is there right in front of you. Often you will butt into it like hitting your head against a brick wall. You know there is a problem but are unable or unwilling to face it and resolve it. Like the square, the opposition is dynamic and forces you to work on self-improvement.

A point to note: a chart with many squares and oppositions describes a person with lots of personal issues to work on. They are, however, hard workers, they have to be, there is no time for them to sit down and relax. No-one will come along to do it for them or clean up after them. Life can be tough for these people but they are generally the 'salt of the earth' types who pitch in and help others. They are the types who help out but never expect anything in return. The opposition aspect allows you to view the problem while the square is almost invisible and therefore harder to resolve.

In Henry's chart the Moon is opposite his Sun and Mercury, as is Neptune opposite Saturn. In the first case the Moon is the faster planet and is separating, that is, she is moving out of orb and away from the exact degree (11° Leo 06') of the slower Sun. This aspect has already spent its energy before birth, perhaps during delivery or while still in the womb. However, the aspect is still quite strong, it is a Full Moon no less.

The other opposition is between the outer planets Saturn and Neptune. Saturn is the faster of the two and is approaching or applying towards the exact degree of Neptune at 5°59 of Aries. This applying aspect is strong, but at the same time is not as significant as the oppositions of Moon and Sun / Mercury, because it is between two generational or outer planets.

△ **Trine - 120° - orb 10°** – two planets 120° from each other but with a 10° orb can be between 110° and 130° apart. This is traditionally a gentle aspect, it is nice and easy flowing. It doesn't need much energy to gain access to the planet's energy.

The problem with trines is that too many can make you overly sensitive to criticism and in some cases it can make you lazy. Life is easy with many trines in your chart. You don't need to make much of an effort to get what you want. However, you generally can't tolerate pain or discomfort at levels that most people can. An excess of trines makes the native extremely sensitive, sometimes it impacts on their health, especially the liver. They suffer when most of us find the going mildly difficult. The trine dominated native may complain bitterly when they have to help out while most of us consider supporting others as just a simple part of life.

People dominated by many trines don't quite understand that they need to co-operate and make an effort in life. They can feel that life owes them a living. They sometimes have an attitude of entitlement that can make them both attractive and repulsive to others who have to serve them. There are many of Jupiter's negative traits in people dominated by trines.

A person with a balance of trines, squares and oppositions, will find that life provides enough of a challenge to be satisfying and yet it is not beyond their strength nor is it too demanding and painful. Too many trines becomes too much of a good thing, but I think that most of us would like a few more, just to ease the load we carry.

In Henry's chart you can see quite a few trines, they form two patterns: a Grand Trine and a Mystic Rectangle. His Moon trines Jupiter and Saturn; Uranus trines Jupiter too; Sun and Mercury trine North Node and Neptune; and Neptune trines Jupiter. The Grand Trine is the big triangle connecting Neptune, Jupiter and Sun/Mercury.

✶ Sextile - 60° - orb of 4° to 6° – the sextile is similar to but not as strong as the trine. It provides opportunities but you will need to put in effort to make it work. The trine provides the opportunities plus the people to make it happen with only minimal effort. Trines and sextiles are most helpful when you have several oppositions and squares in your chart as they ease these harsher aspects. Henry's Mystic Rectangle is formed by two trines (Neptune and Mercury + Moon and Saturn) plus two sextiles Neptune and Moon + Saturn and Mercury.

In Henry's chart you can see sextiles between North Node and Saturn; Saturn and Sun / Mercury; Mars and Uranus; Pluto and Chiron; Moon and Neptune; Moon and North Node. That is a lot, they almost cover the whole chart. Henry, being an ambitious man, obviously made good use of these sextiles to go down the path of building his empire. He capitalised on opportunities and had the energy and drive to make them all come together to achieve success.

⚼ **Quincunx - 150° - orb of 4°** – this aspect is also known as an 'inconjunct'. It is one of initial stress followed by an easing and then its release. For instance, the qunicunx between Chiron and Sun begins as stress which is probably related to Henry's health or the relationship with his father. The stress between these two planets builds as Henry becomes exhausted and run down but going to bed early can bring him back to his old happy self. The tension builds inside Henry until there is a crisis, perhaps he can't get up in the morning. This is followed by some form of release and then things pick back up. The issue is resolved for the moment until the next health crisis tests his Sun's vitality. In some ways you could call it a soft square with a touch of sextile.

These aspects described above are the ones I use all the time in my practice of astrology.

Major Aspects: *strongest is Conjunction followed by Opposition*					
Aspect name	Symbol	°	Harmonic	Orb	Description
Conjunction	☌	0	1	10° Sun Moon & planets	Planets are next to each other - blending their energies, both comfortable and uncomfortable, depends on the two planets
Square	□	90	4	same	Uncomfortable, challenging - two archetypes standing to the side of each other, neither can see the other, they can feel the tension but are unable to recognise where it is coming from, squares make people strong of character
Opposition	☍	180	2	same	Not as harsh as a square but still challenging - both archetypes standing opposite each other, you know who is bothering you, easier to work with
Trine	△	120	3	same	Comfortable, fast energy transfer - too many can make the person too sensitive and perhaps lazy as they don't need to put effort into their lives
Sextile	✶	60	6	6° Sun Moon, & planets	Easy flowing energy, like a small Trine – helps to have a few of these as the person will find that with a little effort much is made easy in life
Quincunx	⚻	150		6° sun, Moon, & planets	Planet energy begins to feel uncomfortable, the tension builds then it is released – tension followed by a release

Table above – Major Aspects

Aspects and Spiritual Development

Aspects also work to your advantage on your mystic's quest.

Conjunctions are always the most powerful influence in your life. This includes planets aspecting house cusps.

Squares are also powerful. They drive you to understand what is happening below the surface of your psyche. With a square your lessons await hidden deep in your unconscious.

Trines are useful in personal growth but it is best when there are just a few. They can act as release points when stress builds. Too many trines can act to bog your mystic quest down in the mud.

Oppositions may be the easiest to work with because the issues are visible, right there in front of you.

Don't think that the aspects in your chart are there to trip you up, they are there to help you. Hard lessons are better than easy ones, the more effort you need to make the better the learning of them. This may seem counter intuitive but from my experience it is the way things need to be.

Name	Symbol	Degree	Orb	Harmonic	Description
Semi-square	∠	45	1	8	Irritating, soft square
Sesqui-square	⚻	135	1	nil	Abrasive,
Semi-sextile	⚺	30	1	12	Helpful, reactive
Quintile	Q	72	1	5	Innate or hidden talent
Septile	S	51.43	1	7	Repercussions, inevitable events
Novile	N	40	1	9	Testing – also called Nonagon
B-quintile	BQ	144	1	nil	Creative, harmonious

Table above – Minor Aspects

Minor Aspects

I rarely if ever use minor aspects, in fact not many astrologers use them unless they have time and a good reason to analyse a chart at that depth. It can take weeks and even months when using every conceivable astrology technique described in the literature. I find that the major aspects provide more than enough information for general readings. Adding more aspects would take me so long to do a reading that I would price myself out of a job. However, many of these aspects still play an important role in astrology and are particularly useful in research. As for you, the student, make up your own mind, do your own research and find what works best for you - and then test what you discover with dozens of charts.

Aspect Orbs

An orb is the degree at which the two planets begin to have an effect on each other. Too far apart and there is no impact, the closer to the exact degree of the slowest planet the more powerful the aspect becomes. Orbs show us the limits or boundaries of influence between planets and house cusps too.

Orbs describe how far apart the two planets can be before they lose impact on each other. This allows you to decide if you need to examine them or not. Note that some astrologers use wider orbs of up to 15° for major aspects.

A point to note: planets close to the angular house cusps (1st, 4th, 7th and 10th houses) are stronger when within about 8° (I prefer to use a 5-7°

orb). This is the orb or the planet's outer limits of influence with the house cusps.

'Wide', 'out of sign' and 'out of house' conjunctions

Look at Venus and Saturn, 22°02 Virgo and 1°31 Libra which is 9°33 away from each other. This is just within my orb of 10°. Although I use a 10° orb for the planets in my readings many astrologers use 8°. If you used an 8° orb in this example, Saturn and Venus are still quite close, but not close enough to form a conjunction. They are, however, close enough to be called a **'wide conjunction'** or a 'mundane' conjunction. This means that the two planets are close enough to influence each other but not close enough for it to be a strong influence. Another thing to note with these two planets is that Venus is in Virgo and Saturn is in Libra, that means they are in different signs called **'out of sign'** so the influence is a little weaker still. Adding to this, both planets are in different houses, so that makes the conjunction **'out of house'**, this also weakens them a little.

Planets conjunct in the same sign and house are the strongest, but when they fall in different signs or houses they aren't quite as strong. In Henry's chart Venus and Saturn are in an 'out of sign' and 'out of house' conjunction. This suggests a minor weakness in Henry's love-life and close friendships. Other indicators of a possible relationship weakness are Venus in Virgo and Venus square Uranus (which is Venus' only major aspect).

When would I consider a conjunction wide using my 10° orb? When two planets are at 12° to 15° apart I would look to see if they are exalted in their own sign or house. This could have a positive or negative impact on the native.

Conjunctions between planets are the single most powerful aspect in astrology which is why it is important to delineate them properly. My rule-of-thumb is: if in doubt always consider a wide conjunction as a proper conjunction.

Chart Shapes

Planets form shapes in the chart. These are named for the shapes that can be seen in the world around us. For instance, Henry Ford has a Splash, a scattered chart, no real shape emerges. Shapes are a visual guide providing information on the chart but by no means are their interpretations superior to that of the individual planet interpretations. You might use them as a general guide. Personally, I rarely consider planetary shapes, they simply do not explain the intricate details that is found in the patterns and aspects formed by the whole chart. Too much information is lost by relying on a single and usually simplistic interpretation.

Splash – rare, all houses have planets in them, a scattered individual or someone that finds interest in many pursuits.

Locomotive – the planets follow each other in a line like a train, the space between the first and last must be no less than 120°. The planet leading in a clockwise direction is the strongest by sign, house and rulership. This person is directed, self contained and purposeful.

Bowl – all the planets must be within 180°; the planet leading in a clockwise direction is the strongest. Like the locomotive above, the native is directed and self contained. The interpretation of these two shapes will vary according to which planet is leading.

Splay – planets are scattered in small groups, this person is organised and orderly.

Bundle – the planets must be bundled together within a Trine or a Square; it is quite rare, this focuses or narrows the person's outlook on life.

Bucket – also called the sling-shot; has 8 or 9 planets within 180° and the remaining 1 or 2 planets are on the opposite side, a bit like a bucket with a handle. This person is single minded and purposeful, often the planet(s) forming the handle is the strongest planet(s).

See-Saw – two groups of planets opposite each other; must have 5 on each side with more than 60° of space between the groups. This person is indecisive but prepared to examine both sides of an argument.

Aspects to the Ascendant and Midheaven

These aspects can have impact on the native though they aren't always used by astrologers. They demonstrate the planetary effect on the person's ego represented by the Ascendant, and the influence or impact on the person's ambitions and achievements as well as their standing in the public eye which is their Midheaven. Use these aspects but only with due consideration for the more important aspects between the planets.

Another reason that they are not commonly used is that an accurate birth time is critical for an accurate Ascendant and Midheaven. You can never be absolutely certain of an accurate birth time. Be prepared to accept that your chart is off by about 2°, this includes all of the house cusps, and that is if you are lucky. Remember this because it may save you from making an inaccurate prediction.

Retrograde (R), Stationary (S) and Direct Planetary Motion (D)

The Moon and Sun never go Retrograde (R), all the other planets do, except for the North Node which is nearly always retrograde and occasionally Stationary (S). The other planets can be in either of three states: Direct (D), Stationary (S), or Retrograde (R).

While all the planets travel around the chart in an anticlockwise direction, Direct, there are times when they will stop S, go backwards R, only to resume their D momentum - in an anticlockwise direction.

Direct planets are true to their nature while S adds a slight emphasis on that planet. However a R planet is moving back to the past signifying that the native needs to learn a bit more according to its nature.

Planets that go R by transit (after you are born the planets continue moving and are now called Transiting planets) are a pain when they sit on sensitive points in your chart. For instance, if Mercury is sensitive or poorly aspected in your natal chart, you may feel affected when it goes R by transit. If you have a R planet then that planet, the sign it is in and its house position, are in need of more attention than usual.

I don't consider a R planet to be much more important than any other planet when I do a reading – unless that planet is particularly conflicted. In this situation I will examine it in more detail.

The influence of inner planet conjunctions with the outer planets Jupiter, Saturn, Chiron, Uranus, Neptune and Pluto

If you read Bill Tierney's *'Dynamics of Aspect Analysis'* you will find that he describes an inner planet (Moon, Sun, Mercury, Venus and Mars) conjunct an outer planet as more powerful than any other planetary combination. The outer planet will always have significantly greater influence over the inner planet. The outer planets are far more psychologically demanding than the inner planets.

Outer planets are dynamic unconscious forces that find expression through their signs, houses and their aspects with the inner planets. A conjunction between 2 outer planets but not an inner planet, can sometimes feel as though they are hidden and not fully engaged in your life. Contact with an inner planet or an Angular house (1st, 4th, 7th or 10th) will help them show their full capabilities. The outer planets need to be exhaustively examined to understand their impact on the native if they only aspect another outer planet.

Nothing occurs in isolation – outer planets are also known as Generational Planets. A whole generation of people, for instance a school year cohort, will have an outer planet in the same sign and in some cases at the same degree. For instance, a whole school grade will have Pluto in Scorpio or a Uranus / Neptune opposition because the outer planets can stand Stationary for years.

The outer planets exhibit the archetypal urges and instincts that influences each generation. However, because they lie deep in the unconscious it is not always easy to recognise their impact on the individual without deep analysis. Outer planet sign and aspects to each other are generational, thus a whole cohort of people of the same age can present with similar traits. The inner or personal planets are much more visible because they are expressed directly as opposed to indirectly as the outer planets are.

When delineating a chart I start with the inner planets, their sign and house position. Be mindful with outer planets though as they will rarely exhibit their sign placement as powerfully as an inner planet. Inner planets are more noticeable regardless of aspects when compared to the outer planets. You will notice a person's Mars in Aries by their drive and aggression and by their lack of social graces. You won't notice Pluto in Aries as much as his house placement and the aspects he forms to house cusps (conjunctions), luminaries and inner planets.

Jupiter is one planet that is commonly seen in school year cohorts. As Jupiter travels through a sign every twelve months a whole class of students can be born while Jupiter is in a single sign. For instance Jupiter is in Sagittarius as I write this book. He entered Sagittarius on the 9th of November 2018 and leaves Sagittarius to enter Capricorn on the 3rd of December 2019. Every child born in that time period will have Jupiter in Sagittarius.

Where and how would each child express Jupiter in Sagittarius most strongly? You can discover this by his house placement, his aspects with the other planets, and if he is within or conjunct an angular house (1st, 4th, 7th or 10th house).

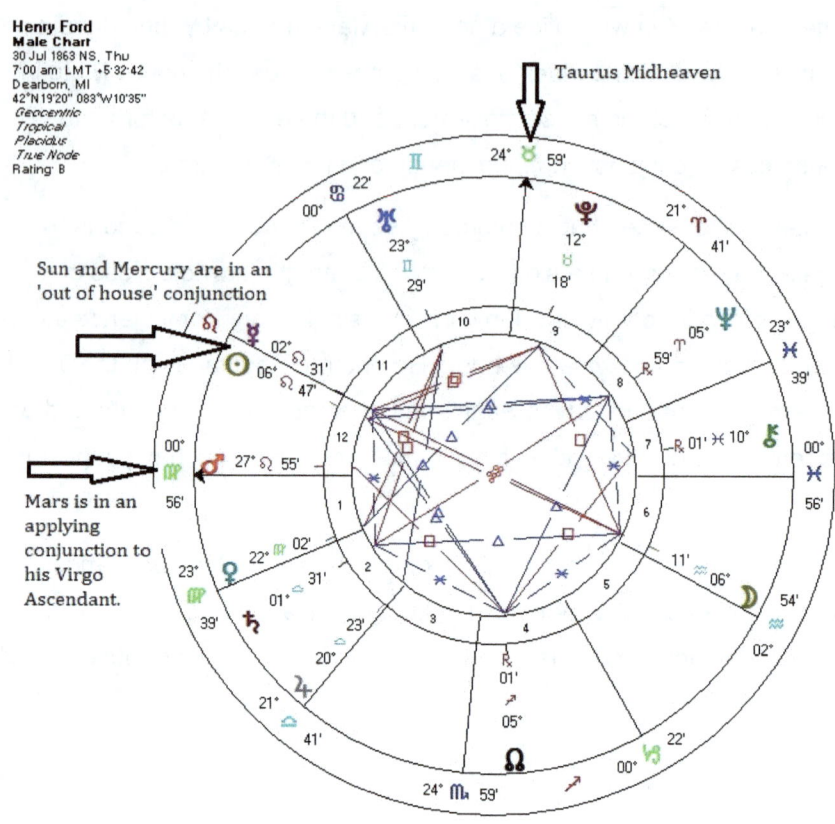

Above chart: Henry Ford showing some of the major features in his chart.

Applying a psychological astrology approach to delineating Henry Ford's chart

I now want to show you how I work with a chart using just two points – Ascendant and any planet that conjuncts it, which in this case is Mars.

Henry has Mars at 27°♌55 (27 degrees and 55 minutes of Leo). Mars is approaching Henry's Virgo Ascendant which is at 0°…56 (zero degrees and 56 minutes of Virgo). Mars is therefore applying to his Ascendant from his 12th house.

This is an incredibly powerful conjunction because the planet Mars is in an applying aspect to the Ascendant. Remember, a planet applying to another planet or cusp is stronger than when it is separating. I use an orb of 7° for planets applying to the Ascendant and 3° to 5° when they are separating. In my experience a planet remains strong throughout its journey in the 1st house. Normally a planet loses impact at around 5° separating as it moves through a house.

Mars is only 3° away from hitting Henry's Ascendant when it will form an 'exact' conjunction. At a distance of 3° Henry is really feeling Mars' power applying to his Ascendant. What does this feel like? Mars' energy is building up to a crescendo so I'd say that Henry has an internal combustion engine, Mars, forcing him to push his accelerator all day and night. He would probably be restless and looking for ways to stay busy and active. If Mars was already in his 1st house and separating it would not be so bad.

How active is Mars in Henry's psyche? I need to now look at the rest of the chart to see if my initial thesis is correct. I need evidence to confirm what I think is happening.

Mars is a singleton, he only has one weak aspect to any other planet, a square to North Node, and as it isn't a planet it is a weak aspect. A singleton is a planet that is not fully incorporated into the rest of the native's psyche. It is a loner, isolated and in some ways avoidant of the other planet and cusp sign archetypes. Mars sits in perhaps the most powerful position in the chart with a significant impact on how Henry thinks, acts and feels and yet it isn't connected to the rest of his astrology community. It appears to me that Henry has some work to do to bring Mars into line with the rest of his psyche.

What else is in his chart? Mars rules the 1st house and the first house cusp, his Ascendant, is Virgo. There is no conflict there because Mars is quite comfortable with the Virgo archetype.

Is there more in the chart that confirms my suspicion that Mars is driving and pushing Henry to be active, perhaps hyperactive, a perfectionist who will stay on a project into the wee morning hours to finish it? Perhaps it causes him to struggle to fall sleep at night because he was always thinking of what to do and how to do it?

Look at Henry's Moon, she is in Aquarius, the sign of worry and she is in the 6th house of hard work, dedication to a purpose and self discipline. Let us make that a double plus for worry, planning and thinking things through on how to get his projects happening.

What about his Sun and Mercury? They should be active too shouldn't they? Well, these two planets do sit happily together as they straddle the 12th house cusp and are opposite the Moon. This suggests he had limited access to these two dynamic planets except in his dreams. Maybe there is something here we could look into, dreams can be creative.

There is enough information now for me to say that Henry Ford was an imaginative inventor. He was also very active and spent a lot of his time working on, thinking and planning his inventions. There is the suggestion that his mind is very active and that this may keep him awake at night.

A point to note: I am sure that most experienced astrologers would agree that there is always more in a chart than they would ever find in a lifetime. I am still finding interesting features in my own chart and will until the day I pass onto the next adventure.

Finding external evidence for my thesis:

"... Ford was the creative force behind an industry of unprecedented size and wealth that in only a few decades permanently changed the economic and social character of the United States."

https://www.britannica.com/biography/Henry-Ford

Here are some details on Henry Ford's achievements:

- Henry Ford took apart and put together his brother's toy just to see how it worked.

- One winter, instead of doing some of his chores (shelling corn) Henry made a machine from scratch that shelled corn.
- When Henry was at school he discovered a book on the principals of steam power.
- At age 16 Henry left his father's farm to go to Detroit to become a mechanic.
- He kept trying even though he failed many times.
- Created the Model T car, the assembly line, the V8 engine, built a car out of soybean plastic.
- His inexpensive Model T was the first car that almost everyone could

afford to buy. *"I will build a car for the great multitude."*
- When Henry Ford introduced the assembly line it could turn out a Model T in 24 seconds.
- Henry built and drove racing cars in his early years.
- He established schools in seven different places in the country.
- During World War Two the Ford Motor Company made jeeps, tanks, and other military machinery for the Armed Forces.

https://henryford88.weebly.com/character-traits.html

Combining the information in the chart and the confirmation from his many biographies I would say that Mars, as it is yet to be fully realised in his psyche, has kept Henry Ford moving, working, inventing and producing. His Virgo Ascendant shows dedication to serve his community and humanity as a whole. Thus we see his Model T Ford, an affordable car for the people. One could say that Henry Ford was hyperactive, imaginative and obsessive. He had a strong desire to serve his community - he was a humanitarian and philanthropist yet he had his faults. His will contained a gift of $205 million to his charity, the Henry Ford Foundation.

A point to note: the above exercise of examining Henry Ford's chart and then checking any background information I can find is one way you can do your own research. Finding validation for your thesis to confirm what you suspect is a great way to practice your delineations. When I write a newsletter or article on someone famous I always check out their biographies from as many sources as I can find. I like to see if I got it right.

Chapter 9 - Elements, Modes and Extra Points

The Four Elements– Fire, Earth, Air and Water signs

The signs are divided into four groups that represent the basic elements of western esoteric tradition: Fire, Earth, Air and Water. Both an emphasis or lack of emphasis on an element can indicate specific strengths and/or weaknesses of the qualities associated with it. Elemental dominance is generally calculated from the number of planets in each sign and house. Some astrologers use the Ascendant, Midheaven and North Node in calculating their elements, others don't. I always consider the houses in my calculations to help me determine if an element dominates the chart or not.

In this chapter you will be analysing the elements and qualities in your chart in a slightly different way than traditionally taught. You will learn to find your own and your client's elemental dominance which will open the chart up like a flower at sunrise.

The early Greeks are reputed to have formalised the four element theory that astrologers and other western occultists use today. The Greek philosophers Plato, Aristotle and Empedocles (450 BC) had a major influence on arriving at these four elements though they were influenced, no doubt, by earlier philosophers like the great Pythagoras. Read the link below on Empedocles, he was quite an amazing person.

https://en.wikipedia.org/wiki/Empedocles

The Elements

I would like to introduce you to the concept of 'types' which I use a lot in my work. In psychology, just as in astrology, we use the term 'types' in a very specific way. We use it to describe certain personality characteristics or groups of characteristics. Fire 'types' have a specific set of personality traits such as energy, drive and are often quite child-like. I also use the word 'dominance' in much the same way. For instance someone with a lot of Water in their chart can be described as having a Water 'dominance' or are a Water 'type'.

In astrology, the Fire dominated person does not have to be an Aries, Leo or Sagittarian to be called a 'Fire type'. Those three Fire signs only describe one single point in the chart – the Sun sign. It does not take into account the Moon sign which is just as significant, nor the presence of stelliums in signs or houses. It does not take into account aspects, chart shapes or planetary patterns, nor the dominance of a specific set of planetary aspects like a dominance of trines or squares.

For example, a Fire dominated person will have a dominance of Fire elements in their chart such as: a stellium in any sign or house; a stellium in Fire houses and/or Fire signs; many trine aspects; plus, the Sun and / or the Moon in a Fire sign or house; plus, Jupiter or Mars significantly placed in the chart.

A point to note: don't rely on a single point in the chart like the Sun sign. Professional astrologers read the entire chart and never rely on a single point to explain their thesis (theory or hypothesis about the person). There is no definitive point in the chart that says everything about you or your client.

Knowing how to calculate a person's elemental dominance is easy once you get used to it. I find that the elements provide my earliest insights into understanding the native. In some cases knowing the native's dominant element is enough to guide your reading in a direction that makes it 'flow' like honey. When you can do a reading like that you truly are on your way to becoming an astrologer of repute.

Fire dominance - Aries, Leo and Sagittarius

Fire dominated people are enthusiastic about everything they do. They have plenty of physical energy and drive, often in glaring contrast with the other elements. There is an emphasis on creativity and charisma which can inspire others to follow their lead. The Fire element prefers to experience things in a physical and energetic way, they are the adventurers of the zodiac.

The element of Fire is like a flame which warms, provides joy and pleasure to those around them. Sometimes that flame can burn - themselves and others. The emphasis is on creativity, inspiration, adventure and they certainly seek attention and acceptance – and they can act out like the drama queen. It is the element of warriors, adventurers, artists, celebrities, romanticists, psychics and leaders. Their negative qualities include aggressiveness beyond normal bounds, selfishness and greed, outrageous behaviour which can put others at risk, egotism and the physical and mental domination of subjects / friends / partners / family or workmates.

Their keywords include: charisma, leadership, assertiveness, aggression, romance, passion, warriors, adventurers, courage, positive and optimistic, dominating, bullying, daring and they always have to be right.

Aries is decisive and adventurous.

Leo leads with courage and nobility.

Sagittarius is the wise counsellor providing advice before and during their adventures, they can also become irresponsible.

You calculate this elemental dominance by examining the sign and house placement of the luminaries (Sun and Moon), Ascendant and Midheaven, personal planets, conjunctions between inner and outer planets and the type of aspects in the chart.

Henry Ford's fire elements:

Ascendant – no.

Midheaven – no.

Planets in Fire signs – Sun, Mercury, Mars, Neptune and North Node.

Planets in Fire houses – Venus in the 1st house and Pluto in the 9th house.

Other - Grand Trine and Mystic Rectangle thus a lot of trines and sextiles.

Henry has a very strong Fire element particularly with Mars conjunct his Ascendant and applying from the 12th house.

Earth dominance - Taurus, Virgo and Capricorn

Earth dominated people provide the organisational support and materials necessary for the Fires to go on their adventure. They enjoy the experience of using their physical body and sensible mindset for the benefit of their community. They have the ability to turn nothing into something as well as provide stability, organisation and structure. Once the Fire signs return from their adventures the Earth signs have a tidy home, hot meal and a warm bed for them to sleep in. A negative Earth is pedantic, impatient, materialistic and can lack an appreciation of spontaneous action.

Their keywords include: perfectionism, attention to detail, gluttony, greed, overwork, traditional, boring, patient and realistic, hardworking, sameness, responsible, determined, resourceful, careful, reliable, practical, hoarders.

Taurus collects and distributes as he establishes the foundations of his workforce.

Virgo analyses and criticises to ensure that her work serves its purpose.

Capricorn organises and manages people and resources to ensure that everything runs according to plan, their plan.

You calculate this elemental dominance by examining the sign and house placement of the luminaries (Sun and Moon), Ascendant and Midheaven, personal planets, conjunctions between inner and outer planets and the type of aspects in the chart.

Henry Ford's earth elements:

Ascendant – Virgo.

Midheaven – Taurus.

Planets in Earth signs – Venus in Virgo and Pluto in Taurus.

Planets in Earth houses – Saturn and Jupiter in the 2nd house, Moon in the 6th, and Uranus in the 10th house.

Other - Venus the passive ruler of Taurus is in the 1st house; there are many square aspects.

There is enough Earth in his chart to ground his enthusiasm into productive action. He has Virgo Ascendant and Taurus Midheaven showing exactly what Henry is famous for: planning and implementing a structured assembly line process to mass produce a useful, fully functional and affordable product – the Model T Ford motor car.

Air dominance - Gemini, Libra and Aquarius

The Air dominated person excels in collecting and sharing knowledge and information. The teaching and educating of humanity relies on these Air qualities. It is through their rational, logical mindset that helps us sift through the lies, fantasies and illusions that abound in our world. They take the Fire signs inspirational ideas and very capably bundle it up to share with everyone. This helps the Earth signs organise themselves to write the manual from which they can then build the product.

While the Air signs 'think' they will often have a problem 'doing'. They tend to spend too much time in their head and not enough providing for their personal and family's needs. Too much Air leads to worry, insomnia and communication problems. Mad scientists and sceptics abound in the Air signs. Negative Air manifests as logic squeezing out the magic and romance from our world. These unbalanced Air types can destroy your spiritual and emotional nature with their drive to reduce everything to a logical and empirical explanation.

Their keywords include: logical, rational, realistic, factual, empirical, intellectual, social communicator, negotiator, conscious thought, denial, mediation, unemotional, eccentric, worrier.

Gemini shares ideas and concepts while encouraging everyone to join them in their social world.

Libra communicates and ensures that others unite rather than oppose, they are the mediators and negotiators.

Aquarius stimulates our world with their unusual and original ideas.

You calculate this elemental dominance by examining the sign and house placement of the luminaries (Sun and Moon), Ascendant and Midheaven, personal planets, conjunctions between inner and outer planets and the type of aspects in the chart.

Henry Ford's air elements:

Ascendant – no.

Midheaven – no.

Planets in Air signs – Saturn, Jupiter, Moon and Uranus. Uranus is both an Air planet and in an Air sign which means the astrologer might want to factor this in when deciding Henry's elemental dominance. Uranus, an Air planet in an Air sign and also in an Earth house might manifest as '*Henry seeks to achieve innovation in his career and business*'.

Planets in Air houses – Chiron in the 7th and Mercury is just within the 11th house, however, as Mercury is sitting on the 12th house cusp I would include him in both the 11th and 12th houses.

Other – Venus is the active ruler of Libra and the passive ruler of Taurus, as such she can behave as both an Air and an Earth planet. Any planet in the 1st house is very powerful. This means that Venus' charm and attraction is strongly projected outwards which can be felt by those around Henry. It would no doubt attract investors to his cause and make him appear far more attractive than if Venus was anywhere else in his chart.

A point to note: Planets that sit within 5° of a cusp are 'applying' to that cusp. In other words Mercury's energy is now directed towards the 12th

house as he is no longer invested in the house he is in. This is common with planets as they pass through a house. The closer the planet gets to the end of the house the less impact they have inside that house.

The Moon is the strongest Air planet in Henry's chart. It sits in the 6th house showing that he has a strong work ethic. Mercury is sitting on his 12th house cusp which might highlight his mercurial mind and perhaps lead to excessive worry and insomnia or excessive dreaming. Uranus has been mentioned already and they all add to his expression of the Air element.

Water dominance - Cancer, Scorpio and Pisces

These signs are emotional, they feel the ebb and flow of emotions in their world much more easily than they can intellectualise about it. They generally need community, friendship and family because they are vulnerable to isolation and loneliness. The Water signs inspire the Fire signs to embark on their romantic quests. The Earth signs provide the physical and organisational means to achieve this vision. The Air signs then rationalise what it is that the adventurers actually experienced and post it on social media like Facebook and Instagram.

Their keywords include: sensitive, sympathetic, emotional, psychic, dreamers, affection, intuitive. Negative Water dominated people can become unstable, abandoned, betrayed, lonely, emotionally manipulative, irrational, addictive, sad, depressed, lonely, emotionally reactive and live with their heart on their sleeve, they experience life but aren't always able to control it.

Cancer draw people close to them so that they don't feel lonely or unwanted, sometimes they manipulate others to keep them safely within the family unit.

Scorpio is also emotionally controlling, they show us that passion can be both constructive and destructive.

Pisces shows the rest of humanity that love is tangible and can easily be used and abused. As the martyr they suffer from loneliness and neglect.

You calculate this elemental dominance by examining the sign and house placement of the luminaries (Sun and Moon), Ascendant and Midheaven, personal planets, conjunctions between inner and outer planets and the type of aspects in the chart.

Henry Ford's water elements:

Ascendant – no.

Midheaven – no.

Planets in Water signs – Chiron is the only planet in a Water sign, Pisces

Planets in Water houses – Sun and Mars in the 12th house, I will add Mercury too since he is sitting on the cusp of the 12th house, North Node is in the 4th house and Neptune in the 8th house.

Other – I consider Chiron as a Water planet and I always take him into consideration. What strikes me about Henry's chart is the very strong 12th house with three personal planets Sun, Mercury and Mars. I would say that the Water element is strong.

In summary all of Henry Ford's elements are powerfully activated and quite well balanced.

How do I use this information? With this depth of information, which is so easily gathered I might add, I can say to Henry that he is an inspired person with a great work ethic (Fire and Earth). He gets stressed at times and loses sleep with worry (Air and Water). His family will at times wonder where he is because he is rarely at home (Earth) but he can make up for that with his enthusiasm (Fire) when he does spend time with them. His 12th house and Moon in Aquarius in the 6th house suggest worry and some anxiety so he should learn to relax.

A point to note: all signs and elements are contained in the natal chart. Most people will have planets in at least three of the elements. More than 4 planets in any one element certainly highlights the personality traits of that element. A lack of planets in any one element can indicate a weakness in that element's qualities. A weakness in any one element may indicate that the native places emphasis on that element to overcome any deficiencies.

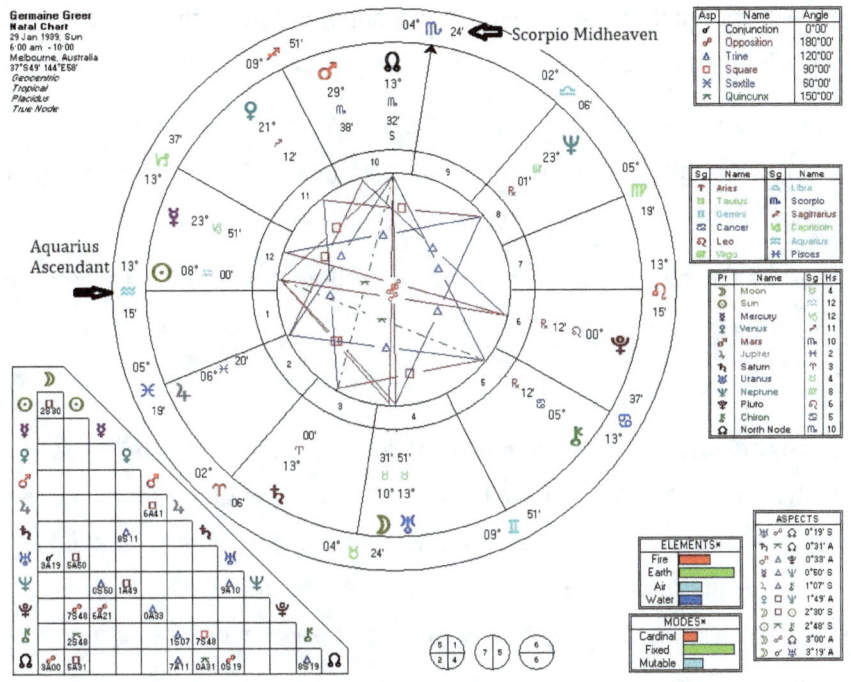

Above chart: Germaine Greer, academic, feminist, free thinker and a rather eccentric person.

Germaine Greer – author, academic, feminist and activist
Elements in Germaine Greer's chart:

Fire - Venus in Sagittarius; Saturn in Aries; Pluto in Leo; Chiron in the 5th house.

Earth - Moon and Uranus in Taurus; Neptune in Virgo; Mercury in Capricorn; Jupiter in the 2nd house, Pluto in the 6th house, North Node and Mars in the 10th house.

Air - Ascendant in Aquarius; Sun in Aquarius; Saturn in the 3rd house, Venus in the 11th house.

Water - Jupiter in Pisces; Chiron in Cancer; North Node and Mars in Scorpio; Midheaven Scorpio; Moon and Uranus in the 4th house, Neptune in the 8th house, Sun and Mercury in the 12th house.

Other – a Grand Trine showing a little more Fire but otherwise a balance of squares and trines.

Germaine Greer's chart has a slight dominance in Earth and Water. She has a slight lack of Air but the Sun and Ascendant in Aquarius exert quite a strong influence in the chart. Germaine's Sun and Ascendant show an Aquarian desire to help others, the less unfortunate's of the world. This is supported by her strong Water and not quite as strong Fire elements.

One way to understand her choice of an academic career is to examine her 10th house. Scorpio sits on the cusp of her 10th house, the Midheaven, and she has North Node and Mars within. A 10th house North Node suggests that she is destined to take control, as does a Scorpio Midheaven, of whatever she desires to do and Mars will support this. The dominant Earth is hard working and gives her the rigour and self-discipline to succeed in the tough world of the academic. Her Water and Fire elements help make her work personable and empowering.

Sun and Mercury tell us that she hides herself in the 12th house but as her Sun is applying to her Ascendant she can sometimes manifest as a Leo, fiery and self confident. Her two luminaries, Sun and Moon, are in Water houses (4th and 12th) which suggests some emotional inhibition due to her upbringing.

Exercise: calculate your strongest and weakest elements and see how they may operate in your life.

Modes – Cardinal, Fixed, Mutable signs

This system divides the zodiac signs into three groupings of four signs.

Cardinal - Aries, Cancer, Libra, Capricorn

These signs show initiative and action as well as reaction. The Cardinal dominated native is like Aries: decisive, fast off the mark and active but will soon become bored and slow down. They are great at starting or initiating a project but they aren't so good at maintaining such a high level of energy to complete it. They could be likened to a match that flares brightly when struck but slowly fades as their energy runs out and they lose interest and enthusiasm.

Fixed - Taurus, Leo, Scorpio, Aquarius

These signs are the stayers, they don't initiate very well but they do stick with it once they get started. The Fixed signs are the ones that are organised and inspired by the Cardinals who enthuse and excite them. The Cardinals can then walk away leaving the Fixed signs to carry on while they go off to start something else.

Mutable - Gemini, Virgo, Sagittarius, Pisces

While the Cardinals start the job and the Fixed work at it to get the work done, it is the Mutables who are the best at finishing the job in a tidy and attractive manner. The Mutables add flair in marketing and selling the finished product.

In a business project you can see where the modes fit in: the Cardinal signs start the project; the Fixed signs are brought in to do the bulk of the work; while the Mutable signs come in at the end to package, market and sell the final product.

Modes in Germaine Greer's chart

Cardinal – Saturn in Aries; Chiron in Cancer; Mercury in Capricorn.

Fixed - Moon and Uranus in Taurus; Pluto in Leo; Midheaven, North Node and Mars in Scorpio; Sun and Ascendant in Aquarius.

Mutable - Neptune in Virgo; Venus in Sagittarius; Jupiter in Pisces.

Germaine Greer is dominated by her Fixed mode. She may not be all that quick at getting started but once she starts something she won't stop. Her Mutable traits may come in after the bulk of the work is done to add the finishing touches with a dash of grace and flair of Venus and Jupiter.

Extra Points in the Chart

Vertex

This is an angle of the chart much like the Ascendant or Midheaven. It is often seen as a karmic or influential point in the chart. When your Vertex is conjunct a planet or point in someone's chart there may be a karmic link with them. For instance, if your Vertex is conjunct your friend's Venus this would show social compatibility and that you may be attracted to them in some way. Another example is that if your Vertex is the same degree of a friend's Mercury then you would probably communicate well together.

Chapter 10 - The amazing Luminaries

The Moon and her cycles

Although the Moon takes 27.3 days to orbit the earth, a New Moon occurs every 29.5 days, this is called the Lunation period or cycle. The Moon travels roughly 13° per day but that can vary between 12° to 14°. The New Moon occurs when the Moon is conjunct the Sun. You won't be able to physically see the moon because the light of the sun is too bright. When the moon moves away from the sun 14 days later it is now in opposition to the sun. This means that it is on the other side of the Earth and fully illuminated by the sun's light.

A New and Full Moon fall in a new house in our chart each month. For example, if the New Moon was in the 3rd house the following Full Moon, 14 days later, will be in its opposite house, the 9th. The next New Moon will then be in the 4th house and the following Full Moon will be in the opposite house, the 10th and so it progresses by house every 29.4 days.

Liz Greene and Howard Sasportas in their book '*The Luminaries*' describe this cycle as the Moon travelling through the zodiac having new experiences so that when she returns to her partner, the Sun, at the next New Moon, she shares her experiences with him.

A point to note: the New Moon is the beginning of the cycle while the Full Moon is its culmination. The New Moon ends the cycle and begins the next one at the same time. The First Quarter represents early experiences on the journey to illumination; the Third Quarter represents expressing or using the knowledge attained during the first half of the cycle.

If your Sun and Moon are within 10°-15° of each other you were born under a New Moon. This suggests that both unconscious and conscious minds are combined often leaving you open to unwanted urges and instincts. This is a passive aspect and one that the native may not be aware of. If Sun and Moon are well aspected in the chart the native usually has a good understanding of themselves.

When the Sun and Moon are opposite each other within an orb of 10°-15° the native is born under a Full Moon. This suggests that they will struggle with unconscious urges and instincts leaking into consciousness. This is an active aspect and unlike the conjunction above the native is often aware of their issues. Being born under a New or Full Moon brings its own advantages and disadvantages but generally it assists the native in developing compassion and empathy for others.

Transiting New and Full Moons

Each month the Moon makes a complete orbit around the Earth and this is reflected in your chart. Its conjunction with the sun in the sky can be observed as the New Moon which is also known as the Dark of the Moon. In this situation the moon is so close to the sun that it doesn't reflect any sunlight back to the Earth. Two weeks later the moon has moved 180° and is now opposite the sun - the Earth lies between the two luminaries. In this position the moon reflects the sun's light back to us. This is called a Full Moon.

The transiting New and Full Moon occur once each month. When an exact New or Full Moon transits an angle or planet in your chart it will remain active until the next New or Full Moon one month later. For instance, when Mars is triggered by a conjunction with the New Moon, within an orb of 1°-2°, you will initiate or begin some sort of Martian project. The transiting Full Moon two weeks later signifies the culmination of the project. A new cycle or project will begin when the lunation cycle ends at the next New Moon. Please understand that these lunar cycles are small and primarily of a mundane or day-to-day nature.

Keep these transits very tight. They can trigger small events especially if the planet or angle is already under pressure natally or it is under transit by another planet. For instance, a Full Moon occurring on the Ascendant would trigger an outward expression of its traits - but only for a very short time, perhaps a few hours. It might manifest as becoming involved in a social event that was planned during the New Moon two weeks earlier. If your Ascendant is already under a transit or progression then the Full Moon falling on its exact degree could trigger greater illumination of the problems it is highlighting.

The Eclipses - Lunar and Solar Eclipses

Eclipses occur four times each year, two Lunar Eclipses and two Solar Eclipses. They occur when the Full Moon or New Moon falls exactly on the Moon's Node.

When the moon is in front of the sun, sitting between you on Earth and the sun in the sky, it is called a Solar Eclipse. The Solar Eclipse is more powerful than an ordinary New Moon as the sun's light or power is eclipsed, or extinguished, causing you to look inwards. It can be challenging when it falls on a natal planet or angle, and again you use a very tight orb of 1°-2°.

The Lunar Eclipse happens when the Earth is exactly between the moon and the sun causing the Moon's energy to be extinguished. The Moon's energy is emotional by nature so you would expect to feel emotionally drained during the eclipse if it falls within 1°-2° of a natal planet or angle.

If an Eclipse falls in your 6th house, for instance, but doesn't aspect any planets or house cusps, it has a weak effect on your health and work relationships. Eclipses have a minor but longer-lasting effect on the house it falls in even if it does not aspect any planets or angles. It has a greater effect, though still quite mild, when it hits an exact degree of a planet of point in your chart.

An eclipse generally lasts for about 6 months, until the next set of eclipses occur. Are eclipses, New and Full Moon's powerful? That is debatable. I recommend you do your own personal research and see how they affect you personally. This type of hands-on research is great experience for all students of astrology to learn more of themselves and how to use specific techniques in their readings.

Moon meditations

I would like to quickly share two Moon meditations that have had significant impact on my life. The first was in a meditation group at a sacred aboriginal water hole on the south coast of NSW about 30 years ago. The place itself was high on the escarpment overlooking the ocean, the energy was almost overwhelming. Carved into the trees along the path to the 'Pool of Peace' were many aboriginal faces. This in itself was an appropriate introduction to an amazing place and experience.

As this was traditionally the aboriginal women's sacred site the meditation was on the cosmic mother represented by the moon. I was present only because the female leaders of the group had first asked for permission for me to be there.

After only a few short breaths to quiet my mind and body I entered a light trance. In my mind's eye I saw the moon high in the sky above us. It then turned into an oval shape, like an ovum, and sped rapidly towards me. It hit me in the navel and buried itself in my abdomen.

It was quite a shock because only a minute or so had gone by. I wasn't expecting anything to happen because I was male and a guest. Instead I had perhaps the most profound experience of the group and of my life. Nine months later that ovum gave birth to my first counselling practice.

Only two years ago I was doing a Full Moon meditation when I had a similar experience. Once again the ovum hit me in the abdomen just below my navel and buried itself there. Nine months later I retired from psychology practice.

These two moon meditations signalled the beginning and the ending of my psychology career very much replicating the lunation cycle in this chapter.

The Luminaries – Sun and Moon

Sun in the chart – the Hero's Quest

There is ongoing debate among astrologers as to which house represents our earthly mother and father – the 4th or the 10th. Liz Greene and Howard Sasportas argue for father as 4th house and mother as 10th. Glenn Perry, in '*Essays in Psychological Astrology: Theory and Practice*', puts forward a solid argument for father as the 10th house and the mother as the 4th.

Father is represented by the Sun, it is fire and it is progressive, expressive and dynamic. Mother is represented by the Moon and is Water, passive, regressive and reflective. The 10th house is ambition and achievement, it is seen as a dynamic house expressing itself forwards and outwards to achieve the native's goals. The 4th house is nurturing and stable, seeking to maintain the status quo. If we place father in the 10th and mother in the 4th house there is a sensible, to me, resolution to the argument. Place father in the 4th and the archetypal themes are in conflict, the same with mother in the 10th.

The father gives his children confidence, self-esteem and the strength to go out into the world to claim their destiny, all 10th house qualities. Mother gives her children nurturing and internal stability so that our 10th house adventures have solid foundations. When you are wounded in your mystic's quest through life you run to your mother for her to make you whole again. Once whole you go back to your father for a renewal of your quest and back into the cruel world again seeking your destiny.

Capricorn, the natural ruler of the 10th house, is ruled by Saturn, old father time. In fact there are too many references to 'father' in mythology to mention here. You can read Liz Greene's *'The Astrology of Fate'* to gain further insights. Cancer, the natural ruler of the 4th house, is ruled by the Moon, which is mother's house and home. Nevertheless mythology does point to mother/father reversals but I leave it to you to come up with your own conclusions.

I stopped using the houses to represent the native's parents early in my astrological career. I still use the Sun as the father and Moon as the mother, or visa versa if the mother is the more dominant parent. Let me explore this theme further because your parents are the two psychological pillars you build your life upon.

The Sun as Father and the Hero's Quest by sign

The Sun plays a dual role, that of the archetypal father and that of your living father. One brings you into the world to assist you to find your life's purpose while the other IS your life's purpose, the Hero's or Mystic's Quest.

The Sun illuminates your spiritual quest or purpose. The nature or type of the quest is seen in your natal Sun's sign. This is determined by knowing the potential of each sign and their polar opposite.

Aries – the deeper purpose of Aries is not to conquer outer monsters but to learn to harness your strength, energy and to harden your will to overcome your inner monsters. Your demons inside require great determination, courage, resourcefulness and self discipline to conquer which is why you are given 70 years to complete this task, it is a lifetime quest. It is also known as an heroic quest.

Taurus – the quest is to use internal resources to conquer boredom and laziness that are barriers to your quest.

Gemini – this sign helps you learn to harness your innate desire to waste time in gossip, to internalise your hard earned knowledge and to then transform it into wisdom.

Cancer – in this sign you learn to nurture yourself, to find the courage to establish a secure internal environment so that you can give to others selflessly with no strings attached.

Leo – the lion's quest is to hold firm in face of criticism and humiliation, to hold true to your spiritual quest despite being torn down by those who are jealous of your charm and generosity.

Virgo – this is the sign of service, however you must first service your own needs so that you better understand the needs of others.

Libra – this sign highlights the necessity of finding balance in giving and taking. If you compromise too much, or take too much, you quickly become out of balance. This makes you vulnerable to manipulation and blackmail by unscrupulous others. Your quest is to find the halfway point in relationships and to give and take responsibly.

Scorpio – transcend your fears by turning inwards and facing them. The journey into hell sees the initiate die to his old life to be reborn as the adept stepping into his true power.

Sagittarius – this sign forces you to face your irresponsible nature, to live a responsible life for the benefit of humanity.

Capricorn – to use your insight and understanding of order and structure to selflessly go with the flow of life. To face life fully resourced allowing disorder to arise without the need to control it.

Aquarius – understanding yourself by being fully engaged with your emotions rather than hiding yourself in your mental world.

Pisces – learning to hold onto reality rather than escaping into fantasy, to stay engaged with the world rather than melting into the void.

These are not absolutes nor are they set in concrete, they are a guide only. I suggest that you seek an understanding of your Sun sign quest from your own research and life experience.

A point to note: please understand that the Sun sign is not the whole story as the other planets play a powerful supporting role in your spiritual quest. I like to think of the Sun sign as the Hero's Quest.

Houses as functions of the Sun

The father is also represented in the house where the Sun resides. It shows where the Hero's Quest takes place:

1st – the quest feels like it is of paramount importance. You are restless and feel a burning urgency to act. However therein lies your quest, to find peace within your body through exercise and meditation.

2nd – you resolve your Hero's Quest by securing your material and emotional foundations. Knowing that you can always return to the safety of this house allows you to conquer your inner dragons.

3rd – your quest is to gain an understanding of the world through knowledge and to then communicate it to the world.

4th – your quest lies in establishing a safe and nurturing home and family environment. A resolution of this quest is in your family's harmony.

5th – your quest is in meaningful expression. Your resolution is found by living a meaningful life every day.

6th – your quest is to thoroughly understand what a life dedicated to the service of others really means. This path requires self discipline and sacrifice as you journey into the world of the Goddess Vesta.

7th – this quest is through others, resolution is found when you are in harmony with your partner and everyone you relate to. This quest requires a deep examination of your Shadow, that part of you that is only awakened by your interaction with others.

8th – this quest is of life and death, only by giving in to the universe can you part the veil that separates the living from the dead. This is best done through the guidance of a qualified and trusted mentor in deep meditation.

9th – this quest involves the selfless expression of wisdom in the service of humanity. No longer can you take from others to use as your own, you must earn the right to this level of wisdom. This quest demands that you live a responsible life.

10th – the quest lies in the outer expression of your instinctual drives and urges. Standing on the firm foundations of the previous 9 signs you can now bring your knowledge and skill to bear fruit from your efforts. This quest lies in manifesting reality by achieving your goals.

11th – this quest is resolved by nurturing others while also nurturing yourself. This quester seeks to fix the world but it often leads to failure because their own failings are left unresolved.

12th – this quest is resolved by dissolving and then returning to the world of the living ready to be reborn into the 1st house. This house is the resting house of the unconscious which I liken to a cave. Your quest is to find a safe manner of living, free of stress where you can prepare to be reborn into your next life purified ready for your next cycle. However, it is not an easy house to journey through as it often requires that you undertake your quest within the cave of your 12th house. Your quest is inwards perhaps through therapy, a monastic experience, a journey guided by those wise to this path. Often psychotherapy is the only way to handle the pressure of this calling. Often there is no father to guide the native through this life thus the need for support from others: a mentor, teacher or benefactor. One needs only look at the 12th house keywords to better understand the pressure to leave, to escape, to let go, to avoid, to dissolve into the great void.

Moon in the chart – the giver of love and life

Where the father Sun gives direction and a reason for living the mother Moon gives the very essence of life itself.

The mother child relationship has been described as the individual's first love relationship. The child is initially part of mother while in the womb. It is now accepted that the fetus grows in its awareness of its environment at around 5 months of conception. At birth the child becomes a separate physical entity thus initiating the individuation process, the process of becoming aware of one's uniqueness.

You never quite lose this initial love relationship with your biological mother and you will seek this same love bond with your own children and partners throughout life. Thus the mother child bond is the most important bond of all. There is no greater love than the love between a mother and her child. However, in some cases there is no love or it is dysfunctional because the mother is wounded in some way. In this situation it sets off a journey for the child to find the love that mother never gave or was unable to give.

You will read throughout your studies in psychodynamic and Attachment theory that the mother child bond is of paramount importance in psychological healing. It is part of my approach in therapy to explore the parenting of the individual – childhood and early upbringing. If there are father or mother issues it can indicate that these issues have permeated the entire life of the native. No other relationship will ever match the power of the parents to influence the psychological development of their children. If there are issues in your client's marriage then look at the relationship between the native and their parents, especially with their mother.

The Moon as Mother the giver of love and life by sign

Like we did with the Sun we will look at the signs to show the relationship between the native and their mother's gift of love and life.

Aries – a childlike mother who loves activity and having fun, on a negative level it can show impatience with conflict and punishment as a way to control the child. The love bond may be built on physical contact particularly sharing the same physical pursuits. Issues can arise in relationships related to the physical expression of love such as sex.

Taurus – a mother who is a good home maker, hard worker and supporter of their children's ambitions. On a negative note mother is demanding and seeks to gain that which the child creates, seeking to materially gain from their child. The native's love is founded on solid material comfort be it food, touch, a comfortable warm bed, good quality clothes and general comfort in all aspects of the home. Issues may arise in relationships when the home lacks that special warmth which comes from being surrounded by material comfort.

Gemini – the mother who shows interest in their child's education and learning while on a negative note mother can worry too much about their children creating tension and anxiety. The native's love is founded on the gaining of knowledge be it buying encyclopedias, demonstrating the value of knowledge and education by reading books to the children and the parent themselves attending classes at night school or university. Issues may arise in relationships when too much emphasis is placed on education at the detriment of intimacy and genuinely engaged conversation.

Cancer – the nurturing mother with an abundance of love, negatively is the controlling and manipulating mother. The native's love is based on home and family, often part of a large or extended family with visitors coming and going. Issues can arise in relationships when the mother is more engaged with family as a collective and fails to engage with the individual.

Leo – a joyful relationship with mother bringing out the best in their child, on a negative note it is the mother who gets a kick out of their child's achievements often pushing them into activities that they may not want to participate in, the movie star mother. The native's love is based on fun and adventure, sometimes too much fun at the detriment of true intimacy. Issues can arise in relationships if the parent seeks attention and recognition at the expense of the child.

Virgo – the careful mother that teaches manners and good protocol, negatively it is a worrying mother who excessively fusses over her children. The native's love is founded on service and responsible action for others. Issues in relationships may arise if the mother capably provides service to the family but loses individual intimacy in the process.

Libra – the mother who gives to her child a taste of life with a good appreciation for beauty. Negatively she teaches vanity and a self centered outlook on life, a superficial mother where as long as it looks good on the outside it is good enough. The native's love is founded on presentation and the setting of personal boundaries with those who wish to take more than they should. Issues in relationships may arise if the mother tends to over-compensate and compromises her or her children's needs for others.

Scorpio – the passionate mother who fights to defend her children's rights. She can dominate and control as well as punish and hinder her child's self development opportunities by refusing to let them take responsibility for their actions, rescuing them from their problems without teaching them to consider and accept the consequences. The native's love is founded on a love of security in the face of deep emotion. Issues may arise in relationships if the mother is unable to demonstrate or teach her child how to set emotional limits.

Sagittarius – makes life an adventure but often forgets to buy food for the children, mother may be so hooked on her own journey that the children don't get what they need from life. They may learn that running off on a new adventure each time the going gets tough is the best solution. The native's love is founded on adventure, wise counsel and charm. Issues in relationships may arise if the mother is unable to set boundaries on her own behavior and demonstrating that using others for self gain is not acceptable.

Capricorn – the stern and unemotional mother, who can also provide the safest home environment. The challenge is emotional expression which if not experienced can lead to detrimental relationships in the future. The native's love is founded on a structured means of living, love forms part of a good house routine, *'clean your teeth and then I'll read you a book'*. Issues can arise when structure is preferred to true intimacy.

Aquarius – a sometimes absent mother who can switch her feelings on and off at will, seeks to provide her children with the opportunities of life but needs to be grounded and in her body more. The native's love is founded on adapting to unusual styles of living, establishing the means of surviving in the moment in a cluttered and disordered household. Issues may arise in relationships when the mother is highly emotional and unable to provide her children with those strategies to survive in a competitive and unstructured world.

Pisces – the fairy godmother, loves everyone, rescues her child's stray friends sometimes to the abandonment of her own children. Needs to get into the real world at times. The native's love is founded on adaptation and self sufficiency. When mother is not quite 'with it' the children can accommodate and make their own breakfast and get themselves off to school. Issues may arise in relationships when they themselves fail to adapt to a changing world which can often be in disarray requiring them to set boundaries and limits to their behavior.

Houses as functions of the Moon

The house placement of the Moon shows where the native needs to be nurtured and supported as well as where she places or finds love.

1st – shows that the native is fundamentally in need of nurturing, it encompasses all aspects of the native's life. This native expresses herself dramatically which can sometimes manifest as moodiness and irritability. Love is freely given and accepted.

2nd – good secure home and relationships, a good support network is needed. The native seeks to create a safe and secure environment for her love to survive. In a world of hardship emotional security becomes a driving force that forces the native to sometimes withdraw to protect her sensitive heart.

3rd – good communication and solid relationships especially with friends and siblings. The native seeks to express her passionate nature in communication and the collection of knowledge. She seeks the safe environment of social support groups, friendship groups and social media.

4th – home and family are the most pressing needs for the native. The native buries herself in home and family to establish a safe place to share her love. Fears of abandonment may arise when the children start to leave home in early adulthood.

5th – friendships and activities that involve lots of friends provide the nurturing and support for this native. They have a need to be accepted and recognized by their peers above most things and will go to great lengths to be noticed.

6th – work is important because it means they feel useful and needed. The native can hide her emotions in service, by being busy she can avoid focusing on her emotional pain. The native can provide her service by also establishing boundaries, routines and timetables to avoid escaping into a meaningless world of work.

7th – love and being in love, sets up all sorts of unpleasant situations when love is more important than safety and self respect, may sell their soul for love. The native seeks to find balance in all things be it friendships or love relationships. This is the house of boundaries and limits so that she can avoid giving too much of herself in relationships.

8th – life is one big emotional crisis, the native needs to learn how to protect their soft and tender emotions from the hard cruel world. Once the native can do this they will then be able to reach in and touch true power. The native seeks to lift the veil that separates life and death, they have a unique connection with spirit and the afterlife. Problems can arise when the native believes that the meaning of their existence is to control their world when in reality it is to control themselves. The Moon in the 8th house is frequently seen in those interested in astrology, tarot and the occult.

9th – studying and exploring the world. Nothing is more enjoyable than exploring new places and new people. This provides them with opportunities to learn service to others without expecting to gain from that service. Often seen in people who are fixated on travel and study.

10th – doing and acting, getting into the world to help others to achieve and move towards their goals. This house shows that the native needs to have goals otherwise they lose direction and become depressed, also shows a tendency to moodiness.

11th – getting out and meeting people, an involvement with charities and other social or environmental organizations. These provide the native with a sense of fulfillment through involvement in humanitarian pursuits. May tend towards involvement but without intimacy or feeling. A difficult house for the Moon to reside in at times.

12th – an absent mother, a mother who was unable to provide the love and nurturing that their child needed. This may be because she was also wounded herself, the mother could have been frequently sick or had mental health issues preventing a solid nurturing bond with the child. Moon in this house suggests the native will need to let go. of the world at times and withdraw to a safe environment like a refuge or healing resort as the stresses of life can become way too demanding on their sensitive souls. Needs a very understanding family and partner.

A point to note: as you can see the Sun's journey is an outer journey that leads inwards to enlightenment as the goal of the Hero's Quest. The Moon's path is initially inwards to provide the native nurturing and emotional support. With the Moon's secure emotional foundations the native is then prepared to venture forth and engage with the Sun on the Hero's Quest. The two luminaries go hand in hand, one without the other can lead to an unfulfilled life.

Sun & Moon in the elements as father and mother

Fire – dynamic and inspirational - impatient and angry.

Water – emotionally honest and nurturing - controlling, moody and smothering.

Air – interesting and knowledgeable - emotionally absent and cold.

Earth – providing comfort and structure - strict and possessive.

And don't forget, if your father is more like your Moon, then chances are that the Moon represents your father more than it does your mother. The same can occur with the Sun which can just as easily represent a domineering and powerful mother.

The cosmic father and mother archetype meditation

I use the Sun and Moon archetypes in situations where there was major dysfunction with either or both parents. At the initial stages of recovery I will introduce the 'cosmic' parents to the native's inner sanctuary. The Sun represents the archetypal or cosmic father and the Moon becomes the cosmic mother. Remember that the Sun might manifest as your mother and the Moon as your father, there is no concrete gender in the world of the unconscious.

I begin by asking you to create a safe place, a sanctuary, like a cottage beside the beach or a cabin in the woods in your inner world. You then call down the Sun and the Moon from the sky and meet with them. This can take several sessions and is best done slowly and gently. Once you feel comfortable with them you can ask them to take your hands in theirs and to send all their love and light into you. This is the start of your healing.

Once you have done many meditation sessions with your Sun and Moon archetypes you might want to experience cosmic father and mother energy at a deeper level.

Imagine that you are a child and allow yourself to be taken into the loving arms of your cosmic father or mother. This meditation can help you experience what unconditional parental love should feel like.

The cosmic mother embraces you in her loving and nurturing arms where you can withdraw to when the world has been unkind. She comforts you when you are wounded by life. You can even imagine yourself as a baby in the arms of your cosmic mother. Allow yourself to fall asleep in her arms.

The cosmic father gives you the confidence and strength to go into the outer world to achieve your goals. Without strong father energy your self-esteem may sometimes falter. When you are ready you can ask to be taken into his arms to experience unconditional father love.

You can re-experience the security and nurturing love of your cosmic parents every day as part of your healing journey.

For those who have had a difficult or even a traumatic relationship with your real parents I have found that this process of working with your cosmic parents is a safe and gentle healing method. I advise that you go very slowly and only proceed when you are ready.

WARNING: if you have psychological issues or feel you need support to do this meditation please speak to a trained psychotherapist first. *I always recommend that you seek out a qualified psychologist or psychotherapist to walk you through these exercises before you try them by yourself.*

When do people seek therapy?

The best time for therapy is when you are ready for it. In my experience it is the applying transits that generally pushes people to seek therapy. Most people complete therapy when the transiting planet begins to separate and moves out of orb of the natal planet or point in the chart.

For example, when transiting Saturn opposites your natal Moon you may experience symptoms of depression, sadness and mood swings. It feels uncomfortable when applying to the exact opposition, terrible when exactly opposite, but then eases off as it separates out of orb and away from the exact transit. As the transiting planet separates the native will sometimes forget how bad things were at the start of the transit. Most people start therapy during the applying aspect and cease therapy after it has begun to separate. Rarely do they leave during the applying or exact transit. I use an applying orb of 2°-7° degrees depending on the transiting and the natal planet or point involved.

The strongest aspects formed by transit to the natal planets and points are conjunctions and oppositions. These transits are similar to natal conjunctions and oppositions and are the most intense. They can sometimes be quite traumatic. The square and trine transits rarely send people for counselling. Trines can cause discomfort especially with Saturn, Chiron, Neptune and Pluto trining a luminary or inner planet. A square transit is often quite internal and is felt more as a discomfort than as a trauma.

I see most people for therapy when they have an outer planet transit such as Saturn, Chiron, Uranus, Neptune or Pluto conjunct or opposite Moon, Sun, Venus or the Ascendant. These, as I have mentioned before, are also the most opportune times for personal growth and insight.

The natal North Node can be tricky. I have found time and again, especially with school children, that when transiting North Node conjuncts their Ascendant, they exhibit symptoms of alienation and social avoidance. Adolescents experiencing this transit will sometimes avoid social activities and may even drop out of school. They often end up sitting in front of the TV or computer, play video games or chat on social media all day and night. This transit has a similar impact to an outer planet transiting the Ascendant. I have not found any correlation with North Node transits to the Midheaven though.

Chapter 11 – Profile of psychopath Doctor Death

Dr Harold Shipman, Britain's most prolific mass murderer.

'During the last quarter of the Twentieth century, Dr. Harold Shipman killed his patients and got away with it. In the process, he became the most prolific serial killer not just in Great Britain but in the Western World. It eventually became known that he had murdered 215 patients and that he was probably responsible for killing another 69, bringing his ghastly total to 284 victims. He may have actually murdered many more…

Kathleen Grundy was 81-years-old when she died five weeks earlier, on June 24, 1998… They called her doctor, Fred Shipman, and he hurried over to the cottage. Shipman gave her a cursory examination and confirmed that she was dead, and that her death was due to a cardiac arrest. When the two volunteers asked what they should do, Shipman suggested that they contact Hamilton's, the local solicitors' office in town.

Although Hamilton's was not Kathleen's solicitors, that morning they had received a will from her. Enclosed with it was a letter, which read: "Dear Sir, I enclose a copy of my will. I think it is clear my intention, and wish Dr. Shipman to benefit by having my estate, but if he dies or does not accept it, then the estate goes to my daughter." The letter went on to request that she be cremated. There was nothing in the will left for her daughter or her grandsons, who she loved very much.

Unhappy with the way they had been instructed, Hamilton's decided to contact Kathleen's daughter, 53-year-old Angela Woodruff, herself a solicitor in Leamington, Spa. Angela usually handled all of her mother's affairs and knew how she wanted the estate to be divided. This new will and the way it had been handled made Angela suspicious.'

http://crimemagazine.com/doctor-death

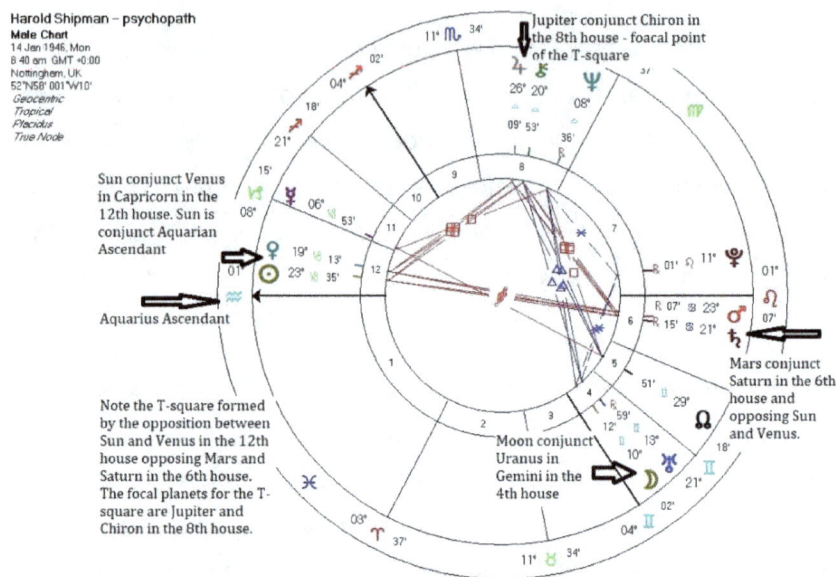

Above chart: Dr Harold Shipman, Doctor Death, showing his T-square, one of the critical features of his chart.

Harold Shipman's chart shows several significators for depression and possibly other psychological issues. His chart contains some classic significators for frustration, anger and arrogance. Does that make him a psychopath?

Working through his chart you can see that he has Sun conjunct Venus in the 12th house. There is nothing sinister with a 12th house Sun, one twelfth of the world's population have their Sun in the 12th house and I doubt many of them have psychopathic tendencies. The 12th house, however, does hide the energy of the planets that reside in it. I consider the 12th house to be a bit like a cave, planets go there to take a break from the world.

You will have already noticed that Sun and Venus are opposed by Saturn conjunct Mars in his 6th house - and the 4 of them are square to his Jupiter conjunct Chiron in his 8th house.

Sun is conjunct Venus and that is always a comfortable conjunction, it shows friendship and companionship. However you can see that their sign, Capricorn, can sometimes suppress the expression of their joyful and harmonious energy. Capricorn is not known for being overly sociable and outgoing. Their placement in the 12th house suggests that these two planets are somewhat withdrawn, perhaps leaving Shipman feeling lonely and isolated. The normally friendly and outgoing Sun-Venus conjunction is therefore inhibited by their house position (12th house) and their sign (Capricorn).

What drew my attention first though, was Mars and Saturn conjunct in Cancer in the 6th house, both planets are retrograde. In conjunction and in opposition these two planets can present as frustration leading to outbursts of anger and aggression. This is a classic combination, elevated in Shipman's chart because they are in the emotional Water sign of Cancer. Both Mars and Saturn aren't comfortable in Water, it slows them down.

Then there is the relationship between the planets. Saturn will always try to suppress Mars' desire to get out and play. Mars gets bored easily and needs to play, to express himself physically. The 6th house is a good place for him, it is a place he can get physical and be rewarded with more work. Saturn, being an outer planet therefore more powerful and controlling than inner planet Mars, will always win in a contest between the two. This is why you will find the words 'frustration' and 'anger' used in relation to a Mars-Saturn conjunction, square or opposition.

The Mars-Saturn opposition to Sun-Venus shows suppression too. Saturn not only has his foot on Mars' throat, so to speak, but he also wants to control and inhibit both the Sun and Venus. Another way of saying this is that the opposition from Mars and Saturn strongly conflicts with Sun and Venus.

All planets have needs to express themselves in their own way and conjunctions, oppositions, squares and trines show us how they inhibit or enhance each planet's relationship. I would say that this single opposition contributes strongly to Shipman's feelings of frustration and anger. Of course a good doctor would never display any negative emotions to the public. In this case Shipman has managed to internalise these feelings. His Sun and Venus are in the unemotional sign of Capricorn and well hidden in the 12th house. This makes it so much easier for him to internalise his feelings of frustration and anger.

Next you can see that Sun, Venus, Mars and Saturn all make squares to Jupiter and Chiron. Jupiter and Chiron are the focal planets of a pattern called a T-square which is formed from the two squares of the opposing planets.

A T-square is a pattern that tells astrologers an awful lot about a person. In this case Shipman's internalised anger and frustration needs release, a means to express itself. But the focal planets for the opposition between Mars-Saturn and Sun-Venus is Jupiter and Chiron - but where are they? Jupiter and Chiron are sitting in the 8th house of death and transformation.

Jupiter is the planet of expansion and expression, he is jovial and generous, a perfect planet to balance the frustration, inhibition, loneliness and anger of the four planets in square aspect to him. But instead of expressing themselves nicely they tie him down, like the sticky threads of a spider's web. These 4 planets plus Chiron have the potential to corrupt Jupiter's naturally positive nature.

Jupiter is conjunct Chiron and we already know that Chiron can represent your birth wound and is psychologically painful. Jupiter needs to expand and express himself but when inhibited he can become rude, greedy and arrogant. Jupiter has similar traits to Mars in that he has plenty of energy, drive and ambition. The problem that you can see building in Shipman's chart is that Jupiter is in pain.

Chiron contributes to Jupiter's anguish by limiting the expression of his normally jovial, outgoing and fun-loving personality.

The focal planet of a T-square is trapped, unable to express itself and so becomes the most inhibited of the planets in that pattern. One keyword for the focal planet of a T-square is 'sacrifice'. Shipman has two focal planets, Jupiter and Chiron, they are therefore called upon to sacrifice their own needs to try and keep the opposition between Sun–Venus and Mars-Saturn from corrupting the native's psychological harmony. Unfortunately, to do that the focal planets are at risk of becoming corrupted in some way themselves.

Think of the opposition, Sun-Venus versus Mars-Saturn, as standing at the two ends of a balance beam, a plank of wood. Now add a barrel in the middle, this represents Jupiter and Chiron. Jupiter and Chiron are now responsible for keeping the planets at each end from falling off the plank. This represents a strong psychological conflict and one that has basically removed Jupiter and his comrade Chiron, from Shipman's repertoire of psychological traits and qualities. That would be enough to trigger episodes of psychological distress (conflict).

As Jupiter also represents morality, once Jupiter is sacrificed or compromised Shipman may lose his sense of morality. I will look further into Dr Shipman's chart in the next chapter on Complexes.

Chapter 12 - Conflict and complexes in psychological astrology

Conflict in the chart

A conflicted planet, sign or house will generally exhibit an excess of that archetype's negative traits. For instance too many planets in Leo can make you excessively fiery, domineering and arrogant, attention seeking and extremely sensitive to criticism. A lesser amount of Leo, however, may present as a more tempered and controlled person showing strong traits of inspired leadership, generosity and creativity.

A psychological astrologer is someone who knows how to locate the key conflicts in a person's chart. Why is this important? Because your conflict is what you spend most of your life trying to resolve. Know someone's conflict and you basically know what frustrates, motivates and drives them. You, the psychological astrologer or therapist, can then develop a specific strategy or therapeutic approach to help your client resolve their conflicts.

We all have conflicted planets or points in our chart, that's why we incarnate, to understand the meaning of our existence. Without a reason to make the effort to grow up we would be quite happy to sit on the beach drinking vodka shots and eating caviar and cream hors d'oeuvres all day long – and that surely is a wasted life.

An example of conflict between two planets: Mercury in Virgo opposed by Uranus in Pisces. Mercury can normally focus on his projects without distraction, but in this opposition may end up struggling to manage Uranus' many interruptions. Uranus in Pisces can become distracted and simply change projects soon after it has begun. This rapid change of pace can place enormous stress on Mercury in the earthy, solid and detail driven sign of Virgo. The conflict between Mercury and Uranus may be experienced as excessive worry and a sense of feeling intellectually unfulfilled. This might manifest as the native becoming worried and depressed when presented with a new project that must be completed within a set time: *"I am such a failure. I can never meet a deadline on time."*

If a house is conflicted you would see it over loaded with planets causing the native to become too focused in trying to express the many urges and needs of each planet. For example, when the 5th house contains a stellium, which is 4 or more planets, the pressure to express each planet's instinctual needs and drives can be overwhelming. Each planet must adhere to the qualities of the 5th house: fun, party, addictions, gambling, friendship, alcohol, flirting, casual sex and more fun. Too much of a good thing can lead to a mental and physical breakdown. In this example the native would become so overwhelmed by trying to satisfy each planet's needs that they could easily become addicted to those negative traits I've just mentioned. Fortunately, the native who is aware of their instinctual needs and drives can decide to channel this towards the positive aspects of the 5th house: imagination and creativity, generosity and gregariousness, sunshine, happiness, leadership and friendship.

Conflict between planets and signs (signs on house cusps and other points in the chart) create ongoing tension between your inner and outer worlds. An example of conflict between a sign and a planet would be Mars in Pisces, a Fire planet in a Water sign. Mars wants to run free, express himself in some type of physical pursuit. Pisces is Water and so is most comfortable in providing the planets various types of emotional experiences. But Mars isn't interested in an emotional experience, he wants action. Look at his arrow, he wants direction and movement. Depending on which house Mars in Pisces resides and the aspects he forms with the other planets, we could say that Mars in Pisces is a minor conflict.

However, if Mars in Pisces is in the 3rd house he would become quite comfortable reading adventure books that involve ships and submarines. Mars would also be quite pleased if the native was a poet who could express this instinctual drive for action in a watery manner – poetry. Mars could also be trine Sun in which case his frustrations with Pisces is mitigated by his interactions with the fun loving and adventurous Sun. When you see a planet in a detrimental sign you must examine many details that includes his aspects to the other planets and his house placement to see if he is indeed in conflict or not.

You would see conflict when planets are in difficult aspects such as an opposition, conjunction and sometimes with trines and squares.

There is no hard and fast rule for what is an internal or external conflict in astrology. Oppositions tend to be external and are more often projected onto someone or something in your environment. External conflict could be your neighbour, manager or partner. *"He made me do it. I hate him."*

Internal conflict is more often seen with conjunctions and squares. This could be experienced as excessive worry, depression, sadness, sleeplessness, unwanted thoughts, loneliness, agoraphobia and anxiety. *"I can't go out because I'm unattractive and hopeless with boys. I'm such a loser."*

These conflicted points in the chart cause you to continually seek ways to pacify them, trying to stop them arising when you don't want them to. Let me give you an example: giving a public presentation can be a terrifying experience especially if you have a conflicted Ascendant, which is your public face to the world; a conflicted Moon which shows your sensitive emotions and desire to avoid stressful situations; or a conflicted Sun which highlights your lack of confidence; then it is possible that these conflicts are the source of your fear of public speaking.

Most people run away from conflict, they seek to avoid and pretend it doesn't exist. Conflict doesn't just go away of itself but psychotherapy can help to access your unconscious conflict to make it visible so that you can work on it in therapy and at home in meditation. You could also do this by looking at your chart to locate the planets, signs and houses that are conflicted.

Let me use the example of public speaking and a conflicted Ascendant. Imagine that you have an Aquarian Ascendant. Aquarius is bright, intelligent and quite often loves being in the public eye. Those qualities do not make you fearful of public speaking. But what if the ruler of Aquarius, Uranus, is in poor aspect with Venus? The conflict between Venus, your social self, and Uranus, your public self, may create internal conflict - anxiety.

What if Neptune was sitting right next to your Aquarian Ascendant? Neptune can make you experience episodes of dreaminess, forgetfulness and confusion causing a loss of confidence. This kind of analysis is how you find conflict in the chart.

Conflict causes pain and most often that pain is internalised. But sometimes the pain is so deeply hidden (repressed) in your unconscious that you simply don't notice it but everyone around you does. Once someone has the courage to tell you that you are behaving strangely you can then examine your chart to find the source of your conflict and start healing.

When conflict is not easily resolved it may, and this is quite rare, it may constellate into a complex.

What is a complex?

"A complex is a core pattern of emotions, memories, perceptions, and wishes in the personal unconscious organized around a common theme... Primarily a psychoanalytic term, it is found extensively in the works of Carl Jung and Sigmund Freud... Complex existence is widely agreed upon in the area of depth psychology, a branch of psychology that asserts the most significant parts of one's personality are derived from one's unconscious. It is a way of mapping the psyche, and is a crucial theoretical item in therapy. Complexes are believed by Carl Jung and Sigmund Freud to influence an individual's attitude and behaviour."
https://en.wikipedia.org/wiki/Complex_(psychology)

A complex causes disruption in the native's ability to have their psychological needs met. This might manifest as an inability to relate with others in a normal or appropriate manner.

Everyone has minor psychological issues that tend to surface at times, but serious internal conflicts that constellate into a complex is quite rare. A complex might also be described as a constellation of internal belief patterns manifesting as external behaviours that limit the person's engagement and enjoyment in life. A psychological astrologer may consider the possible existence of a complex after a thorough examination of conflicted planets and points in their client's chart. Complexes amplify the conflict you have between the natural flow of your internal urges, needs and instincts and how they are expressed.

A point to note: trying to describe a complex is a real pain. Sometimes it is better to just think of it as 'serious psychological issues'. Astrologers see conflict in the chart all the time but when there are so many that it has corrupted the native's ability to function appropriately in society then it MIGHT become a complex.

Dr Harold Shipman - God Complex

'...Shipman's belief in his own superiority grew. He became more arrogant, convinced that he could never be wrong. In effect, he developed a "God Complex," not uncommon among doctors, but in Shipman, this was highly developed. So sure he was of his own superiority, he now began to attack other doctors and colleagues of equal standing, and even stood and attacked professors at lectures. Many doctors, embarrassed by Shipman's actions, now avoided him. Yet his patients loved him...' http://crimemagazine.com/doctor-death

Dr Shipman's acts of murder have been described, in some instances, as acts of mercy, he being the 'Angel of Mercy'. He murdered his victims, it is believed, because they were ill and suffering, an act of euthanasia. However, it appears that some were either a nuisance and annoyed him while others provided him with extra income. He stole money and jewellery and in one case he tried to inherit the estate of a victim. Interestingly, although he was said to be arrogant and abusive to his staff and other doctors, his patients were devoted to him.

Shipman eventually developed a taste for drugs leading him to commonly prescribe pethidine (demerol, pethidrine), an opioid pain killer, to his patients. His patients never saw the drug, he used it himself.

In the crimemagazine.com article, Shipman was said to have developed a **God Complex**.

God Complex: *'A god complex is an unshakeable belief characterised by consistently inflated feelings of personability, privilege, or infallibility. A person with a god complex may refuse to admit the possibility of their error or failure, even in the face of irrefutable evidence, intractable problems or difficult or impossible tasks. The person is also highly dogmatic in their views, meaning the person speaks of their personal opinions as though they were unquestionably correct. Someone with a god complex may exhibit no regard for the conventions and demands of society, and may request special consideration or privileges.'*
https://en.wikipedia.org/wiki/God_complex

A God Complex is composed of traits that are basically the same as Narcissistic Personality Disorder and many of the Antisocial Personality Disorder. These were previously called Psychopaths and Sociopaths. The difference between a narcissist and a psychopath is that the psychopath crosses the line to commit violent criminal acts. A narcissist is more inclined to bully and steals from their employer or employees. They also excel at what is called 'white collar crime'.

Do narcissists also have a God Complex? I would say that many do. The traits listed fit each category quite snugly, like a hand in a glove. However, some narcissists may not exhibit the same god like behaviour of the God Complex. Those with a God Complex act out their omniscience while a narcissist does not necessarily act out to that extent. There is only a subtle difference between the two. You would be more inclined to see the diagnosis of a God Complex used to describe someone in the era in which Shipman practised medicine which is the mid 20th century.

The narcissist's symptoms include: self-interest, greed, self importance, a misplaced sense of entitlement, bullying, perceive themselves to be omniscient and omnipotent, a total disregard for the well being of others, a complete lack of empathy, selfish, a sense of superiority, arrogance, judgemental, immoral, amoral, unethical, addicted to power, indiscriminate use of power for self gain, and they lie through their teeth and think nothing of it.

You will see many narcissistic types in your workplace and in the news. They are experts at climbing to the highest levels of management where they soon abuse their position and those who work beneath them. Over many years as a therapist I have counselled many hundreds of their victims.

These traits are seen in politicians, corporate directors and CEO's, workplace managers, public service, lawyers, in the military, managers of private charities, religion and in every hierarchical organisation. They gravitate to the top quickly and easily by ingratiating themselves with other narcissists in positions of power above them.

A God Complex in this context ably describes the doctor of the early to mid 20th century when Shipman practised medicine in his community. Doctors were worshipped as gods, only one step below that of priests – and we now know where that led to.

Shipman's conflicted Jupiter contributes strongly to the narcissistic traits listed above. Jupiter is the head of the pantheon of Roman gods and goddesses. Jupiter is known as Jove, or Zeus in Greek Mythology. Because the traits above are strongly configured in the negative traits of Jupiter, a God Complex could also be referred to as a 'Jupiter Complex'.

It might be said that Shipman's patients became the worshipping and adoring public that Jupiter enjoys having around him. His staff and fellow doctors, however, became the servants to Jupiter's alter ego – the narcissist.

A point to note: these narcissistic traits form many of the negative traits of the Air Fire Phenomenon and are not limited to Jupiter but are shared by all of the Fire signs Aries, Leo and Sagittarius as well as the Fire planets Mars, Jupiter and Sun. They can also be seen in the Air planets, Uranus and Mercury, and to a lesser extent, with the Air signs Gemini, Libra and Aquarius.

Shipman's T-square was the first pattern in the chart that I examined - it really does stand out. It highlights the impact this pattern has on his Jupiter. There is another weak T-square in Shipman's chart. Mercury and North Node are opposite each other and both square Neptune. This places Neptune in a compromised situation that in some ways limits his natural expression. This will affect his ability to support the Moon which I will examine below.

The Air element dominates his chart with Moon, Uranus and North Node in Gemini; Aquarian Ascendant; Mercury in the 11th house; Neptune, Jupiter and Chiron in Libra; and Pluto in the 7th house. The powerful Air signs Gemini and Aquarius plus the Fire planet Jupiter, appear to have contributed to his sense of authority, superiority and lack of empathy.

There is little emphasis on Fire signs however Jupiter is the main Fire contributor. The conflict within his Water 4th, 8th and 12th houses are strong and definitely contribute to his disturbed mind. These all point to a constellation of conflicts.

Jupiter is a Fire planet and resides in the Water house of death, the 8th house. The T-square places pressure on Jupiter as its focal planet to sacrifice his normally positive expression of joviality, generosity, morality and wisdom. In some ways this placement corrupts Jupiter causing him to manifest many of his negative traits. Chiron is the planet of 'anguish' and as such impacts Jupiter too though not as powerfully as the T-square pattern itself.

Shipman's Sun and Venus are in the generally unemotional Earth sign of Capricorn. That in itself is certainly no indication of psychopathy, not at all, even though they are both in the hidden 12th house as well. This placement suggests that Shipman feared abandonment which reinforces the trauma of the loss of his mother at such an early age. He also has his Sun and Venus opposed by Mars and Saturn. These conflicts strongly suggest social isolation, fear of being assaulted plus it is highly possible that he was a victim of bullying. I also suspect that he had traits of Autism Spectrum Disorder.

Let's keep looking because what we have so far does not confirm that he is a narcissist nor does it convince me that he has a God Complex.

His Ascendant is Aquarius which is Air, eccentric, unusual, aloof and sometimes unemotional. It also suggests that he is out of touch with his emotions. However, we all know that an Aquarian Ascendant does not suggest psychopathy. What I am guiding you to consider though is a more powerful contributor to his conflicted psyche, which is his Moon. Shipman's Moon is conjunct Uranus the ruler of Aquarius. The planet that rules the Ascendant sign is called the '*Lord of the Chart*'. This makes Uranus a very powerful planet.

Both the Moon and Uranus are in the Air sign Gemini. Again let me remind you that a Gemini Moon conjunct Uranus may suggest a lack of empathy but does not of itself suggest psychopathy.

Gemini is one of the happiest and personable of signs. Gemini's just love chatting, socialising and sharing, they delight in social engagement. There is nothing inherently wrong with a Moon–Uranus conjunction, a lot of people have it and live with it quite comfortably. Let me examine these two planets in Gemini in more detail.

The conjunction between Moon and Uranus in Gemini in the 4th house adds an extra dimension to Shipman's personality. This is not a warm conjunction even though it resides in his 4th house of home and family where the Moon is naturally exalted. It suggests detached and / or aroused emotions in the family home. It also says something about his mother and their relationship. Mother is represented by the Moon and the 4th house. His mother died at the age of 43 years when Shipman was just 17 years of age.

As you read this section please note that Uranus is an Air planet, this is important. Moon and Uranus are in Gemini which adds the second layer of Air to Shipman's chart. It is my experience that people with an Air dominance sometimes exhibit symptoms of worry, a racing mind, insomnia and disturbed negative thoughts. Don't forget that he was addicted to opioids which he may have used to calm his racing mind so that he could sleep.

Shipman's Moon and Uranus in Gemini suggests that his mother was probably an intellectual, unemotional and aloof. Perhaps they had a purely functional relationship. There was no doubt they communicated a lot as this is high on the Gemini list of desirable activities - communicating.

When you also consider that his Sun and Venus are in Capricorn in the 12th house it suggests that there were very few hugs between mother and son. Overt signs of affection were probably at the lower end of their relationship spectrum. However, the Sun's placement may better reflect his relationship with his father who appears to have been unemotional, absent and unavailable.

Shipman's Moon is trine Neptune and Chiron, a trine between Moon and Neptune can signify unconditional love. The trine with Chiron suggests an interest in the occult and healing. The Moon may use these easy flowing trines to ease her discomfort with Uranus.

Does the Moon succeed in easing Shipman's moodiness and racing negative thoughts through these trines? Perhaps she does. Shipman remained married until his suicide which appears to have been so that his wife would receive a decent pension. Perhaps the relationship with his wife eased his conflicted mind. The lovely trine between Moon and Neptune certainly suggests love and affection and perhaps this was reflected in his marriage in some way. However, we need to remember that Neptune is the focal planet of Shipman's second T-square. This position suggests that Neptune is distracted as he must sacrifice his energy to manage the opposition between Mercury and North Node. It appears that he was unable to share the unconditional love of Moon trine Neptune with others beyond his immediate family.

Chiron's trine to the Moon does not appear to have eased the T-square from Sun-Venus and Mars-Saturn.

A point to note: as you can see I am examining each layer of conflict, or possible conflict, for you to better understand how I delineate a chart of this nature.

"Shipman... was the favourite child of his domineering mother, Vera. She instilled in him an early sense of superiority that tainted most of his later relationships, leaving him an isolated adolescent with few friends."
https://www.biography.com/people/harold-shipman-17169712

"She (Primrose, Shipman's wife) stood by him throughout the trial, and even continued writing him love letters when he was locked up."
https://www.thesun.co.uk/news/6107400/primrose-oxtoby-dr-harold-shipman-wife-murder-kids/

"The couple were 'childhood sweethearts' and met after he had started studying at Leeds University Medical School in 1965. They had been travelling on the same bus up to Leeds. Primrose had been working as a window dresser at a department store at the time. It was a whirlwind romance and the pair were married, with Primrose pregnant, while Shipman was still in his first year of university. The couple went on to have four children together." https://www.mirror.co.uk/tv/tv-news/inside-harold-shipmans-family-loyal-12430802

"Friends say that Shipman was everything to his wife, that she was devoted and submissive to a man commonly remembered as moody and domineering. He has been described by many as forceful, clever, enigmatic; she was barely literate and highly impressionable. They married when she was very young and six months' pregnant, a lapse for which her parents allegedly never forgave her."
https://www.theguardian.com/world/2004/jan/16/gender.uk

Summary of Dr Harold Shipman's chart

T-square – Sun-Venus opposing Mars-Saturn with both square Jupiter-Chiron: tension builds on the focal planets, Jupiter and Chiron, possibly corrupting Jupiter's positive traits. This allows his negative traits to dominate Shipman's psyche. This is quite a complex and disrupting planetary pattern particularly with the tension from Mars and Saturn who dominate the other four planets. The opposition between Sun-Venus and Mars-Saturn suggests that he was a victim of bullying and was fearful of being assaulted. Without the Mars-Saturn conjunction the pressure on Jupiter would be significantly less.

T-square – Mercury opposing North Node both square Neptune: although aspects to the North Node don't seem to be as strong as those involving a planet I will include this T-square in my analysis. It suggests that Neptune needs to sacrifice his role in the chart to help keep Mercury and North Node in balance. That would certainly inhibit the promise of spreading unconditional love to his Moon. As suggested earlier the trine from Neptune to the Moon would normally manifest as unconditional love particularly for his wife and family. From the news articles I've quoted it is evident that there was love and affection in his marriage.

Sun conjunct Venus in Capricorn in the 12th house: both the sign of Capricorn and the 12th house combine to inhibit the free expression of his Sun and Venus traits. It suggests an unavailable father, fear of abandonment and psychological trauma perhaps brought on by his mother's cancer and death.

Air dominance: 7 points in Air signs. Aquarian Ascendant, Moon and Uranus, the Lord of the Chart, strongly placed in Gemini, and Moon and Uranus in the 4th house. This suggests that he experienced mental tension in the family home and had issues with an unemotional mother.

They also suggest the Air Fire Phenomenon which is explained in an earlier chapter.

Water houses: Jupiter and Chiron in the 8th house of death are the focal planets of the T-square; Moon and Uranus in the 4th house of home, family and childhood; Sun and Venus in the hidden 12th house. This highlights his psychological conflicts.

Pluto in the 7th house: I haven't mentioned this previously but it does play its part. The 7th house is 'others' which include his patients. Pluto is well aspected suggesting that he was seen to demonstrate compassion for his patient's well being. Pluto is the most positive planet in his chart and may be part of the reason why his patients adored him.

Neptune trine Moon: this unconditional love aspect suggests that Shipman was capable of love which appears to have manifested itself in his longstanding marriage to his wife, Primrose. After the trial Primrose and her family were given new identities to protect them.

Before I would diagnose Shipman with narcissism, psychopathy or a God Complex I would need to examine his background. I want confirmation that he also had the necessary precursors I'll outline next.

How are psychopaths created?

In my work and study I have come across certain characteristics that contribute to someone developing Antisocial Personality Disorder (also known as a Psychopath). It is important to understand that the psychopath is both a product of their genetic inheritance and their upbringing:

* they have ample opportunity to practice bully or torturing of others. Sometimes this begins with torturing animals like the neighbour's pet. I

am unaware if Shipman tortured animals, his siblings or bullied his school mates. However, as a doctor he had ample opportunity to bully his staff and those he disliked. He also clearly demonstrated that as a trusted doctor he had many opportunities to access vulnerable patients. His position of authority gave him tacit 'permission' to do things to them that was definitely psychopathic - such as killing them. It does appear that he was a bully in the workplace and perhaps home.

* another characteristic is to gain materially from his actions. Shipman certainly did gain from his deceased patients often stealing their belongings and money. In the one case we know of he forged a patient's will so that he gained her entire estate.

* there is a slight possibility that they were raised by overly permissive parents who spoiled them into thinking that they were special and gave them a sense of entitlement. These may turn into school and workplace narcissists and bullies but rarely psychopaths like Shipman. From the background material we have it is possible that his mother spoiled him and treated him as special.

* those who were raised by dysfunctional parents in a household that associated with drug and alcohol abuse and a strong association with criminal gangs may also develop these traits.

* unresolved trauma which has created serious psychological dysfunction. His mother contracted cancer and he was her primary carer up to when she died at 47 years of age, Shipman was 17 years old at that time. I am quite confident that this was a very traumatic period of his life. This helps validate his Sun-Venus conjunction in Capricorn in the 12th house which suggests a fear of abandonment.

* a predisposition to violence. I have no material to support this apart from the violent act of administering drugs to commit murder.

* in some cases of psychopathy the right orbito frontal cortex of the brain is damaged. In this situation the cause of their psychopathy is neurological dysregulation leading to an inability to inhibit their urges. In other words when they have a tantrum they are unable to stop it from escalating into violence. This is particularly seen in those with narcissistic and psychopathic personality disorders. I have no supporting evidence that Shipman suffered a brain injury or a dysregulated right orbito frontal cortex. However, there is growing scientific evidence that some forms of mental illness are correlated with damage to this area of the brain.

The psychopath learns how to appear normal

I have worked with enough psychopaths to know that they are clever, very clever. Unless the psychologist is experienced in working with psychopaths they can appear quite normal. A psychopath will grasp the mind of the therapist within about 3 minutes and know exactly how to manipulate them.

Their psychological profile shows that they have no remorse but they can learn how to pretend to be empathic and compassionate. A psychopath who wishes to fit in will study the social routines, norms and cues used by the 'normal' population. They learn how to fit in like an actor learns his lines.

"When I meet someone I put out my right hand this far... I wait for the other guy to grasp it and then I squeeze his hand but not too tight. I then move it up and down three times before I let go. Then I ask him in a mild tone, 'How are you? How is the family?'"

I believe that there is a strong neurological feature in the narcissist that must first be triggered in a specific way to turn him or her into a psychopath. One day in the future a neurological predisposition to mental illness will be found by examining specific features of the EEG of the brain. EEG is measured using an electroencephalograph.

The transition from an Air and Fire dominance into a Personality Disorder is extremely rare and the pathway is very complex. Dr Shipman had some of these rare features, for instance, his mother died when he was 17 years old from cancer. He was her main carer and confidante from an early age. His mother's illness and death appears to have contributed to his experiencing bereavement and psychological trauma. His opportunities certainly came once he began practicing as a doctor and had access to patients and drugs. Yet he didn't exhibit overt violence, his violence was covert, hidden, like his 12th house planets. He was verbally abusive and critical to his children and the staff who worked for him. Indeed, these are narcissistic traits, but the next big step, to psychopathy and murder, only arrives through a complex combination of internal conflict, opportunity and life experiences.

Just as an aside, bullies can be seen as early-stage narcissists. With the right opportunities and rewards they can make that transition to psychopathy by bullying for pleasure and material gain. Once they have crossed the moral threshold to believe that they can do no wrong they too may be capable of cold-blooded murder. That, I believe, describes Dr Harold Shipman. There is evidence in his chart that suggests he had a predisposition towards developing a Narcissistic Personality Disorder, the God Complex.

Are people with a God Complex psychopaths and murders? Not at all, you will see them in any hierarchical organisation as mentioned earlier. What concerns me are world leaders with a God Complex. At any moment they could order their military forces to reduce a city of civilians to ashes. The thought of consequences never enters their unempathic heads.

A point to note: although I will discuss this point in detail in later books a dominance of Air and Fire rarely manifests as severely as narcissism or psychopathy. It is, interestingly, commonly seen in successful people be they astrologers, chefs, authors, scientists, academics, business men and women, sports people and in every arena of human endeavour. A strong Air and Fire chart can manifest as driven behaviour leading to success but it can sometimes manifest as an over-bearing and bullying monster. Please don't think that Air and Fire dominance causes people to become a psychopath, it simply doesn't. These two elements are just an expression of the drives within us which rarely corrupt into psychopathy. If you are interested to know more please watch out for my future publication on this amazing Air Fire Phenomenon in my upcoming book, *'Psychological Astrology and the Signs of The Zodiac'*.

Does Dr Harold Shipman have a God Complex

If I were to single out the most probable astrological planets and signs that contribute to a God Complex I would include Jupiter, Sagittarius, Uranus and Aquarius as the most likely suspects. It is extremely rare to find the Sun involved in this complex. The Sun is unique in that he will always manifest in as positive a manner as possible.

Shipman's T-square formed by the opposition between Sun-Venus and Mars-Saturn with their focal point on Jupiter and Chiron; his conflicted Moon-Uranus conjunction; his Air sign dominance; and his strong Water houses suggest that Shipman did have a God Complex. This diagnosis can only be given in the context of his meeting most of the environmental opportunities discussed previously.

Would I have diagnosed Dr Harold Shipman with a God Complex, a Narcissistic or an Antisocial Personality Disorder from his chart? Not at all. Astrology describes possibilities, it does not diagnose, at least I don't use it that way. His conflicts could just as easily have manifested in a multitude of ways many of which could have been positive and empowering given the right environment.

What would you tell Mrs Shipman if she brought 10 year old Harold to you for an astrology consultation?

I'll help you out. Obviously there is significant conflict in the chart which makes your response quite simple: *'find a good psychotherapist and arrange counselling for your child'*. This is non-judgemental, empathic and provides clear advice fulfilling your ethical requirements. My advice is that if you see conflict in a chart that makes you feel uncomfortable then always advise your client to seek counselling.

I would also suggest to Mrs Shipman that she harness Harold's active mind to help him learn how to calm his mind and his fears. This will be especially useful at bed time. It might include self-hypnosis audios so that he learns to physically relax. I would also suggest she have a series of fantasy based audio-books that will guide him into sleep in a nice, safe fantasy environment.

Because it appears that he is the victim of bullying and has some autistic features in his chart I would suggest she speak with his teacher and principal about providing a safe place at school for him to spend his recess and lunch breaks. As he gets older I would recommend she involve him in activities where he feels that he can achieve a level of mastery, perhaps chess, tennis or ten pin bowling. I would not try to push him into group sports. Maybe you could add your own thoughts to this list.

Chapter 13 - Putting your chart together - chart delineation

The word 'delineate' means to interpret or explain. Astrologers traditionally use this word when we describe the chart to our client. There are many ways to go about delineating a chart so I will begin with the basic combinations of the three key elements - planets, signs and houses.

An understanding of the planets, their rulerships and how they operate in the elements (Earth, Air, Water and Fire) is critical in delineation. Some planets operate best in Fire signs like Mars, Sun and Jupiter; others prefer Water like the Moon, Pluto and Neptune; others prefer Earth like Saturn, Venus (passive) and Mercury (passive); and some planets prefer Air like Mercury (active), Venus (active) and Uranus. Always be mindful that planets and signs have a tendency to break the rules too.

The Golden Rule is now VERY important

Planets are WHAT – the planet archetypes themselves.

Signs are HOW – the planet's personality.

Houses are WHERE – the stage where the planet archetypes act out their performance.

Planet / sign delineations – some practice

Astrologers begin to delineate a chart by putting the planet + sign keywords into sentences. Here are some examples:

Venus + Cancer = a warm person with a need for emotional support, loves being with family and entertaining at home.

Mars + Gemini = interested in everything and possibly thinks they know everything too, talks a lot, is chatty and sometimes mentally and physically hyperactive, needs to channel his energy into physical activity, can be argumentative.

Sun + Aquarius = an inspired person who has many interests, is quite intuitive in problem solving, they can sometimes become stressed and nervy.

Saturn + Pisces = someone who processes their feelings constructively but can also be restricted emotionally; alternatively someone that can create some remarkable and inspired works of art both as a tradesman and professional artisan.

Planet + sign + house delineations - combining the keywords of all three:

Venus + Cancer + 3rd house = loves being at home with family, also has a strong need to communicate with her family.

Mars + Gemini + 7th house = a driven person, talkative and loves chatting with prospective partners, someone that just wants to talk but may become argumentative with those close to them, may not be able to focus on emotional issues, prefers physical and intellectual relationships to emotional ones.

Sun + Aquarius + 4th house = someone with an inspired mind that enjoys teaching and encouraging his children to learn about the world. Also feels a great need to move house, feels restricted by physical & emotional attachments. Requires physical and emotional space at home.

Saturn + Pisces + 5th house = enjoys water skiing and having fun at the beach, a committed ocean adventurer, may feel restricted with children and unable to control them, restricted in making close friends, once they have friends they won't let them go.

Summary of combining keywords

1) Combining two points:

* Sun in Capricorn = happiness / saviour / generosity / resourcefulness / father / discipline / structure.

* Sun in 11th house = happiness / fun / confidence / giving / sharing / hopes / humanity.

* Moon in Gemini - mother / mental processes / society / socialising / empathy / communications / worry.

* Moon in 5th house - friends / mother / fun / warmth / partying / older women / creativity / imagination / empathy.

2) Combining all three points:

* Sun - vitality, happiness, generosity, direction, father, salvation.

+ Capricorn - solid, determined, disciplined, direction, stubborn, earthy, order, structure, scaffolding.

+ 11th house - humanity, giving, hopes, dreams, wishes.

Combining these keywords into a sentence - *"The native is compassionate, resourceful and disciplined, gives generously to those in need."*

* Moon in Gemini in the 5th house - *"The native has fun with friends and family sharing emotions, socialising and communicating."* Or *"The native

enjoys being part of a community that shares their feelings in a safe and educational environment." Or *"The native enjoys being with older women who share their feelings, enjoys socialising and having fun while teaching others."* Or *"The native is nervy often worrying about what their family and friends think about them."*

* Mercury in Capricorn in the 12th house - *"The native prefers to stand back from the crowd and will only communicate when they feel safe to do so."* Or *"The native dreams of having a strong intellectual bond with others."* Or *"The native communicates from a deep sense of self; they don't waste words, they cut right to the chase."* Or *"The native prefers to listen, rarely offering their opinion unless given a secure environment to do so."* Or *"The native harbours deep seated worries and may sometimes suffer nightmares, headaches or escape the stress in their lives by sleeping excessively."*

Every professional astrologer started their practice by studying the keywords for each planet, sign and house. In each reading they would build keyword combinations, slowly and painstakingly, until they have the best description which fits what they see in the chart.

A point to note: a single planet can be expressed in many different ways as you can see from the sentences above. How do you know which sentence is the correct one? You do that through diligent practice of combining keywords until they start to confirm what you see in the entire chart. An astrologer sees a person as the product of their whole chart, not as bits and pieces.

Planet	Rulership Sign	Rulership house	Exalted	Detriment	Fall
Sun	Leo	5th	Aries	Aquarius	Libra
Moon	Cancer	4th	Taurus	Capricorn	Scorpio
Mercury	Gemini + Virgo	3rd + 6th	Virgo	Sagittarius + Pisces	Pisces
Venus	Taurus + Libra	2nd + 7th	Pisces	Aries + Scorpio	Virgo
Mars	Aries	1st	Capricorn	Libra + Taurus	Cancer
Jupiter	Sagittarius	9th	Cancer	Gemini + Virgo	Capricorn
Saturn	Capricorn	10th	Libra	Cancer	Aries
Uranus	Aquarius	11th	Scorpio	Leo	Taurus
Neptune	Pisces	12th	Cancer	Virgo	Capricorn
Pluto	Scorpio	8th	Leo	Taurus	Aquarius
Chiron, dwarf planets and asteroids	nil	nil	nil	nil	nil

Table: planets and their Rulerships, Exaltation, Detriment and Fall

What to look for when you delineate a chart

Rulerships

Rulerships help astrologers understand how the planet is affected by its placement in a sign or house. Each planet has a preference for various signs and houses. Some signs can make the planet weaker or stronger, the same for houses. Use the Rulership table above to examine your own chart.

Every planet rules a sign and a house, this is called Rulership. The sign or house where it is most comfortable is called Exalted. However, if the planet is uncomfortable in a house or sign it is said to be in Detriment or Fall. These are but part of what you will find in the chart. Sometimes it is important and sometimes not. I don't use exactly the same terms used in traditional astrology very much these days. I think of planets as experiencing varying degrees of comfort and discomfort in the signs and houses. These grids, however, are invaluable when starting out as an astrologer. Learn the planet rulerships, they are important, then allow your intuition to guide you.

Knowing how well a planet relates with other planets, signs and houses will come to you with practice. Using the example in the previous chapter, Dr Harold Shipman, his Sun and Venus are going to be comfortable with each other basically no matter where they are in the chart.

I mentioned that because Shipman's Sun and Venus were in Capricorn and somewhat subdued by their 12th house placement. Of course, what would you expect given the nature of Capricorn? Capricorn is traditional and conservative, he is also pragmatic, he wants to know what he can do, not what he can think or feel.

For example, Venus brings a pretty flower to show Capricorn. She is thinking how beautiful it would look sitting in a vase in his kitchen.

Capricorn says, *"Harrumph, can I eat it? Can I sell it? How can it improve my fuel economy?"*

There is no sign that will make Sun and Venus feel extremely uncomfortable with each other. After all, they spend a month in each sign and each house as they travel through your chart.

In the sign of Capricorn, Sun and Venus will function quite well. Capricorn will teach them discipline and how to be better organised. Capricorn makes the Sun and Venus clean up their mess after they've been playing in the lounge room; he gets them to make their bed each morning; and he shows them how to brush their teeth properly. There is nothing wrong with Capricorn. If it is hugs that the Sun and Venus want then they would wait until they had arrived at Cancer's home.

I had said previously that Shipman's Sun and Venus were in the 'hidden' 12th house. This is where they are structured (Capricorn) and make pretty things (Venus) and he can express his self esteem (Sun). But it all happens inside a cave, the cave of the 12th house. It isn't freely available to Shipman, it is hidden, deep inside his psyche.

You may have heard the saying, *'Don't hide your light under a bush.'* It means that if you have a talent don't hide it, show it off proudly. In Shipman's case that bush is the 12th house, his light was hidden inside a cave where he would have struggled to experience or express it. What did his patients see? They saw the manufactured outer shell of the cave front and his humanitarian Aquarian Ascendant. He could only access the beauty of his Capricorn Sun and Venus if he ventured bravely into the cave of the 12th. That might prove way too frightening for him because this placement can indicate fear of abandonment, loneliness and isolation. This might lead to depression and anxiety and possibly manifesting as symptoms of the Autistic Spectrum.

To understand the impact of the sign and house in Shipman's example I also looked at the aspects that the Sun and Venus made with other archetypes namely: Mars, Saturn, Jupiter and Chiron. I saw that Shipman was so preoccupied with trying to remain psychologically stable that his Sun and Venus remained hidden in their cave. You can imagine that with the level of conflict in his chart it made them too afraid to come out. In the end their lack of positive input appeared to have contributed to his psychological dysfunction and eventual acts of murder.

Perhaps Shipman could have accessed his Sun's self esteem and power by using the cave metaphor in psychotherapy.

Your planets, signs and houses form the road map to your psyche. Fortunately those holes in the road, your negative or hidden qualities, can be accessed and repaired in many positive ways. As an astrologer and therapist you could develop suitable approaches to raise awareness of these 'less than comfortable' points in your own and the charts of others. That is where archetypal meditations can be very helpful.

What do I call a planet in conflict or discomfort?

I see the planets and signs of the chart as a community complete with relationships formed by their aspects - conjunctions, oppositions, squares, trines and any other aspects I considered important. An example would be Venus and Saturn who wouldn't normally get along too well, but they could if there were other features in the chart that suggested so. If Venus was conjunct Saturn in Scorpio it could be interpreted as an intense and perhaps uncomfortable relationship. If this occurred in the 2nd house you could help reduce the native's internal conflict by recommending they see a financial advisor. This will help them order and structure their material and financial affairs. If it occurred in the 7th house you could recommend marriage counselling so that they could better understand and manage their love life and friendships. If in the 11th house they might want to join a humanitarian organisation.

Every negative has a flip-side in astrology. As the saying goes: *'every cloud has a silver-lining'*. Find this silver-lining by using your understanding of astrology and psychology. You can then help your client create strategies to manage the conflicts you have highlighted in their chart.

A point to note: if you don't have training in psychotherapy please refer your client to someone who does. This is the professional ethics part of an astrology practice – refer when you need to, don't take risks with people's lives.

Planetary shapes & patterns

The shapes that the planets form in the chart can provide vital clues too. What strikes you first may not always be the most important feature of the chart so be careful when you interpret these shapes. Looking at Dick Smith's chart below you will see that it is strong on the Western side (the right side of the chart), it makes a slight Bucket shape and contains a Grand Cross pattern. Let's examine his chart and see what those shapes and patterns mean to Dick.

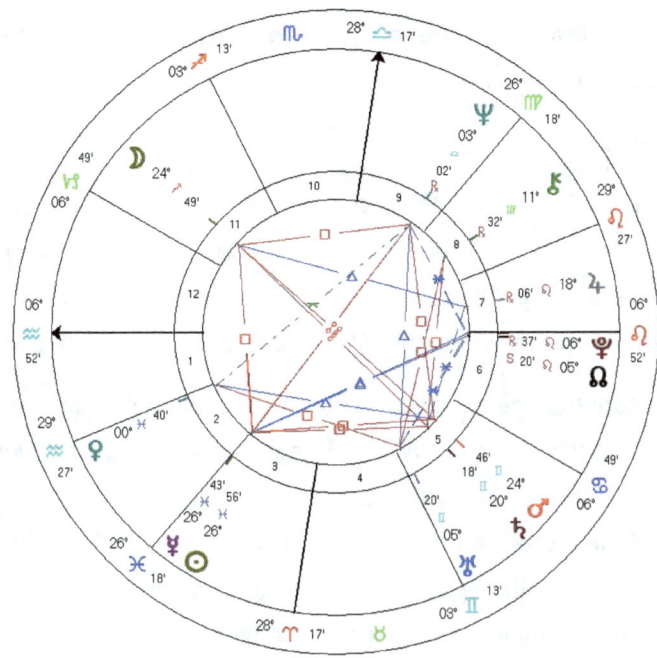

Above chart: Dick Smith, entrepreneur, electronics whizz kid, pilot, eccentric.

Dick Smith - entrepreneur, adventurer, pilot, electronics whizz kid, outspoken eccentric

Rulerships

Mercury Rules the 3rd house + is in Fall in Pisces – Mercury is in his favourite house, the Airy 3rd house of communication (he rules Gemini which rules the 3rd house); but, he is not happy being forced to communicate through the Watery and dream-like sign of Pisces.

Mercury thus becomes conflicted by his placement in Pisces yet he loves being in the 3rd house WHERE he is allowed to communicate as much as he wants. Unfortunately, he is limited by his sign position, Pisces, in HOW he expresses his mercurial traits. This tells the astrologer that Mercury is both happy and in conflict. Such an important planet as Mercury certainly needs further examination.

Venus Rules the 2nd and 7th houses - a happy Venus in the 2nd house which she passively rules through her rulership of Taurus.

Venus is Exalted in Pisces which means that Venus is quite happy in the sign of Pisces.

Venus in Pisces and Neptune in Libra are in Mutual Reception - they share certain qualities because they share the other's sign.

Venus, therefore is nicely placed by sign and by house. We would next look at her aspects with the other planets: a square to Uranus which is difficult and annoying; a nice trine to Mars, her lover; and a minor aspect, a quincunx, to Neptune.

Chart Signature

The next thing you do is take note of each of the elements and modes for each of the main points in the chart like the Ascendant and the Midheaven; and each planet's sign. By adding them up you can determine the chart signature.

Sign Elements – include planets, Ascendant and Midheaven

Fire   - 4 (Moon in Sagittarius; Jupiter, Pluto and North Node in Leo).

Earth - 1 (Chiron in Virgo).

Air   - 6 (Mars, Saturn and Uranus in Gemini; Neptune and Midheaven in Libra; Ascendant in Aquarius).

Water - 3 (Sun, Mercury and Venus in Pisces).

Dick's strongest element is Air with 6 points and his weakest is Earth with only 1 point.

Sign Modes

Cardinal - 2 (Neptune and Midheaven)

Fixed   - 4 (Jupiter, Pluto, North Node, Ascendant)

Mutable - 8 (Moon, Sun, Mercury, Venus, Mars, Saturn, Uranus, Chiron)

Dick's strongest mode is Mutable and his weakest is Cardinal.

Signature: Dick Smith has a dominance of Mutable Air which is Gemini (6 points in Air and 8 in Mutable). His weakest signature is Cardinal Earth which is Capricorn. You can determine from this that Dick Smith has a polished and personable approach to sales, marketing and promotions. He isn't so good at the hard work of structure and organisation, he would no doubt outsource this to someone with a strong Earth sign to balance his lack of Earth.

Planet emphasis

What planets are emphasised in Dick Smith's chart?

The Moon does stand out and it may be something to examine in more detail.

Are there any retrogrades? Yes, apart from the North Node who is basically always R, he has Jupiter, Chiron, Neptune and Pluto in R. They are generational and not something I would look at early in my reading.

Are there powerful personal planets which will make them more relevant? Yes, Mercury is conflicted but also quite powerfully placed.

Are there any strongly placed outer planets? Yes, Pluto is retrograde and powerfully placed applying to the cusp of an angular house, the 7th; Jupiter is retrograde and also in a powerful angular house, the 7th; Neptune is retrograde in the 9th house and part of his Grand Cross pattern.

Are there any planetary patterns? Yes, a Grand Cross involving Neptune, Moon, Sun, Mercury and Mars. I would add Saturn even though he is 'out of orb' to Neptune. I would call him a wide conjunction to Mars and draw him into the pattern.

This quick delineation method shows which planets and points may need further analysis.

House emphasis

Is there an emphasis on angular houses? Yes, the 7th house. This is important for obvious 7th house reasons, especially if the client came for advice on relationship issues.

Is there any other house emphasis? Yes, the 5th house has a mini-stellium of three planets, one personal and two outer planets. It is of some importance in relation to his creativity, interests and friendships.

Next I would look at the house placement of the two luminaries, both are in Air - his Moon is in the 11th house (Air), and the Sun is in the 3rd house (Air). This shows where Dick is most conscious (Sun) and unconscious (Moon). They direct his attention towards major areas of his life. His Sun gives him meaning and the Moon shows where he needs or gives nurturing. Please note that these two houses reflect his signature – Air.

Sign emphasis

Do any signs stand out? Pisces does with three of his personal planets: Mercury, Sun and Venus. Leo has three planets: Pluto, Jupiter and North Node and they are all involved with his 7th house, an angular house, and within the 8° to 15° orb of influence to its cusp. Gemini has three planets: Mars, Saturn and Uranus. Gemini is also his chart signature. I would focus on all three signs: Pisces, Leo and Gemini.

Element and Mode emphasis

Fire is emphasised because of the angular 7th house with three planets in Leo; the 5th house has a mini-stellium of 3 planets; and the Moon is in Sagittarius.

Water has Sun, Mercury and Venus in Pisces.

Air is strong with a Gemini signature and a mini-stellium in Gemini; Aquarius Ascendant and Libra Midheaven; Sun and Mercury Exalted in the 3rd house.

Earth is weak with only Chiron in Virgo.

Reading a chart requires that you notice these planets, signs and houses that are the most emphasised in the chart.

Remember that a heavy emphasis will always suggest conflict - and conflict is what the native will focus on throughout their life. A weakness in a mode or element is both a conflict and a strength because the native will often over-emphasise it to bring themselves into balance.

Dick's Gemini 5th house is one I would definitely look at – can you see what I am seeing? His signature is Gemini; Gemini's ruler, Mercury is conjunct the 3rd house cusp and the Sun and those 3 planets in Gemini are in the dynamic and creative 5th house. When we add his Aquarian Ascendant and Sagittarian Moon in the 11th house we have a flamboyant salesman and entrepreneur.

Planetary Aspects

Planetary Patterns:- the planets that form a Grand Cross - Sun conjunct Mercury + Mars conjunct Saturn + Moon + Neptune. Interestingly it is this pattern that provides Dick with the drive and resilience to achieve fame and fortune. Why? Because it is painful and we always seek to relieve our pain.

Odd things to look for

Was he born at a New or Full Moon? No.

A point to note: delineating a chart is extremely demanding in time and skill. Astrologers only get better and faster when they delineate a lot of charts, and by that I mean hundreds of charts. That doesn't mean that they all have to be your clients. You can read charts of friends and family, celebrities and people from history. The more you study the better you will become.

Chapter 14 - Transits – an introduction

Although transits and progressions are beyond the scope of this book I think you need to know a little about them. Consider this a basic introduction to transits.

Your natal chart is a snapshot of where the planets were at the exact moment you took your first breath of life. That snapshot remains your natal chart, the blueprint of your personality and of your destiny.

The planets don't stop moving when you are born, though, they keep moving. Within 6 hours of your birth the Moon has moved 3°, the next day the Sun, Mercury and Venus have moved 1 degree, and after 1 year Mars has moved half way around your chart. Everything continues to move, this is called 'progression'.

I like to examine the transits in someone's chart when they come for therapy. A transiting chart shows me where the planets are at any point in time and what the native's lessons are. Transits are what triggers people to seek therapy, to change their diet, or even to start a new career.

Looking at the Pluto's Cave chart you can see a biwheel - the natal chart is the wheel in the middle, and on the outside wheel is the transit chart. That outer wheel shows where the planets were at the date and time I chose (11th December 2018).

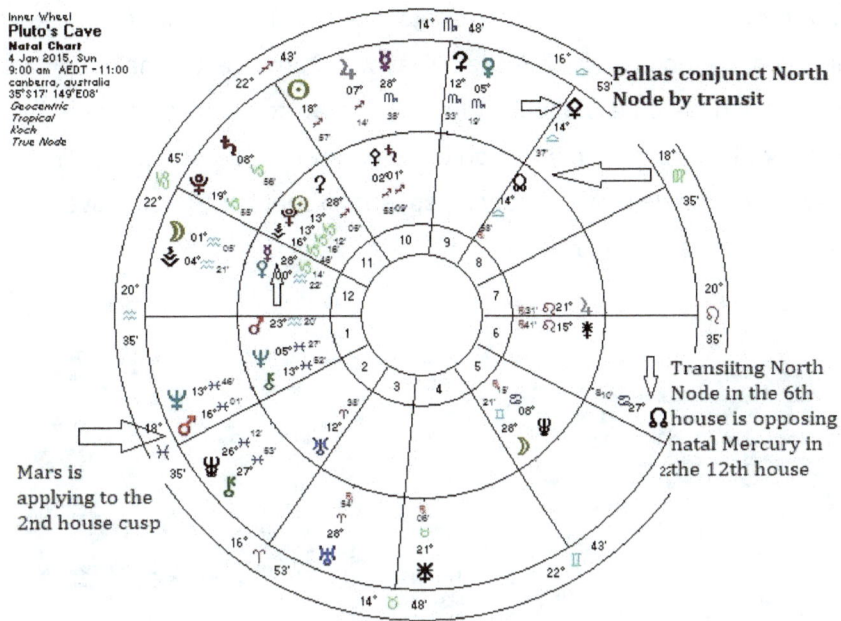

Above chart: outer wheel shows the transits of Pallas, Mars and North Node; the inner wheel is the natal chart for Pluto's Cave.

You can see in this biwheel that transiting Pallas, an asteroid goddess, is exact conjunct the chart's natal North Node - 14°37 of Libra in the 8th House. That is an exact conjunction by transit.

Transiting North Node is opposite natal Mercury but it is not exact, it is 2° from exact. Don't forget, the North Node is the only planet that travels clockwise around the chart.

Transiting Mars is applying to the 2nd house cusp by 2°.

A point to note: the transiting planets move in an anti-clockwise direction (except the North Node). They will, from time to time, stop moving and become Stationary; then they may go backwards, Retrograde; and then they will go back to moving forward again, Direct. Transiting planets move at varying speeds except the Sun, it moves at the same speed every day.

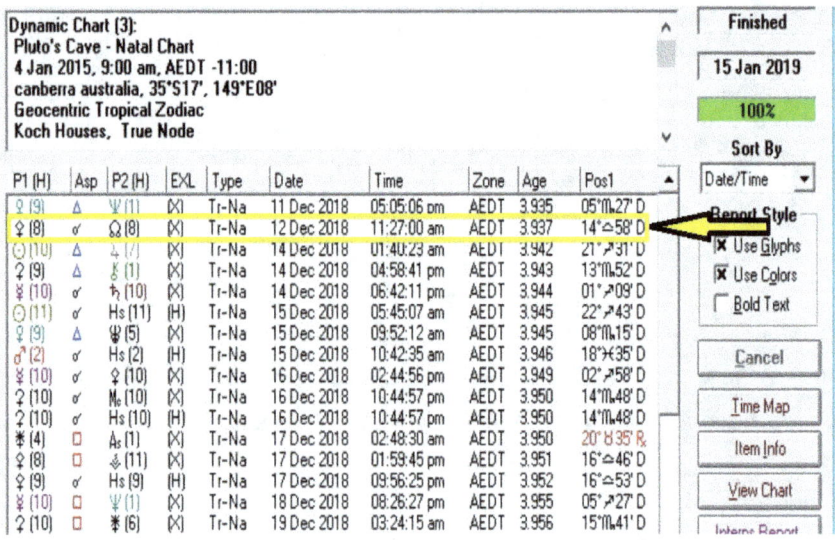

Grid above – shows transiting Pallas exact (X) conjunct natal North Node.

Exercise

An exercise you might want to do is to write down all of your transits for this month. Make up a grid showing the transiting planet, the aspect it makes and the natal planet affected. You can also note each time a planet crosses a house cusp too.

Keep this to exact transits, 0°, and record how you feel, what happens and how you think the transiting planet has impacted your natal planet or house cusp.

You can use the same format as the grid I've copied with my software. You could also create your own transits grid from your chartsubscriber.com account.

Transit meditations, a form of Active Imagination, are an excellent way to learn about your natal and transiting planets. Pluto's Cave would meditate on Pallas and the North Node three times, writing down each meditation and the conversations he had with the two archetypes, he has a few days for this meditation because this is a slow transit.

This is how you do alchemical magic, this is psychological astrology in action.

I recommend that you limit your transit meditations to conjunctions to begin with. If you try to do every transit at once you will never have time for anything else. Record everything, every meditation as well as how the day itself went. Fast meditations like the Moon only have a window of a few hours, but Mercury, Sun and Venus have a nice window of 1 degree which is one day. You have about a week for your meditations with Mars while Jupiter can sit on the exact degree for several weeks. Outer planets can last for months without moving.

There is nothing that can top having a direct, personal experience with your astrology archetypes, it truly is making magic.

Chapter 15 – Active Imagination and the archetypes in your chart

"Active imagination is a matter of allowing the natural mind time and freedom to express itself spontaneously… This is a knack which, given patience, anyone can acquire. Active imagination requires a state of reverie, halfway between sleep and waking. It is like beginning to fall asleep but stopping short before consciousness is lost and remaining in that condition. It is often helpful to adopt some little ritual as a rite d'entrée: Jung imagined he was descending into a cave…" Anthony Stevens (1990). *'On Jung'*, page 202.

"Without this playing with fantasy no creative work has ever yet come to birth. The debt we owe to the play of the imagination is incalculable." Carl Jung (2016). *'Psychological Types'*, p.88, Routledge.

Active Imagination

This term was coined by Carl Jung in his early work using psychodynamic therapy. It was how he accessed his unconscious world recorded in his famous 'Red Book'. It describes the very simple technique of 'imagining'. I use it with the archetypes both astrology and tarot and it is an extremely effective method for gaining insight from the archetypes themselves. Just close your eyes and imagine you are with the planets or signs and just go with the flow. Don't try to push it along, just give in and let the meditation and imagery or sensations flow through you.

Planets as archetypes

When I say the word 'dwarf' what comes to mind? Is it Gimli from '*Lord of the Rings*'? Perhaps other dwarves popped into your head like characters from the books you have read, cartoons you have watched and the toys and figurines you've seen and played with. Each of these are forms of the 'dwarf archetype'.

In this example your planet is the dwarf (WHAT); his mannerisms, the clothing he wears and his speech patterns are the sign (HOW); where he is at the moment is the house (WHERE). In this example your planet is a dwarf but his appearance and setting define him much better than that single word - dwarf.

The planet archetypes are raw energies, they are yet to be refined and polished to suit your individual life-needs for this incarnation which is the role of the signs and houses. Jung said that archetypes existed before humanity evolved and thus helped shape our physical, material and spiritual evolution on this planet, they are our primary energy forms.

The fundamental psychological traits of the individual are filtered through the planets, this is pure archetypal energy. For instance, the Sun represents self-esteem, confidence, vitality, heroic courage and joyfulness. These traits can be seen by others, sometimes you will notice them within yourself.

A point to note: archetypes form our myths and our myths are projected back to us via TV, radio, the movies and in our books every day. We eat and breathe our mythological archetypes all the time.

Archetypes arise from the Collective Unconscious: Jung stated that every culture in the world share these common archetypes. There are many archetypes in your world, for example, the hero archetype - your father is your first hero which is astrology's Sun archetype. When you don't get enough father / hero energy (not enough attention from your father, the hero), you need to go into the world to find one. Thus many boys and girls worship sports stars, rock stars and movie stars. 'Stars' is a good choice of word for it is archetypal, like the planets.

When an archetype is unformed, for example when your father is absent through your formative or early years, then you experience a burning desire to find a replacement father archetype. This desire or need may be so great that you push beyond societies boundaries and choose unacceptable heroes. For example, boys who worship the Nazi movement are seeking a father figure outside society's limits. Their need for their father's attention is so distorted that they have swung, like a pendulum, to the other side of society's acceptable norms.

Another example is the mother archetype, the Moon. This is generally the unconditional loving mother archetype which is sometimes also considered the lover because mother was your first source of love, suckling from your mother was your first sensual experience. You can find more on this in Psychodynamic and Attachment theory.

Men and women who didn't experience their mother's love and affection in a balanced way seek the Mother in their lovers. Sometimes they are so dependent on this archetype that they can become distorted in their needs for her.

Those with terribly out of balanced needs for a father or mother figure can seek to control their lover's every move, thought and emotion. You, as an astrologer would see this in their Sun and Moon sign and house position and their aspects to the other planets. This unbalanced person's behaviour often destroys their object of love when he or she can't fulfil their nurturing needs.

This is sometimes the situation with overly-dependent mothers. They love their children so much that they create a dependency for and from their children. Their children may grow up expecting the same co-dependency in their lovers. They fear such things as abandonment and betrayal and will do anything to avoid being alone.

Planets are archetypes, they are the raw energy form that you can see reflected in the real world. Look at each planet and you will see their counterpart around you:

Mercury = communication, the TV news presenter.

Venus = love and social occasions, you see her in lovers as well as others when you share a cup of coffee with a friend.

Mars = drive, fathers and mothers who are driven to succeed often working 16 hours a day to achieve their goals, others may be sports stars or soldiers.

Jupiter = expansion, you see him in your generous friends, a manager who likes a drink, the gambler, academic and considerate wise older people.

Saturn = consolidation, you see Saturn when you are helped on a project to get it just right by a teacher, the clerk who tells you to wait in line, it is your societal rule on good manners and obeying road signs.

Chiron = wounds and healing, you see him in the doctor on TV, the concerned teacher, the naturopath, the psychologist.

Uranus = freedom, you see him as the activist, the seeker of justice when a person or race is persecuted or more of our precious environment is destroyed.

Neptune = the somewhat unrealistic idealist, you see him or her in the new age movement, the magician in fantasy books.

Pluto = the cool dude with the dark glasses sitting with you in meditation circles, the killer in movies who brings vengeance on those that get in their way.

Signs highlight the archetypal personality

The planet archetype must have some way to express its primary personality and this is through its sign placement. Mars in Aries is a dynamic and rash form of energy, the archetype of the child with ADHD, hyperactive with a short attention span. Mars in Cancer is less rash, in fact it is not so comfortable acting out because Mars is Fire and Cancer is Water. When expressed in a positive manner Mars in Cancer will seek to nurture and will expend its energy caring for others.

Another way to understand this is in Liz Greene's explanation that the sign is like clothing. The planet is the person and the sign is his/her clothing which highlights their personality. Moon in Scorpio would dress rather darkly, a secretive hood to cover her face and her sexually alluring aura. Moon in Pisces would dress colourfully, mostly greens and blues, like the sky and ocean appearing a little spaced-out. Venus in Capricorn would be dressed conservatively in earthy colours appearing slightly cold and aloof. The archetypes need expression and the sign gives it just that, an outward form and a personality that we can relate to.

Houses showcase where the archetype's action takes place

Now that you have the archetype clothed and with a personality you need to know where they are going to act out their particular traits the most often. Where is the archetype of Moon in Sagittarius being generous and wildly emotional? Where is she most erratic and having fun in an adventure and knowing that she will walk away as soon as her partner asks for commitment?

You can see this by the house that the planet is in. For example, Moon in Sagittarius in the 1st house expresses her avoidance of commitment (and love of partying) as part of her basic ego and personality. The 1st house is where planets are most readily expressed, so the Moon in Sagittarius struggles to manage her desires to be flamboyant, irresponsible and moody. If she was in the 8th house it would be sexual, a predator perhaps if poorly aspected, or a teacher of tantric sex and involved with every form of the occult.

Glenn Perry, in his book, '*Introduction to AstroPsychology*', uses the analogy of houses as 'stages', the scene where the planet acts out. The stage is a place where your emotions, frustrations, strengths, interests and your weaknesses are played out for all to see.

By placing the archetype, the planet, in appropriate clothing or costume and on a particular stage setting you can witness a powerful demonstration of the themes and plots in that person's life. Imagine each house as a stage, the planet as the actor and the sign as the costume then you will begin to understand the native's conflict and their psychological strengths and weaknesses.

Chapter 16 - Introducing the five main asteroid goddesses

Although there are thousands of asteroids that astrologers could use in their delineations I have chosen to include just these five female asteroid goddesses in my readings. They are: Juno, Vesta, Hygeia, Pallas, Ceres and one male, Chiron, whom you have already met in previous chapters.

The asteroid goddesses orbit the sun in the asteroid belt, between Mars and Jupiter. The asteroid belt is said to have once been a planet, Marduk. According to some the Marduk race interfered with the Martian race threatening their very existence. The Martians were fed up with the Mardukians so they harnessed some kind of power and blew the entire Marduk planet up. The far side of Mars that faces outwards, towards Jupiter, is a kilometre thicker than the sheltered side and is made up of enormous boulders. This is said to be the residue of the exploding Marduk.

If you are interested in really weird stuff then watch this Youtube clip introducing the above story. I am impressed with what Dr Courtney Brown has done with his amazing remote viewing team:
https://www.youtube.com/watch?v=fBt1Nq7qIBw

Back to astrology, the asteroids take roughly 4 and 1/2 years to orbit the sun, so that means they are in each sign for a little over 4 months. These feisty girls can trigger or awaken the qualities of your natal planets and points as they wander through your chart in transit.

Astrologers tend to stick to the basic planets - Sun, Moon, Mercury, Venus, Mars, Jupiter, Saturn, Uranus, Neptune, Pluto and the North Node. I have always used Chiron in my readings because my astrology teacher, Chris Turner, taught her students to use Chiron in all our readings. She even named her astrology school after it: The Chiron School of Astrology in 1977 - the year of its discovery was the year she opened her school.

By adding more planets to your charts you would expect it to increase the quality of information contained in the chart. However, there is a good reason why astrologers limit the number of planets in their readings: it makes for a clearer and more focused reading. The more points placed in a chart the greater the chance of making a mistake. Adding too many extra points just makes your chart a jumbled mess of lines and symbols.

I've seen people add so many extra points to a chart that it was impossible to read. I will usually see this with beginners who think that the more points the better. Don't stress, I was like that once too.

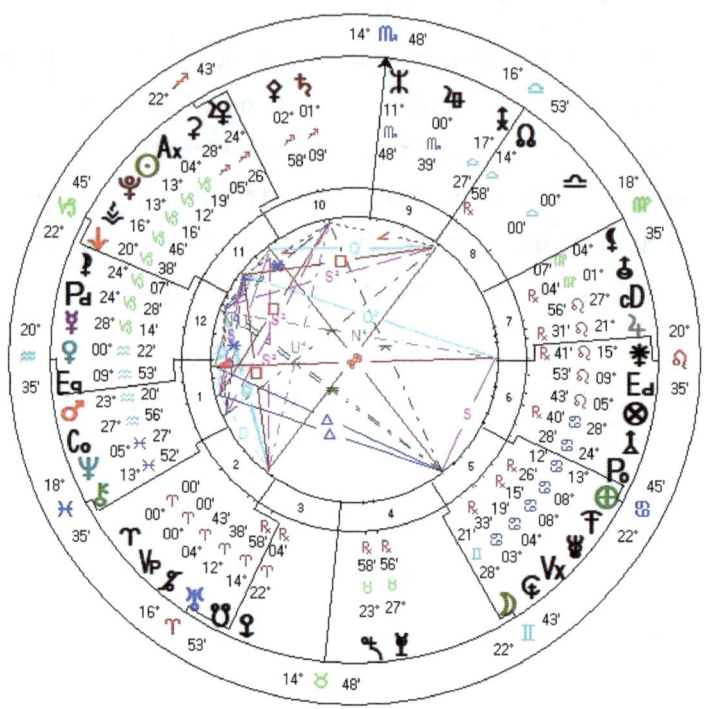

Above chart: a very crowded chart.

If you want to add extra points like the Vertex, Black Moon Lilith, Eris, Sedna, the Centaurs, or other asteroids and dwarf planets, I suggest that you do it as a series of separate charts. I will sometimes create several charts each with the basic planets plus maybe 4 or 5 of these extra points. This is also how you do research on specific asteroids, dwarf planets and theoretical planets.

There are good reasons why I add the five female asteroids Juno, Vesta, Hygeia, Pallas and Ceres – one reason is because astrology's traditional planets are mostly male. There are only two females among the planets we traditionally use: Venus and the Moon. I find that these 5 asteroid goddesses add an extra dimension to my readings.

However, remember from your lessons on the planets, every planet can manifest as either gender - male or female - even the asteroid goddesses can change gender. You don't get to choose how they present in your psyche, it comes from deep within your unconscious.

The female asteroid goddesses are all feisty girls who enjoy expressing their feminine qualities, they can be a bit of a handful too. Just ask some of my students who meditate with them. One student wanted to be in a relationship so much that they quickly manifested it for her - within two weeks of asking she was in a full blown relationship. After some months it turned out that Mr Right was OK but he really wasn't her soul mate. When she confronted the asteroid goddesses in her next meditation they said, *"Well, isn't that what you asked for, a boyfriend?"*

Don't forget to study up on your Greek Mythology. Understanding the myths behind every astrology archetype helps enormously in your readings. This is also valuable when working with them in meditation.

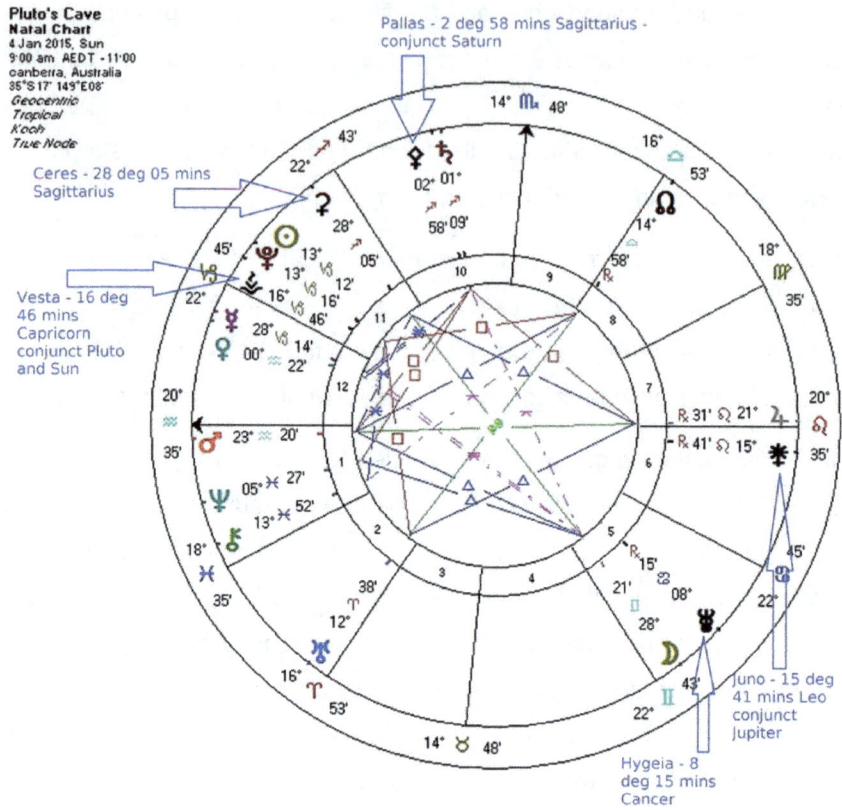

Above chart: the five Asteroid Goddesses

The five Asteroid Goddesses

Ceres - her Greek name is Demeter, the Goddess of fertility and the mother of Persephone. Ceres rules fertility, the harvest and all things that make a house into a home.

The myth: one day Ceres' beautiful teenage daughter, Persephone, went walking in the fields but failed to return home. She had disappeared as though swallowed by the earth itself. Ceres wandered the earth looking for her beloved daughter. In despair Ceres sat on a rock, crying. Just then a young farm boy, Triptolemus, saw her and asked why she was crying. After he heard her sorry tale he told her that he had seen the earth split open at Persephone's feet while he was working in the fields. Out of the earth emerged a fearsome god riding a chariot. The god snatched up the young girl in his arms and then returned to the earth with her.

Ceres was incensed, she knew exactly which god had abducted her daughter and went straight to Jupiter (he is known as Zeus in Greek mythology). There she demanded that his brother, Pluto, hand her daughter back. When Jupiter confronted his brother, Pluto, the God of the Underworld, Pluto stated that he loved Persephone and refused to hand her over. In frustration Ceres told Jupiter that if she didn't get her daughter back then she would stop the harvest - which she did. No more did the sun shine to ripen the crops. Soon the weather grew cold and snow began to fall. The people of the earth began to starve. Bitterly they cursed Jupiter for abandoning them.

Eventually Jupiter gave in to public pressure and again called Pluto to his throne room. He inquired if Persephone had broken the 'rule of the dead'. This rule stated that if a living soul ate the food of the dead then they must stay in the Underworld. Pluto had only just learned that Persephone, in desperate hunger, had partaken of a few pomegranate seeds.

Jupiter was now frightened. Ceres had the power to destroy all living beings on Earth. He asked Pluto to compromise, to negotiate, offer something in return so that Ceres would not destroy the world. When Ceres heard that Persephone was doomed to remain in the Underworld she was heartbroken. Eventually she agreed to allow her daughter to remain underground with Pluto as his wife for 2 seasons. The other 2 seasons she would live with her mother above ground. There are many variations to this tale in Greek mythology.

Ceres is a very powerful goddess determined to help her loved ones, as a mother would. What happened to the farmer boy? She rewarded him by introducing him to the secret Eleusinian Mysteries and gave him the power to grow anything he wanted - a fitting gift from the Goddess of agriculture, cereals, fertility and the harvest.

In the Pluto's Cave chart - Ceres is in Sagittarius, in the 11th house and opposes the Moon. This tells us that the generosity of Ceres, her fertility and power, is associated with Sagittarius allowing her to manifest her wise and adventurous spirit; with Ceres in the 11th house we see that she is driven to fertilise humanity with her wisdom. The opposition to the Moon shows Ceres will sometimes clash with the Moon, a practical mind versus an emotional need to nurture. Ceres will remind Gemini Moon not to get too carried away socialising with friends on social media.

Pallas (also known as Pallas Athene - a Greek goddess who was known as Minerva by the Romans) - rules feminine wisdom and intuition, the virgin warrior goddess.

The myth: Her father, Jupiter, the king of the gods, was in the habit of eating his children when they were born. But Pallas wasn't going to have anything to do with that. One day Jupiter woke with a headache when suddenly, without warning, the fully grown Pallas emerged from his head.

From that day Pallas ruled women who were independent and no one's plaything. She refused to allow anyone to dominate her mind, body or soul. I have a wonderful friend who has Pallas sitting on her Ascendant, she was the first female engineer in the country and eventually she sat as head of the university engineering department. She has enormous strength of character and wisdom. Her manifestation of Pallas is seen in her love of all forms of mythology, esoteria and she has made a second career as a healer. Like Pallas she certainly doesn't tolerate idiots. She epitomises the goddess Pallas in so many ways.

In the Pluto's Cave chart, Pallas is in Sagittarius in the 10th house and conjunct Saturn. Her 10th house placement shows that she is very interested in leading her students in the right direction. Her conjunction with Saturn shows that she wants to share the responsibility of directing the business side of Pluto's Cave. Pallas guides Pluto's Cave with wisdom and in consultation with Saturn.

Vesta - this Roman goddess represents dedication and devotion to a higher purpose. The main Roman Temple of Vesta for the Goddess of the Hearth, is surrounded by The Sacred Grove. This was a temple of spirit and as such its devotees were required to attend its sacred flame. The Vestal Virgins, there were up to six at any one time, was a priestesshood with magical powers who devoted thirty years of their life to the service of the goddess Vesta. Everyone in Rome was entitled to light their hearth from the sacred flame.

The Vestal Virgins presided over many religious ceremonies and kept the wills and official records of Roman citizens. It was said that the fortunes of Rome was linked to that of the Vesta Temple. Look at your own chart to find where Vesta resides and you will see where you are most loyal, devoted and dedicated.

In the Pluto's Cave chart Vesta is in Capricorn and resides in the 11th house of other people, humanity and helping to meet the hopes, dreams and wishes of the community. Vesta is also conjunct Pluto and Sun which tends to elevate her above the other goddesses. The conjunction suggests that Vesta works directly with the God of the Underworld, Pluto, and with the Sun, who is life itself. I would sum this up by saying that Vesta dedicates herself to serving the needs, hopes, dreams and wishes of the Pluto's Cave community.

Juno - in Greek mythology she is called Hera, Jupiter's wife. Long did Juno suffer with her womanising husband who took great pleasure in mounting females in many forms - from cows and swans to humans and goddesses. Juno represents the matriarchal ruler of humanity and as such she is one goddess the people of ancient times turned to when things went bad in marriage and at home.

She was wise, motherly, gentle, personable and a counsellor for those seeking advice and support. She ruled mothers, motherhood and mothering. She was also a wise elder to whom people turned to when in financial trouble as she also ruled money and anything to do with running a household.

In the Pluto's Cave chart she is in Leo in the 6th house and applying to the 7th house. This suggests that Pluto's Cave seeks to be a responsible and disciplined mother type nurturing students (the 7th house is 'close others' which includes students). Juno does this with a generous and fun loving spirit but she wishes she were in the 7th house where she would rule relationships directly rather than indirectly from the 6th house. Juno can be a little overbearing and judgemental at times so I think it is just as well that she isn't fully in the 7th house.

Hygeia - the Goddess of healing is the daughter of the Greek god of medicine, Asclepius. Hygeia is another powerful goddess who is responsible for your ongoing health. In the chart she shows where you need to apply healing for daily management of your health. Her name is still used today - 'hygiene'. She has the medical symbol of her father, a staff with a snake curled around to symbolise the rising energy of life.

In the Pluto's Cave chart she is in Cancer in the 5th house where the Moon also resides. They form a wide conjunction. This shows that Pluto's Cave seeks to understand and heal in a social, friendly, fun-loving and creative manner.

Exercise

There is little research material on these asteroid goddesses for astrologers to draw upon. I tend to base my readings on personal experience with them and from their Greek and Roman myths. Therefore I suggest that the best way for you to understand how they operate in your own chart is to study their myths in as much depth as possible.

You might want to go to your chartsubscriber.com page and add these five asteroid goddesses to your natal chart.

Further information on the asteroid Goddesses here:
https://en.wikipedia.org/wiki/List_of_asteroids_in_astrology

Chapter 17 - Meeting the asteroid goddess archetypes in meditation

Juno (called Hera in Greek mythology) - goddess of motherhood and relationships

I am still working to better understand these goddesses at a personal level, so please be patient with me. I believe that the best way to understand the archetypes is to examine them in hundreds of charts and as many transits. I also recommend that every astrologer get to know their archetypes intimately by meditating with them.

Juno is the Roman name for the Greek goddess, Hera. Juno is Jupiter's wife, and if you know your Greek mythology, Jupiter or Jove is the Roman name for Zeus, the King of the Gods.

Juno was a dutiful and devout wife, holding the family together as wives and mothers do. She represents the security of belonging, being accepted by your family, as well as to be in a committed, long-term relationship secure in love and respect. Despite her husband's frequent philandering, flirtations and affairs she remained by his side. Certainly she was angry and jealous, certainly she sought revenge and sometimes she punished the innocent victim of her husband's attentions.

When Jupiter was too busy to entertain a prospective courtier, those waiting to see him would often try to get close to him by flattering his wife, Juno. She enjoyed playing gatekeeper to the King of the Gods. As you can see Juno was in an incredibly powerful position as the Queen of the Gods.

Her influence was far above that of the other goddesses, she got what she wanted just as her husband did. And they did love each other, apparently. There must have been affection and commitment, perhaps even some passionate lovemaking, but I think that only happened after the birth of his very last child, Dionysus, god of the grape-harvest.

These gods and goddesses are a reflection of our earthly world: our families and friends, workmates, our lovers and finally of ourselves. They reflect back to us what we struggle to see in our day to day life. We see them, however, in the myths of life, in our movies, our books, our heroes and heroines in sports, at our workplace, at school and in the theatre. The gods and goddesses are alive and well and all around us.

Juno is no exception. You will see her at the library answering questions and queries, running her empire professionally with only a little favouritism. Juno, like her husband, had her favourites. *'Do you wish to speak the King? Yes? Well then, you'd better flatter the Queen who can by-pass all that annoying protocol and red tape'.*

Juno is no fool, she enjoys her power yet she is also wise, perhaps the wisest of the goddesses. Not just because she is a queen but because she has faced hardship and survived. She has found strategies to cope with grief and loss, jealousy and betrayal.

Pallas may have been born of Jupiter's head and considered the wisest of all the female goddesses, yet she can be very one-sided. Pallas is asexual, she lacks the desire for playing those complex games of emotional blackmail so common in royal courts. Juno, though, will flirt just as wildly and outrageously as her husband yet doesn't cross the line. She has morals, principles and values gained from life experience.

In the astrology chart she is powerful, she exhibits where and how your feminine power and life experience expresses itself. She is said to rule marriage, commitment and things related to marriage and family but I'd extend that to include all feminine traits and qualities. In fact, all the female archetypes exhibit much the same traits as each other but are slightly attuned to specifics like 'marriage' for Juno.

Vesta is 'devotion to a purpose'; Pallas is 'feminine wisdom'; Ceres is 'all things fruitful'; and Hygeia is 'healing'. But they are still strongly feminine in how they express these specific qualities. Maybe I see them as very similar because I am male.

Juno is found in the asteroid belt between Mars and Jupiter taking 4.36 years to make one orbit of the Sun. Look for her Return every 4 and 1/3 years for greater insight into how she operates in your psyche (chart). Her transits to sensitive points in your chart will illuminate her role in your natal chart.

My meditation: *I see her floating in the clouds above the Elysian Fields. I have met her there before, many years ago. The first thing that strikes me is her perfume, so alluring, so desirable. Her flowing white gown makes her seem relaxed and approachable. She likes what I've written about her, she loves flattery. Juno calls me but I know that she is not interested in playing games today. She enjoys conversation and is genuinely interested in people. As dispassionate as she is at times she does enjoy helping, it makes her feel wanted, very much a Lunar or Cancerian trait.*

I ask her how she operates in my psyche and she tells me that she helps with her charm, feminine wisdom, intuition and compassion. She also helps me break rules by pushing my compassion beyond the limits of traditional boundaries.

These asteroid goddesses have their own rules. They aren't magical or mystical, they just play it as they see it, but, beware the wiles and ways of the goddesses.

The Queen of the Gods smiles as she strokes my hair, she is so much wiser than I could ever hope to be, and she knows it. She enjoys our conversation and my interpretation of her character. Juno is never malicious, but don't ask her for help if you aren't prepared to accept the consequences.

In transit she will assist, similar to a Venus transit but it lasts much longer. All the goddesses will try to help in some way. Just be warned, she can cause things to fly out of control if you don't set boundaries. These goddess girls have no respect for tradition or convention.

And so, with a giggle, she tells me that it is time for me to leave her. She has had her fun and enjoyed our conversation but it's time for me to go to bed.

Ceres (called Demeter in Greek mythology) - Goddess of fertility and the harvest

Ceres is the Roman name for the Greek goddess, Demeter, she is the mother of Persephone, the young lady kidnapped by Pluto and taken into the underworld. Persephone is another goddess of power, she rules Hades, the underworld, with her husband, Pluto.

I sometimes see Ceres as the Empress card in the tarot major arcana. She represents feminine power, the power to create, to give life, to birth. She also represents warmth, family, dedication to family and friends, love and loyalty. In fact, if you study the goddesses you will see this common thread, they all love and they are all creative. Ceres seems to be able to manifest this in our outer world with greater clarity - what she does is make things real.

I have Ceres in my natal 12th house, for me that is a cave on the beach and inside sits the one-eyed Cyclops. I first met the Cyclops when I was writing my first psychological astrology book on the twelve houses. He and I sometimes sit together in my meditations where I curl up in his arms. He is like the BFG, the Big Friendly Giant. He says that he protects me from the wild world outside his cave. As he says, *'it's dangerous out there'*.

My meditation: *I decide to visit Ceres in the 12th house during one of my meditations. I saw her sitting at a large loom weaving a shawl, like a big fishnet that some women wear around their shoulders. The wool was soft like cashmere. I had to ask her what it was for.*

She handed it to me and told me to wear it. It curled around me like a cocoon and I fell into a deeper trance. I use it sometimes when I meditate. I am still amazed that it works.

I also met Ceres in a dream. Over several nights I programmed my unconscious to meet with her in my dreams and finally it happened. It was a little weird because I was dreaming an ordinary dream when I found myself walking past an attractive, bright-eyed, auburn-haired woman. She looked directly at me. I was mesmerised by her gaze and so I stopped right in front of her. I was in a shopping mall surrounded by a crowd of people milling about and this particular woman just stood out. Where everyone else was busy she was serene and present. I'm sure that I've seen her before, somewhere…

Ceres looked into my eyes to make sure that I was paying attention and told me that I would achieve everything I wanted in this life, 'and more'. It seems that even astrologers need a second opinion and she had answered the question I wanted to ask her.

Ceres is very special to me. I've met her a few more times since and each time I come away feeling validated and accepted, nurtured and knowing my journey continues '*as it should*'. Perhaps you too could visit your Ceres and ask a few questions - what does she say?

Recommended reading in psychology:

Joseph Campbell - *Hero with a Thousand Faces*

Robert Bly - *Iron John*

Stephen Biddulph – *Manhood*

Allan Schore - *Affect Regulation and the Origin of the Self: The Neurobiology of Emotional Development*

Polly Young-Eisendrath - *Female Authority: Empowering Women through Psychotherapy - A Jungian Approach*

Mara Liberman - *Eating Disorders and Myths: A study of the symbolic meaning of eating disorders*

James Hillman – *Re-Visioning Psychology*

Germaine Greer – *The Female Eunuch*

Naomi Wolf - *The Beauty Myth: How Images of Beauty Are Used Against Women*

Liz Green and Howard Sasportas – *all their books*

Recommended astrology podcasts:

http://theastrologypodcast.com - Chris Brennan

http://www.holestoheavens.com - Adam Sommer

Thank you for reading my book. I hope it has inspired you to learn more about the psychology of astrology. If you found that this book has helped you in your studies please leave me a review.

You are welcome to email me, I'll do my best to respond in a timely manner. Don't forget to subscribe to my newsletter, it's free.

Wishing you good fortune in your study and practice of astrology,

Noel Eastwood

June 2019

Canberra, Australia

Books by Noel Eastwood

Psychological Astrology series:

Psychological Astrology an Introduction – 2019 (also available as an audio-book)

Psychological Astrology and the Twelve Houses – 2015 (also available as an audio-book)

Psychological Astrology and the Signs of the Zodiac - due for publication in 2019

Psychological Astrology and the Planets of Power - due for publication in 2020

Psychological Astrology, Jung and the Mystic's Quest - due for publication in 2020

Also by Noel Eastwood:

Astrology of Health - 2016

Self Hypnosis Tame Your Inner Dragons: clinical and psychic use of trance – 2016 (also available as an audio-book)

The Fool's Journey Through The Tarot series:

The Fool's Journey Through the Tarot Major Arcana - published 2017 (also available as an audio-book)

The Fool's Journey Through the Tarot Pentacles - published 2018

The Fool's Journey Through the Tarot Swords - published 2018

The Fool's Journey Through the Tarot Cups - due for publication in 2019

The Fool's Journey Through the Tarot Wands - due for publication in 2020

What readers are saying:

Psychological Astrology and the Twelve Houses

'Most helpful book on psychological astrology - As a psychotherapist who is relatively new to the field of astrology, my skills have really benefited from listening to this book! Noel Eastwood dives into the deep waters in an organized and digestible way. The tone of this book is friendly and conversational and filled with great explanations and examples. He makes what can be an overwhelming language seem approachable.' D

'Great examples for reference - great for the students of astrology and of self awareness towards growth. A very good read.' T

'A very informative book which guided me through the maze of astrology. It was like Noel was with me showing me things I would not have by myself. Noel made things clear and easy to read which gave complete understanding of the subject matter, with great examples. I cannot wait until Noel`s next book is published.'

"I was very excited to read his book because it takes on some intensely personal subject matter from a psychological perspective, which Noel is uniquely qualified to write about, since he is that rare combination (that I wish we had more of in the astrological world), a practicing psychologist and astrologer. His areas of expertise are Jungian and archetypal psychology, astrology, Tarot, and Taoist meditation, so he's well-versed in the realms of the psyche. My first impression, once I got started reading, is that this book is an ideal blend of serious subject matter handled with respect for the reader, with just enough astrologese for the basic-to-medium-advanced astrology student. Noel does not overwhelm you with the level of detail that is automatically off-putting for the beginner. You won't be scared picking up this book, in other words, if you aren't an astrology expert. This is book is for the person who (in my opinion) would be dissatisfied with the superficial or cookbook style astrology book and is looking for something that goes deeper, that explains the pieces of the self we don't usually discuss, even in the astrological world, but most people who want to understand their own (and others') psychology wish could be discussed with some depth and understanding of what's really going on in our psyches as expressed through our natal charts. Speaking as a professional astrologer, I personally got the most out of the very end of the book, where Noel discusses 'houses as psychological defenses.' If you read this book for nothing else, get it for the series of meditations Noel asks you to do; those on their own are very valuable (and I would suggest keeping a journal as you go, to capture your responses). A valuable book for the person looking for psychological self-awareness." AG

"Nice looking book about to read it but it is not cheaply made and is on the exact topic I was curious about. Astrology is such a vast topic I'm trying to delve deeper into the meanings of each aspect and the houses and signs in them are a little confusing to me so this is exactly what I was looking for." KS

"I have studied astrology for years and buy a new book every now and then to enhance my understanding. This book is the first in a long time that really had me intrigued and learning (had my highlighter out!!). Eastwood's combination of astrology and psychology knowledge/experience makes the content easier to follow and provides a much deeper foundation on how to interpret the 12 houses, what's in them (and what's NOT) and other key influences. Looking forward to the next two books in this series!" J

"This book is exactly what I was looking for! Excellent information presented in an entertaining and logical way. For the serious student only, I would advise. I've been on the metaphysical road pretty much since birth & have studied astrology charts for over 25 years. This book truly helped me synthesize an enormous amount of facts and data that constantly swim around in my head. Noel Eastwood...Thank you, sir, for taking the time and making the effort to help students (like me!) on our sometimes strange and difficult (yet always amazing) personal journeys. For me, healing is the goal, knowledge is the path and application & practice are the keys. This book makes a great contribution and I look forward to more from this author / teacher." AS

Astrology of Health

"Noel Eastwood is an amazing astrologer and gifted writer! I have never found so much good information about the astrology of health in any other book."

"Beautifully written book that looks at individuals likely health issues through their predominance of the elements in their charts. It looks at whether one has a Fire, Earth, Air or Water Dominance in their Natal Chart. Depending upon the leading element the individual has, they will have certain strengths and weaknesses health wise. Written in an interactive conversational way between student and teacher it is entertaining and teaches the reader gradually over a number of lessons. Along the way it makes use of a number of case study charts to illustrate the lessons of elemental predominance with regards to Health. I know the elements are one of the cornerstones of Astrology. In understanding more about how their emphasis relates to one's health I found the book highly useful." DK

"I have just completed reading "Astrology of Health." I literally could not put it down. I learned so much!! By envisioning myself as silent observer at the table with Eastwood's student, I participated in each lesson. I am not an astrologer. Yet, I felt I examined each chart. I could clearly see the relationship between each astrological influence and how those influences manifested in each person's life. I had never thought about medical astrology at that depth nor had I clearly understood how generational charts reflected genetic, familiar medical and psychological themes and spiritual lessons. I was educated, informed, excited, and amazed!" CC

"This work by Noel Eastwood is a vital and necessary tool for all astrologers, beginners and professionals alike. His description of the Signs and their Elements (Air, Fire, Earth and Water) is exceptionally illuminating and unique, especially the way in which he describes the defences each element tends to erect. To know our weaknesses is surely one of the best tools we can possibly have at our disposal, and the clarity with which Noel describes and explains these weaknesses is without doubt, the most insightful and enlightening available. But he doesn't stop there. He goes on to discuss and explain the various planetary and luminary effects that these have on our psychology and health, as well as giving vital information about the Angles (Asc./Desc., Midheaven/IC) with regard to health matters. In the 'Lessons' areas, peppered with actual charts, his discussions with his students are 'hands on' which gives even more clarity to this subject; and his style is 'natural', which is an invaluable quality that makes it easy reading. And be sure to read the Appendices, which are a true treasure of knowledge and understanding of this subject." S

'The Fool's Journey' series

"I'm not sure how often you get messages like this but I just wanted to say I absolutely loved Fool's Journey through Major Arcana & Pentacles which by accident I read 1st. I'm now going to read the Swords and then The 12 Houses. I can't wait for the next 2 books in the series to come out. You helped me tremendously with my Tarot Readings. I'm on your mailing list so I do hope you will send out a notice once they are published. I so appreciate you very much for you talent, your creativity and for sharing it with the world." TS

"In October of 2009 Carl Jung's Red Book was released for the first time. Chronicling the great psychoanalyst's venture into his own subconscious, revealing fractal universes and personifications of unconscious material. A whole new world of it's own. One that is not unlike the universal symbology embodied in the Major Arcana of the Tarot. Noel Eastwood's delightful book, "The Fool's Journey through the Tarot Major Arcana," is unlike any other tool for learning about this centuries old symbology and how it can be meditated upon, and used to relate to the workings of our daily lives, and our own subconscious. It is a free-flowing, progressive adventure of the Fool through all of the other cards. Taking the simple Spirit he was conceived with, the Fool advances as he encounters each force and personality. A true "Hero's Journey," and one that every spiritual adventurist will love and recognize. The story sucked me in, and only spat me out at the end. I recommend this series as a companion to the works of Carl Jung, Anna Wise, Joseph Campbell, Paul Foster Case, J. Nigro Sansonese, and my own." FK

"Deceptively simple but deviously deep! One might be tempted to under estimate the power of this little book to change lives; it is filled with the wisdom of the ages! Those on a hero's journey of personal growth, such as Follin, would do well to meditate on each lesson until it illuminates the next step and course of action. Noel uses ageless, effective simplicity to harness the power of parable to transfer wisdom." CC

'Fantastic story. Fantastic narration. Loved it!! - I thoroughly enjoyed listening to this book today. The narration is excellent and the content is amazing. It takes you to a deeper understanding of the Major Arcana. I highly recommend this book no matter how experienced or inexperienced a Tarot reader you are!' LY

www.ingramcontent.com/pod-product-compliance
Lightning Source LLC
Chambersburg PA
CBHW071858290426
44110CB00013B/1203